Education, Social Status, and Health

JOHN MIROWSKY

CATHERINE E. ROSS

ALDINE DE GRUYTER
New York

About the Authors

John Mirowsky is a Professor in the Department of Sociology and Population Research Center at the University of Texas at Austin.

Catherine E. Ross is a Professor in the Department of Sociology and Population Research Center at the University of Texas at Austin.

ALDINE DE GRUYTER
A Division of Walter de Gruyter, Inc.
200 Saw Mill River Road
Hawthorne, NY 10532

This publication is printed on acid-free paper ∞

Library of Congress Cataloging-in-Publication Data

Mirowsky, John, 1949–
    Education social status and health / John Mirowsky and Catherine E. Ross.
        p. cm. — (Social institutions and social change)
Includes bibliographical references and index.
    ISBN 0-202-30706-9 (hardcover : alk. paper)—ISBN 0-202-30707-7 (pbk. : alk. paper)
    1. Education—Social aspects. 2. Educational sociology. I. Ross, Catherine E., 1953– II. Title. III. Series.
    LC191.M576 2003
    306.43′2—dc21

                                                                    2003000319

Manufactured in the United States of America

10 9 8 7 6 5 4 3 2 1

Contents

Acknowledgments   vii

Introduction: A Rediscovery   1
    Chapter Previews   6

1 Education as Learned Effectiveness   25
    Education, Learned Effectiveness, and Health   26
    Education and Socioeconomic Status   28
    Education as a Root Cause of Good Health   30

2 The Association between Education and Health   32
    Defining Health   32
    Measuring Health   34
    Education's Correlation with Health Measures   35

3 Education, Personal Control, Lifestyle, and Health   50
    Education and Human Capital   51
    Designing a Healthy Lifestyle   52
    The Sense of Control Links Education to Healthy Lifestyle   60

4 Education, Socioeconomic Status, and Health   71
    Economic Resources   72
    Productive Activities   98
    Education, Socioeconomic Status, and Health   124

5 Education, Interpersonal Relationships, and Health   126
    Education, Marriage, and Social Support   126
    Marriage and Health   129

6   Age and Cumulative Advantage   140
    Accumulating Effects   141
    Amplifying Effects   146
    Decline Slowed or Only Delayed?   158
    Education's Cumulative Advantage   168

7   Specious Views of Education   170
    Education as Credential   171
    Education as Reproducer of Inequality   174
    Education as False Satisfier   182
    Education as Spurious Correlate   185
    Education, Inequality, and Health   193
    Education: The Solution, Not the Problem   195

8   Conclusion: Self-Direction Toward Health   197
    Learned Effectiveness Tops Access to Lucrative Positions   198
    Learned Effectiveness Provides Control over Lifestyle
        and Circumstances   198
    Education Has Pervasive, Cumulative, Self-Amplifying Benefits 200
    Lack of Education Turns Low Income into Privation   200
    Structural Amplification Concentrates Problems   201
    Resource Accumulation and Substitution Imply
        Structural Amplification   203
    No One Loses When Someone Gains Control   204
    Education: The Answer   206

9   Data and Measures   207
    ASOC: U.S. Nationwide Survey   207
    CCH: Illinois Statewide Survey   213

References   215

Index   235

Acknowledgments

The Aging, Status and the Sense of Control (ASOC) survey was funded by a grant from the National Institute on Aging (RO1-AG12393) to John Mirowsky (principal investigator) and Catherine E. Ross (coprincipal investigator). The Community, Crime and Health (CCH) survey was funded by a grant from the National Institute of Mental Health (RO1 MH51558) to Catherine E. Ross (principal investigator) and Chester Britt (coprincipal investigator). The sampling, pretesting, and interviewing for the surveys was conducted by the Survey Research Laboratory of the University of Illinois. The National Institute on Aging and the National Institute of Mental Health supported our analysis and writing with the grants named above, and with a grant from the National Institute of Mental Health to John Mirowsky (principal investigator) and Catherine E. Ross (coprincipal investigator) to study parenthood and well-being (RO1 MH56543).

We are indebted to the National Institute on Aging and the National Institute of Mental Health for support of our research and writing. We thank the Ohio State University for the sabbatical that gave us time for writing. We worked with Paul Hu, John Reynolds, Marieke Van Willigen, and Chia-ling Wu on various parts of the research reported in this book. We thank them all.

Introduction: A Rediscovery

Education forms a unique dimension of social status, with qualities that make it especially important to health. It influences health in ways that are varied, present at all stages of adult life, cumulative, self-amplifying, and uniformly positive. Educational attainment marks social status at the beginning of adulthood, functioning as the main bridge between the status of one generation and the next, and also as the main avenue of upward mobility. It precedes the other acquired social statuses and substantially influences them, including occupation and occupational status, earnings, personal and household income and wealth, and freedom from economic hardship. Education creates desirable outcomes because it trains individuals to acquire, evaluate, and use information. It teaches individuals to tap the power of knowledge. Education develops the learned effectiveness that enables self-direction toward any and all values sought, including health.

For decades American health sciences acted as if social status had no great bearing on health. The ascendance of clinical medicine within a culture of individualism probably accounts for that omission. At the heart of it, American culture rejects the class and caste systems that many of our ancestors escaped or overcame. Americans might respect the abilities and contributions of aristocrats like Thomas Jefferson and George Washington, but they take inspiration from the achievements of self-made individuals like Ben Franklin and George Washington Carver. This orientation at times becomes a reluctance to face facts about gradations of advantage, wealth, power, prestige, or ability. We remember the cautionary stories about this reluctance told to us when we were studying sociology in graduate school. Jerry Myers, one of our professors then, told us about his own days as assistant in the late 1950s to August Hollingshead and Fritz Redlich, who were writing a book titled *Social Class and Mental Illness* (Hollingshead and Redlich 1958). Myers did fieldwork and data analyses for the project. He told us that, prior to publication, Hollingshead and Redlich expected scholarly criticism for describing mental illness in the context of community and class culture. Their approach departed greatly from the Freudian analyses of intrapsychic processes and close family relationships that dominated

1

psychiatric literature then. Instead they were barraged with editorial and public umbrage over the book's delineation of social strata in New Haven, Connecticut. Apparently the idea that social classes existed in New Haven offended many, to whom it sounded misleading, provocative, and un-American.

The national ideals of equality and individualism may have enhanced the ascendance of clinical medicine, with its ideal of the physician acting as agent scientist on behalf of each individual patient and seeking to identify a specific disease as the proximate cause of the individual's symptoms and signs. Regardless of social background, everyone with, say, tuberculosis has the same disease requiring the same treatment. A case might involve a strain of the bacillus resistant to specific antibiotics, and some individuals may have allergies or other conditions that rule out specific treatments. Such details refer to the disease and the individual as organism and not to the person, much less to the person's social status. Once the disease has been identified, the medical procedures indicated are essentially the same for everyone. That fits nicely with the ideals of equality and individualism. In clinical medicine the individual's social background and standing easily get relegated to a minor role. Perhaps they make the physician lean toward the diagnosis of a disease that is relatively common among persons with social attributes similar to those of the patient. Perhaps they make the physician see compliance with a demanding, unpleasant, or expensive regimen as more or less likely. Nevertheless, the clinical setting and the physician's role as agent for the individual who comes there obscure the role of social status in regulating the risk, severity, and consequence of disease. A river of disease and disability flows through the clinic daily. Realistically, clinical medicine cannot do much to change a patient's social status or personal history that led to the episode at hand.

Medicine's traditional focus on the distinct causes of specific diseases deflects attention from forces that create more or less disease of many kinds. Much of contemporary medical culture originated in the scientific breakthroughs of the nineteenth century, particularly the discovery of microorganisms as causes of disease. Those discoveries led medicine to seek a unique necessary cause for each distinct disease. Remove that cause and you prevent or cure the disease. So, for example, the spirochete *Treponema pallidum* causes syphilis, a disease that progresses through three stages characterized by local formation of chancres, ulcerous skin eruptions, and systemic infection leading to general paresis. Killing the spirochete with extracts from the blue *Penicillium* mold cures the disease. Avoiding exposure to the organism through sexual discretion or the use of condoms prevents the disease. Regardless of a person's social background and standing, they will not get the disease without infection by the organism, and treatment that kills the organism cures the disease.

The logic and power of many infectious-disease examples crystallized twentieth-century medicine's organization around the search for the distinctive causes of specific diseases. Those same concepts and assumptions that propelled advances in the fight against infectious disease became early obstacles to understanding and controlling many chronic diseases. For example, researchers and physicians often were reluctant to accept that cigarette smoking caused a specific disease because smoking seemed correlated with many different diseases but not essential for any one of them, including heart disease, stroke, emphysema, chronic bronchitis, and several types of cancer. Richard Doll's demonstration of the unusually high correlation between cigarette smoking and lung cancer helped give legitimacy to its role as a cause of disease. Even so, the complexity of smoking's effects created much confusion, because no single one acts as the sole necessary cause. Smoking prompts the production of mucus, paralyzes the cilia that normally clear the mucus, and delivers a tar containing fifteen or more cancer-causing substances. In the process it degrades the structure and function of the lungs, giving the smoker's blood too little oxygen and too much carbon dioxide, creating inflamed regions pooling mucus, meanwhile depressing the activity of the immune system's macrophages, thereby greatly increasing the risk of lung infection. Confusion over the variety of smoking's effects was compounded by confusion over the variety of causes contributing to each smoking-related disease. To this day smoking kills more Americans through heart disease than through lung cancer. Smoking is only one of several major factors contributing to heart disease, along with the high blood pressure and high fractions of circulating low-density cholesterol that result most often from exercising too little and eating too much. Eliminating smoking would not eliminate heart disease, although it would cut the rates considerably. Eliminating smoking would not even eliminate lung cancer, although it would come close.

Chronic disease research over the last half of the twentieth century forced science to think differently about the causes of disease. Despite the institutional and cultural forces focusing medical research and theory on distinctive proximate causes of specific diseases, researchers were forced to look over their shoulders, back toward more distant causes of many diseases. Some turned their orientation a full 180 degrees, looking for the origins of that river of disease and disability flowing daily through the clinics. Researchers who head back up that stream rediscover the effect of social status on health.

American sociology, epidemiology, and public health said surprisingly little about the effects of social status on health for decades. Partly that is because the effects are so pervasive that socially oriented health scientists take them for granted. A sociologist studying the effects of undesirable and uncontrollable events on health, for example, would recognize that such events probably happen more often to lower-status individuals. The researcher would take precautions to avoid mistaking other effects of low status among individuals experiencing undesirable and uncontrollable events for effects of the events themselves. Typically that would involve statistical adjustments for education, occupational status, and household income. Those adjustments would mathematically correct for any differences in health across levels of events that might actually result from other health effects of the status differences. Social scientists refer to the procedure as estimating the effects (in this case, of stressful life events) holding social status constant. An epidemiologist studying the effect of sedentary lifestyle on heart disease or a public health scientist studying the effect of condom use on rates of sexually transmitted disease would take similar precautions. There is nothing wrong with this. Indeed, good scientific practice demands it. Every once in a while, though, the scientists should remember why they need to make these adjustments and should consider the implications. Researchers habitually make such adjustments because social status affects just about everything that affects health.

Perhaps health scientists had an additional reason for paying little attention to the effects of social status on health: the unexamined assumption that those effects soon would vanish. During the twentieth century the advanced industrial nations made enormous progress in public health programs that benefit all citizens, especially workers and the poor. Everyone benefits from public supplies of monitored and treated water, the testing and regulating of private wells, public sanitary sewers and sewage treatment, regulation of private septic systems, removal of trash and garbage to sanitary landfills or incinerators, rat control, mosquito control, fire control, flood control, safety standards for buildings, environmental and occupational health and safety standards and programs, transportation safety standards and agencies, the regulation of food purity and vitamin content, the evaluation and regulation of product safety, the evaluation and regulation of dangerous medical interventions, programs that mandate or promote vaccination against childhood infectious diseases, and agencies that scan ceaselessly for the outbreaks of epidemics, combating them as early as possible. Health scientists know the value and effectiveness of these systems. Perhaps that knowledge encouraged a complacent assumption that the disparities in health across social strata were fading and would soon vanish. In the United States it took a long while before researchers began to question that assumption and examine the evidence for or against. The results were a surprise and a wake-up call: although mortality rates are going down, the differences in mortality rates across social strata are growing. At first the American researchers suspected that the absence of a U.S. national medical care system might explain the disparities. However studies in Canada and England also found substantial and growing differences in mortality rates across social strata. Some countries such as Sweden apparently have enhanced average life expectancy at birth by constraining the range of socioeconomic differences. To our knowledge, though, no country has eliminated the effects on health of the differences in social status that exist.

In the United States the growing recognition of persistent socioeconomic disparities in health led several of the National Institutes of Health to outline research needed on the topic. In 1998 the institutes announced a program to encourage and support research on "Socioeconomic Status and Health Across the Life Course." The announcement makes the following observation, summarizing the core issues well:

> The relationship between socioeconomic status (SES) and physical and mental health, morbidity, disability, and mortality has been long and extensively documented. While the overall relationship of SES to mortality may attenuate in older ages, socioeconomic position continues to be linked to the prevalence of disability and chronic and degenerative diseases, including cardiovascular disease, many cancers, and Alzheimer's disease. Low SES may result in poor physical and/or mental health by operating through various psychosocial mechanisms such as poor or "risky" health-related behaviors, social exclusion, prolonged and/or heightened stress, loss of sense of control, and low self-esteem as well as through differential access to proper nutrition and to health and social services. In turn, these psychosocial mechanisms may lead to physiological changes such as raised cortisol, altered blood-pressure response, and decreased immunity that place individuals at risk for adverse health and functioning outcomes. (National Institutes of Health 1998)

That program announcement was followed a few years later by a request for applications from researchers for funding to study the biological and behavioral mechanisms that link social and physical environments to health disparities (National Institutes of Health 2000). Together those documents outline research that the U.S. national health institutes would like to see over the coming decades. They herald a renewed and explicit attention to the effects of social standing on health.

Our own interest in the effects of social status on health predates the announcements described above. In many ways, this book and those announcements grew out of the same crystallizing realizations. Much of the material in this book reports the results of our ongoing national survey of aging, social status, and the sense of control over one's own life, begun in 1993 and funded by the National Institute on Aging. Some of it reports the results of our other projects, particularly a statewide Illinois survey in 1995 and 1998 of community, crime, and health across the life course, funded by the National Institute of Mental Health. Much of the material, though, goes well beyond merely reporting our results. In the chapters that follow we report what we think, beyond what we have observed. Much of the material represents our best answers, as of 2003, to the scientific questions that stimulated the program announcement and request for applications mentioned above. We expect that this book will be one of many by scientists from various fields contributing their observations and thoughts on why and how social status affects health. In giving our best current answers we draw on findings and ideas from many sciences, including demography, economics, social psychology, biopsychology, medicine, human physiology and endocrinology, and cellular molecular biology. At heart we are survey researchers trying to understand why and how social status affects health, and why education apparently acts as the core aspect of social status with an enduring, consistent, and growing effect on health.

CHAPTER PREVIEWS

Chapter 1 summarizes the main elements of our view of *education as learned effectiveness* that enables self-direction toward health. It introduces the concept from economics of human capital, which is the productive capacity developed, embodied, and stocked in human beings themselves. Education develops human capital by helping individuals become more effective. The real skills, abilities, and resources developed through education help individuals achieve a variety of personally valued ends, including health. Education makes individuals better at acquiring or creating effective means. The chapter delineates education as a distinct aspect of socioeconomic status. We argue against the common practice of treating education, occupation, and economic well-being as merely three manifestations of a single dimension of social status. Understanding how social status affects health requires a careful differentiation among its elements, looking at the relationships among them and at their distinctive connections to health. Chapter 1 ends by arguing that education acts as a root cause of good health, because it gives people the resources to control and shape their own lives in ways that protect and foster health, regardless of the kinds of health risks faced in their time and place.

Chapter 2 describes the *association between education and health*. We begin by defining health as the word appears in English and American usage, both common and scientific. For our purposes we define health as feeling sound, well, vigorous, and physically able to do things that most people ordinarily can do. We continue the standard practice of using the word health to mean three distinct things depending on context: a dimension graded from very negative (unhealthy) to ideally positive (very healthy), an individual's current status or place on that dimension, or the apex of that dimension—the ideal state of health. Next we describe how social scientists measure health in surveys of the general population. We point out that surveys need to compare general levels of health across social categories or strata. Unlike clinicians, survey researchers do not need a detailed description of each individual's biological status that reveals the distinctive nature of that person's problems. Likewise, unlike clinical researchers, we do not need large sets of measures that reveal average differences across treatment groups in the progress of a specific disease or condition. Instead, survey researchers need measures of health that are plain, comparable, concise, general, and common. We describe the five types of health measures used in surveys: individual reports of subjective health, physical impairment, vitality and well-being, diagnosis of serious chronic disease, and expected longevity. We describe the strengths and weaknesses of each type of measure, and show how each correlates with education. Health, by any definition and by any measure, increases with the level of education.

Chapter 3 describes the relationships among *education, personal control, lifestyle, and health.* We restate our view that education improves health because it increases effective agency, enhancing a sense of personal control that encourages and enables a healthy lifestyle. We begin the chapter by reviewing the theory of human capital and its relationship to education. Formal education develops skills and abilities of general value. An individual who acquires an education can use it to solve a wide range of problems. Some are the problems of productivity that concern employers and economists. Some are problems in which economic prosperity is one of several means toward a more basic end. Health is one of those basic ends.

Next in Chapter 3 we describe how education helps individuals to design and assemble a healthy lifestyle, summarizing the beneficial effects of education on smoking, exercise, overweight, and drinking. Education encourages and helps individuals to assemble a set of habits and ways that are not necessarily related except as effective means toward health. Purposeful individuals weave together a healthy lifestyle from otherwise incoherent or diametric practices allocated by subcultural forces. Usually, individuals tend to do whatever others like them do, particularly if it distinguishes the people they identify with from the ones they do not. Some of those things make health better and some make it worse. For example, men exercise more frequently than women, but women restrict body weight more closely than men; young adults smoke more than older adults, but also exercise more. Individuals putting together a healthy lifestyle must adopt the healthy habits of men and women, young and old. In doing so they create positive correlations among traits that otherwise are unrelated or even negatively correlated.

In the rest of Chapter 3 we show how the sense of control over one's own life links education to a healthy lifestyle. We define what we mean by the sense of control, showing how we measure it and how it relates to other concepts such as locus of control, self-efficacy, helplessness, and subjective alienation. The sense of personal control is a learned, generalized expectation that outcomes are contingent on one's own choices and actions. We describe how education boosts the sense of control, and how that in turn shapes a healthy lifestyle. We present statistical models integrating these elements and showing how they articulate to connect education to health.

Chapter 4 details the complex of relationships among *education, socioeconomic status, and health*. In it we show how education acts as the preeminent aspect of social status that affects health. The chapter has two main parts, detailing education's impact on health through economic resources and through productive activities. In the first section, on economic resources, we begin by describing important aspects of education's effect on household income. Notably, the average increase in household income associated with an additional year of education gets larger at higher levels of education. In our data the average household income increases by an additional 11 percent for each additional year of education. We think this compounding exists because each newly acquired ability multiplies the effectiveness of previously acquired ones. Empirically, education increases household income largely by increasing the likelihood of employment and of marriage (often to someone who is employed), and by increasing both personal earnings and other household income.

Although education's effect on income compounds, income's effect on health follows a law of diminishing returns. Additional income of, say, $5,000 improves the average level of health considerably among persons with incomes in the bottom third, but it has little or no effect on health among persons in the top third of household income. As always, each additional dollar makes the biggest difference to individuals who get the fewest dollars. We argue that education's interaction with income accounts for much of income's diminishing incremental effect. Education moderates the effect of income on health. Higher education reduces the harm associated with lower income and conversely reduces the health gains from higher income. In essence, the well-educated tend to be healthy regardless of income. Because persons with high incomes tend to be well-educated, differences among them in income have little effect on health. On the other end, persons with low incomes tend to have low levels of education, leaving them more vulnerable to the health effects of differences in income. This is an example of what we call structural amplification, a phenomenon that Chapter 6 describes in detail.

Chapter 4 goes on to show how education operates as an effective substitute for income on multiple levels. Economic hardship, in the form of difficulty paying bills and buying food, clothes, medical care, or other household necessities, mediates much of lower income's association with poorer health. Education moderates the effect of income on economic hardship. The well-educated tend to avoid economic hardship at all levels of income. Low income increases the risk of economic hardship mostly among the poorly educated. Once again, we see a pattern of structural amplification. Low education makes individuals more likely to have low income and less able to avoid economic hardship given low income.

Household composition partly explains why low income creates greater economic hardship for the poorly educated than for the well-educated. Other things being equal, persons raising children and persons without partners experience more economic hardship at any given level of income. The combination, raising children without a partner, greatly magnifies the risk of economic hardship. By our estimates, an unmarried person raising a family needs 2.3 time more income than two married persons raising the same number of children in order to have the same low risk of economic hardship. Better-educated individuals generally have fewer children and begin raising them later in life when jobs are more secure and better paid and relationships are more mature and stable.

We continue Chapter 4's section on economic resources by arguing that material privation and risky exposures probably account for only part of the effects that low income and economic hardship have on health. In wealthy countries such as the United States, few families go without the basic minimum of food, clothing, and shelter needed to stay alive and functioning, even when experiencing economic hardship. When extreme privation does occur it generally comes and goes as an episode rather than forming a persistent damaging and lethal status. More commonly, low income and economic hardship limit housing options to dilapidated buildings, frequently in squalid and threatening neighborhoods. We list many ways that personal and neighborhood poverty expose individuals to biological, chemical, and physical risks of illness, disease, and impairment. Economic hardship, however, typically means something other than a leaky roof or rats in the walls. Even for the great majority of adults in their comfortable homes and decent neighborhoods, economic hardship is a taste of inadequacy and failure laced with a threat that what one has may be lost. Biomedical research shows that threatening situations produce physiological responses that impair health in several ways: by creating symptoms experienced as illness, by increasing susceptibility to pathogens and pathological conditions, and by accelerating the degradation of critical physiological systems. Economic hardship poses a direct threat to the

well-being of oneself and one's family. As a result, people exposed to economic hardship probably experience frequent, intense, and prolonged activation of the physiological stress response, with negative consequences for
their health.

We go on to argue in Chapter 4 that greater access to medical care does
not account for the association of economic well-being with better health.
We argue that health is not a commodity that can be sold or bought.
Although difficulty paying for medicine or medical care is one indication
of the economic hardship that erodes health, it is the hardship and the circumstances that give rise to it, rather than the lack of medical care, that
cause the health problems. Aggregate measures of health such as life
expectancy or infant mortality mostly depend on social and economic
resources such as average levels of education and gross domestic product
per capita rather than on the prevalence of medical resources such as doctors and hospitals per capita. Many countries such as Great Britain and
Canada instituted national health care systems providing universal access
to treatment. Doing so reversed the social gradient in the use of services,
but did not reduce the socioeconomic gradient in health and survival.
Despite the absence of universal medical coverage in the United States,
lower-status Americans also now use more medical services than higher-
status individuals do. In the United States as well as elsewhere, this has
not diminished socioeconomic differences in health.

Like it or not, health is not something that can be bought. People cannot
just buy medical services that make them and their families healthy. Businesses cannot just buy medical services that make their employees healthy.
Governments cannot just buy medical services that make their citizens
healthy. Some of the clearest evidence of this comes from research examining the effect of medical insurance on health. Perhaps the best kept secret
of American health science is that having medical insurance does not
measurably improve health. The existing studies compare individuals in
three broad categories: those with private medical insurance provided as
a benefit of current or past employment (including the spouse's) or purchased directly (including supplements to Medicare), those with public
insurance from Medicaid (which goes primarily to the poor or medically
indigent) or Medicare (available to seniors) with no private supplement,
and no medical insurance. All of the studies find essentially the same
thing. People with private medical insurance have the best health, those
with only public medical insurance have the worst, and those with no
medical insurance are in between but close to the privately insured. This
pattern holds for the full range of health measures, from subjective health
to mortality rates.

The better health seen among individuals with private medical insurance results entirely from their high levels of education, employment,

marriage, and economic well-being, which preserve and improve health directly and also increase the likelihood of having private medical insurance. Our results find no differences between those with private medical insurance and those with no medical insurance in their changes in subjective health, physical impairment, and diagnosed chronic conditions over a three-year period. In other words, private medical insurance shows no sign of preserving or improving health. The one benefit of medical insurance that we could find is that it helps protect the household from economic hardship. That small and indirect beneficial effect is not large enough to account for a significant share of the effects that education and income have on health.

We end Chapter 4's section on economic resources by looking at the sense of control as a mediator and amplifier of income's effect on health. Money cannot buy health, but it can reinforce a sense of control that encourages healthy behavior and makes things seem less threatening. Not surprisingly, greater household income increases the sense of directing and regulating one's own life. A sense of control over one's own life improves health two ways. The most important is that it encourages efforts to find ways of staying healthy. When people feel effective and able, they believe they can find things to do that will create a long and healthy life. That in turn encourages them to discover healthy ways of living and to change themselves and their lives to be healthier. The second way a sense of control improves health is by making life seem less threatening. In humans, perceived threats to well-being, status, self-esteem, marriage, friendship, and so on stimulate the body's response to physical attack. Individuals with a firm sense of control feel confident of their ability to judge risks accurately and deal with threats effectively. Events and situations seem more benign to individuals who believe they can avoid most problems and correct or manage the rest. Other things being equal, that perception reduces the triggering of physiological alarm.

Health and the sense of control have what causal analysts call a deviation-amplifying reciprocal effect. A strong sense of control improves health and functioning, and good health and functioning strengthen the sense of control. Unfortunately this works both ways. A weak sense of control degrades health and functioning, which further weakens the sense of control. Over time these reciprocal effects push individuals in different directions. That has two consequences. It enlarges the differences among individuals in health and in the sense of control. It also increasingly combines poor health with a low sense of control in some individuals and good health with a high sense of control in others. The deviation-amplifying reciprocal effect enlarges the disparity among individuals while making some of them the beneficiaries of multiple advantages and others the bearers of multiple disadvantages.

Economic well-being forms a major link between education and health, but the nature of that connection is not what it might seem. Ability and effectiveness create the link, more than money itself. Income enhances the ability to achieve ends, but the well-educated with low income can achieve the same outcomes through other means. Economic resources and economic well-being constitute a major path from education to health. They in turn link to education through employment, occupation, and work, which influence health through additional pathways.

The second part of Chapter 4 looks at productive activities as links between education and health. The biggest misconception about social status and health is that money is what counts. Paid work contributes to health in various ways. Higher levels of education lead to jobs that are more rewarding in themselves, as well as better paid. Moreover, higher education changes the nature of pay from compensation for sacrificed autonomy to reward for productive creativity. Prosperity, autonomy, and creativity all contribute to health, and all characterize the work of the well-educated.

We begin the section on productive activities by describing the four kinds of measures social scientists use when studying productive activities. *Employment status* refers to categories of labor force participation or nonparticipation: employed full-time, employed part-time, keeping house, retired, unable to work because of a disability, temporarily unemployed or laid off, in school, in the military, or in an institution (generally a prison or asylum). Individuals with paid jobs or looking for paid jobs (other than the military) are considered in the labor force. *Occupations* are official categories of paid activity with distinctive requirements and demands, such as cook, elementary school teacher, medical assistant, or cab driver. *Occupational status* generally refers to the occupation's prestige implied by the average levels of education and income of persons in the occupation. More broadly, occupations are graded along a variety of dimensions that describe aggregate conditions, such as the typical degree of danger, physical labor, environmental extremes, repetitiveness, closeness of supervision, or complexity of work with people, data, or things. *Work* is an activity directed toward production or accomplishment. The work a person does may pay well, poorly, or not at all. It may be varied, engaging, and enjoyable, or repetitious, tedious, and oppressive. It can be high, low, or middling in a chain of command, or not in one at all. Most importantly, work can be self-expressing, or self-suppressing. Some people see work as the things they would not do if they did not have to. Others see it as they way they create things of value.

In the rest of Chapter 4 we detail the relationship of education and health to each measure of productive activity, beginning with employment status. Education brings more people into the labor force, and keeps more people in, at the highest level of participation: full-time employment. The increases in full-time employment across levels of education require corresponding decreases in the other categories. Three other categories account for most of those decreases: keeping house, unemployment, and inability to work. Education's positive impact on full-time employment and negative impact on unemployment combine to reduce the unemployment rate, which is the fraction of persons in the labor market but not currently employed.

Full-time employment and better health go together, but why? There are two possibilities: causation and selection. In causation, something about employment status affects health. For example, full-time employment may promote health through economic well-being and independence, personal development, and healthier lifestyle. In selection, health influences the employment status individuals can be in or choose to be in. In our research we find evidence of both causation and selection in the relationship between employment and health. We find that full-time employment helps to create and maintain the higher levels of health and functioning that make full-time employment more likely and more stable. Employment in the United States today typically does *not* act like a "meat grinder," taking in healthy young workers, wearing them out at an accelerated rate, and then ejecting them old and used-up before their time. Employment and health have something like a symbiotic relationship: each helps create the conditions beneficial to the other.

Next we describe occupation as a link between education and health. The more arduous, dangerous, and unpleasant an occupation, the lower the average education of persons doing it for a living. Even so, differences in those qualities of occupations account for very little of the differences in health across levels of education. Partly that is because hazardous occupations often require physical activity that benefits health. Mostly, though, it reflects the success of occupational health and safety regulations and practices. Even though some occupations are much riskier than others, the overall levels of occupational risk are so low that differences in health associated with occupations generally vanish against the background of health differences created by other socioeconomic forces. Workplaces today are remarkably safe. While some of this reflects the shift from industrial to service occupations, much of it reflects the precautions taken in stable, indoor work sites such as factories, warehouses, stores, hospitals, and offices. In terms of fatalities, today's twenty riskiest occupations mostly involve outdoor work at changing locations using vehicles or power tools. Today's factories and offices create so little risk to life that, for most occupations, the workers face greater risks to life at home, and much greater risks on the way to and from home.

We find that, with one exception, the qualities of occupations measured by the federal government do not account for differences among workers in their health after adjustment for individual qualities such as age, sex, education, earnings, household income, and history of unemployment and economic hardship. We find only one occupational attribute that consistently predicts individual differences in health, apparently because it measures the occupational constraints on individual productive creativity: the percentage of workers in an occupation who must perform repetitive work, doing the same thing according to a set procedure, sequence, or pace.

We conclude the section on productive activities by describing the qualities of work that promote health: autonomy and creativity. Work is physical or mental effort or activity directed toward the production or accomplishment of something. Employment is paid work. Employment almost always trades some degree of freedom for income. In a market economy everyone needs money to get things they require or want, and most people must work for the money. The balance in that trade depends as much on the amount of freedom given up, and the burden of the work, as it does on the pay. Often when people think of the burden of work they think of time spent, physical and mental strain endured, risk taken, and harm suffered. The true burden lies in the denial of self-expression and the inhibition of autonomous action—the stifling of free will. Humans need to work, and not just because they need the money. Directing physical and mental effort toward production and accomplishment is to humans what running is to horses. Work is so deeply enmeshed in our species' mode of survival that humans do it in the absence of immediate need, like a riderless horse galloping for no reason except the desire to run and the joy of doing it. Humans take pleasure in work, and must do it to be whole, hale, and healthy. The burden of employment results from the loss of independent choice and self-generated action. Education lifts this burden. It minimizes the loss of independence, maximizes the opportunity for creative self-expression, and transforms pay from compensation for surrendered freedom to reward for productive accomplishment.

We end Chapter 4 by stating our four main conclusions about socioeconomic status and health. First, health does benefit from economic well-being. Destitution, privation, and the exposures and strains of dilapidated housing in decaying and threatening neighborhoods account for some of the health problems found near the bottom of the economic ladder. Far more of it comes from repeated or prolonged economic hardship, which undermines health by evoking dread and hopelessness, stimulating physiological responses felt as sickness that also reduce the effectiveness of the immune system and degrade other critical systems through a variety of mechanisms. Second, education greatly moderates the association between economic resources and health. The effectiveness learned through education, and the confidence based on that effectiveness, operate as an alternative resource that substitutes for money if money is in short supply. Higher levels of education make individuals less dependent on money for solutions to their problems while also reducing the likelihood of problems and increasing the reserves and flows of money available to address them. Third, money cannot buy health. Some amount of money is necessary, but no amount is sufficient. Health is not a commodity. No product or service one can buy will provide it. Individuals who deliberately try to prevent health problems generally will be healthier than those who let the problems develop and then rely on medical intervention for remedies. Finally, productive self-expression nourishes health. Creative work challenges the mind, exercising and developing it. Education makes workers better able to find engaging, enjoyable, and challenging things to do that others reward.

Chapter 5 looks at *education, interpersonal relationships, and health*. We begin the chapter by documenting the positive effect of education on marriage and social support. Education increases the probability of being married, largely by decreasing the probability of being divorced. The better-educated also have a lower probability of being widowed by any given age because their partners tend to be better-educated too and thus live longer. The well-educated enjoy greater marital stability because they marry later in adulthood under more favorable economic conditions, and because they have happier and more satisfying marriages. The well-educated have more supportive and equitable relationships than those with less education because schooling helps partners understand and negotiate with each other, see more than one side of an issue, and respond flexibly with attempts to understand the other's position and to arrange something that is mutually satisfactory. In addition, education helps individuals avoid the interpersonal strains produced by economic hardship. Education increases household income, but also reduces economic hardship substantially for other reasons too. In particular, the better-educated delay parenthood and have smaller families, and also manage better within the limits of the household's income.

Marriage protects health and decreases mortality rates. Compared to married people, the single, divorced, and widowed have more physical health problems, including more acute conditions, chronic conditions, days of disability, physical impairment, poor subjective health, and higher mortality rates from coronary heart disease, stroke, pneumonia, many kinds of cancer, cirrhosis of the liver, automobile accidents, homicide, and suicide, all of which are leading causes of death. Why does marriage improve health? Lower economic hardship seems to be the main reason. Married persons have higher household income and lower rates of economic hardship at any given level of household income, particularly when there are dependent children in the household. Married persons also have greater perceived social support, which indirectly improves health by reducing depression and anxiety. They also have a more orderly lifestyle than the nonmarried, which benefits their health. Married persons are less likely to smoke and to drink heavily, and the men in particular are less likely to go out to bars, get in fights, drive drunk, drive too fast, take illegal drugs, engage in risky sports, get in trouble with the law, or be sexually promiscuous. Unfortunately, married persons do not exercise or control body weight as much as others, which cancels some of the health benefits of marriage. Married persons do go to the doctor for checkups and screening tests more regularly than others, but there is no indication that doing so improves their health much. Overall, the health benefits of marriage mostly come from improved economic well-being and a safe and orderly lifestyle.

In Chapter 6 we describe education's heath effects relating to *age and cumulative advantage*. Education's varied and enduring consequences produce health advantages for the better educated that accumulate and grow over the life course. To fully understand education's positive impact on health one must envision that benefit unfolding across the lifetime. Education's health-related effects are present at every age. They accumulate and compound over a lifetime, producing ever larger health differences between persons with different levels of education who entered adulthood about the same time. A cumulative advantage is a benefit acquired by successive addition. Education's cumulative health advantage rests on three underlying phenomena: permeation, accumulation, and amplification. In the other chapters of this book we discuss a range of things influenced by education that in turn affect health, including habits, interpersonal relationships, family responsibilities, employment, occupational exposures and opportunities, economic sufficiency and security, neighborhood qualities, autonomous and creative activities, and a sense of controlling one's own life. In Chapter 6 we define and describe the other two forces behind education's cumulative advantages: accumulation and amplification.

Accumulation refers to gathering many smaller effects into a larger one. Some accumulations benefit health and others harm it. Education tends to speed or advance the beneficial accumulations and slow or delay the detrimental ones. Accumulation occurs when consequences, once present, tend to stay present. The health-related consequences of education accumulate on many levels. We give examples from the socioeconomic (job experience and seniority, percentage pay raises, wealth) and behavioral (habits such as smoking or exercising, beliefs such as perceived control over one's own life, personal relationships) to the biological (body fat, blood pressure levels, cholesterol levels, insulin resistance, aerobic capacity, joint deterioration, arterial fatty plaque) The socioeconomic and behavioral accumulations necessarily influence health through biological mechanisms. Some undesirable biological accumulations get defined as diseases or medical conditions when they progress beyond a clearly dangerous point. Some undesirable accumulations eventually provoke damaging and deadly crises such as embolism, fibrillation, heart failure, infarction, hemorrhage, stroke, shock, or respiratory arrest.

Most of the better-understood biological accumulators influenced by education reflect elements of health lifestyle such as smoking, diet, and exercise. However differences in the levels of stress over the lifetime probably influence biological accumulators directly apart from health lifestyle. As used here, the word "stress" refers to a specific neuroendocrine reaction, called the stress response, to external events or conditions, called stressors. Much current biobehavioral research examines "allostatic load," which is the impact of intense, recurring, or chronic stress on neuroendocrine accumulators that influence health. The changes represent learned, habitual responses of the hypothalamus-pituitary-adrenal axis that expose the entire body to hormones such as epinephrine, aldosterone, and cortisol. That exposure over time affects the state of accumulators such as resting blood pressure, body fat, and insulin resistance. Education reduces allostatic load by giving individuals the skills, resources, standing, and confidence to master their own lives and cope with its challenges effectively and efficiently.

Education's amplifying effects form the third element of cumulative advantage. In Chapter 6 we next describe how those consequences often influence each other or regulate each other's effects on health. Feedback amplification occurs when the current state of a system produces effects that lead to more changes in the same direction. For example, body fat makes individuals less inclined to exercise, and the less they exercise the faster they accumulate fat. On the other hand, regular exercise slows the accumulation of fat, and a trimmer body makes exercise more enjoyable. Over time, deviation-amplifying feedback has two effects. First, the differences among individuals grow. Second, the beneficial accumulations get increasingly paired in some individuals, whereas their detrimental opposites get increasingly paired in others.

The feedback between physical functioning and the sense of control over one's own life amplifies one of the most important links between education and health. A low sense of control increases the accumulation of impairments, and impairments decrease the sense of control. That "double-negative" feedback magnifies over the life course the advantage in sense of control and in physical functioning enjoyed by the better-educated. It increasingly concentrates good physical functioning and a firm sense of personal control together in the better-educated, while concentrating physical impairment and a weak sense of control together in the less well-educated. It also amplifies the effects of short-term random shocks to each of the two accumulators. The effects of psychosocial crises such as layoffs, bouts of unemployment, or episodes of economic hardship get enlarged when a weaker sense of control slackens the brakes on the accumulation of physical impairment, further degrading the sense of control. Likewise, the effects of health crises such as injuries, infections, flareups of chronic diseases, and critical events such as heart attacks and strokes get enlarged when the increased physical impairment undermines the sense of control, thereby undermining efforts to lessen or reverse the resulting physical impairment.

Next in Chapter 6 we detail the phenomenon of structural amplification, which is summarized in earlier chapters. Problems faced by the poorly educated more often than by the well-educated frequently also degrade health more severely for the poorly educated. Often the same thing that would make a situation less destructive also helps individuals to avoid or escape the situation, so it is not common among those in the situation. Conversely, the same thing that makes a situation more destructive often leads individuals to be in it, multiplying the damage. Higher education helps individuals to avoid risky situations and, failing that, to get out of them sooner while limiting the harm done when in them.

Education makes individuals more resourceful in two senses of the word. It makes them better at acquiring whatever they need, and better at improvising with what they have. Education makes individuals more adept at what we call resource substitution, which means using one thing in place of another, and finding ways to achieve ends with whatever materials, relationships, and circumstances present themselves. Resource substitution and the structural amplification of disadvantage are, in many ways, opposite faces of the same phenomenon. A capacity for resource substitution makes the absence of any one standard resource less harmful for the better-educated. Conversely, lower education leaves individuals less adept at acquiring and inventing resources, increasing the individual's dependence on each standard resource.

Structural amplifiers often stack up in cascading sequences. The capacity for resource substitution helps the better-educated to avert problems or ameliorate outcomes at each step. In contrast, the relative lack of resources and resourcefulness among the poorly educated exacerbates the outcomes at each step.

The same resources and resourcefulness that can soften the impact of difficult but avoidable circumstances can soften the impact of unavoidable or random ones too. Even though a particular risk to health may be unavoidable, and perhaps even equally common across levels of education, its effects still will be worst among the poorly educated. That adds to the concentration of problems among the poorly educated, often setting in motion deviation-amplifying feedback and cascading structural amplification that further concentrate problems.

We end Chapter 6 by stating our view on a current scientific debate about whether the effect of social status on health diminishes in old age. Some researchers and theorists think that differences in socioeconomic status get smaller in old age as the average levels of income and wealth decline. Smaller differences in income and wealth in old age would seem to imply smaller education-based differences in health. We point out that, contrary to what many believe, the amount of inequality in income and wealth does not get smaller in old age in the United States. Social Security income exerts some equalizing effect, but not enough to overcome the differences based on savings, investments, private pensions (often keyed to peak lifetime earnings), and government-sponsored programs such as IRA and 401k plans that allow tax-deferred saving. Some individuals also assume that Medicare and similar programs reduce health inequalities in old age by assuring access to needed medical care for all retirees. Supposedly that somehow counteracts the cumulative differences in health resulting from a lifetime of differences in exposures, behaviors, incidents, and stress. That expects a lot, and there is little reason to think Medicare does or ever could meet those expectations.

Social scientists often assume that biological forces of senescence take over in old age, making the social forces that operated over the lifetime less important to health. Most young persons enjoy good health, and most old ones bear disease and disability, seemingly regardless of their socioeconomic status. Nevertheless, among seniors of the same age, the ones with lower levels of education have declined in health longer and farther. Current biological theories and studies of senescence imply that the differences among individuals in cellular-level biological decline increase with the age of the survivors. The most important biological aging clock ticks at a variable speed determined by the rate at which cells and tissues must repair themselves. The process has three properties: it acts as an accumulator on the level of molecules, cells, and tissues; it is advanced by disease and in turn eventually increases susceptibility to disease, thereby creating deviation-amplifying feedback; and it makes individuals with a history of exposures and problems more susceptible to the acquisition, progression, and debilitation of disease, thereby structurally amplifying health disadvantages. Given all we know, it seems likely the biological aging clock ticks faster for the poorly educated, making them biologically older than the well-educated who were born about the same time.

Researchers sometimes mistake the historical trend toward bigger effects of education on health for a decline in education's effect in old age. The rising breadth and quality of knowledge makes education more useful and effective. The oldest Americans lived their lives when humankind knew less about staying prosperous and healthy. Under those circumstances education had less of a positive effect on health throughout life.

That is one reason why the effect of education might be smaller among the very old even though it continues to increase as they grow older. The advantages or disadvantages in health associated with level of education accumulate during all of adulthood, over many areas of life, and at all levels of organization from the socioeconomic down to the molecular. Education's pervasive, accumulating, and amplifying effects create the cumulative advantages and disadvantages in health that emerge and grow over the lifetime.

Chapter 7 takes a critical look at four *specious views of education*. In the chapter we contrast our view of education as learned effectiveness with four alternatives: education as credential, as reproducer of inequality, as false satisfier, and as spurious correlate. The four critical and disparaging views of education share one element in common that distinguishes them from the human-capital view. They deny that education's apparent benefits result from the productive skills and habits of general value that people learn in school.

The credentialist view maintains that education produces an artificial effect. It has real consequences, but only as a mark of status. Education's effect is purely symbolic, acting as a token that opens social gates, and not by imparting anything of inherent and general usefulness related to worker performance. According to credentialists, persons in power control access to lucrative jobs, choose which credentials to demand for access, and favor credentials that distinguish persons similar to themselves from others. Gatekeepers require academic credentials in order to reserve the best positions for persons like themselves.

Another set of critics portrays education as a reproducer of inequality that merely copies social status from one generation to the next. They argue that the educational system encourages and promotes children based on signs of family social status, and trains them to accept their status and behave in ways appropriate to it. Marxist and neo-Marxist scholars often emphasize education's relatively explicit tracking according to social class. They say that school policies and personnel reproduce the inequality by sorting, segregating, labeling, tracking, and differentially socializing students according to social origins. Schools train upper- and middle-class students to be independent, creative, and ambitious, while training the lower- and working-class ones to be obedient, punctual, quiet, and submissive. In doing so, education empowers students from high social class origins but oppresses those from working-class and lower-class backgrounds, thus reinforcing the status quo.

Post-Marxist European social criticism also portrays formal education as a system for reproducing inequality that imparts nothing truly productive. However, it emphasizes the affinity that individuals of similar status have for each other because of shared culture, rather than the domination of one class by another as a result of conflicting economic interests. Implicit tracking occurs when high-status individuals and their cultural agents in the academic world select and promote students based on interests and activities cultivated in the family and consistent with those of high-status adults in general. The educational system merely selects and promotes prestigious cultural interests learned at home. Cultural capital embodies the culture of the dominant class: its behavior, habits, tastes, lifestyles, and attitudes. Cultural self-development requires time and money, so the resulting knowledge and ability act as forms of conspicuous consumption. Much of cultural capital's social value results from its apparent lavish impracticality. Because the possession of this cultural capital is a sign of being from a higher social status, children from high-status families get rewarded by teachers and encouraged at school. As a result they do well in school, complete high school, and go on to college.

A third view of education sees it as a system for getting members of all social strata to accept their relatively advantaged or disadvantaged positions. American society justifies inequality by reference to individual ability and effort. The system of formal education persuades members of all social strata to accept the inequality in autonomy, authority, income, wealth, and quality of life as proper and fitting. Schools do not have to exhort students to accept their advantages or disadvantages. The process itself carries the message, to the extent that the desirability of the jobs individuals get is proportional to the length and difficulty of their studies and the quality of their grades. In the critical view, the educational system produces acceptance of inequality even though the academic competition is unfair and irrelevant to the skills needed in the desirable jobs, and even though the best jobs get rewarded out of proportion to the value they produce.

A fourth set of critics argue that the length of schooling reflects an unmeasured factor that produces education's seemingly beneficial effects. Portrayed as a spurious correlate, educational attainment merely stands in for the unseen factor that actually produces the benefits. Critics of education speculate on a variety of possible hidden factors. Some argue that the real determinants of success are family *social* origins. In such views, wealthier and more powerful families send their children to school longer, embed them in more influential and privileged networks, get them more enjoyable and lucrative positions, and transfer wealth to them. Others argue that family *genetic* origins determine both educational attainment and adulthood outcomes. The competition for educational attainment reveals the genetically preordained intelligence that really produces what seem to be education's beneficial consequences.

After rebutting the critical views we try to explain why so many social scientists might want to argue that education imparts nothing of intrinsic effectiveness. We trace the critical views of education to discoveries made in the 1960s and 1970s. Research in that period found that educational attainment predicted subsequent occupational status, personal earnings, and household income among U.S. males, apparently acting both as a main avenue of upward mobility and as the nearly exclusive link between the social status of one generation and the next. Critics of social inequality often saw these findings as implicit justification for the social and economic inequalities that exist. If education develops abilities that enable individuals to achieve better outcomes, then the resulting inequality might seem inevitable, functional, and fair. The wish to delegitimize social and economic inequality stimulated attempts to discredit education's real value, portraying it instead as a system of channels and barriers that at most teach acceptance of and conformity to one's rank.

Attempts to discredit education generally presume that education's value lies in providing access to lucrative social positions. They erroneously equate money with well-being and disadvantage with dispossession. The money fallacy is that earnings, income, and wealth are the sole or central aspects of prosperity. In our research we repeatedly find that money is only one means of achieving well-being and health, and generally not the most powerful one. By developing effective skills and habits, education develops the capacity for resource substitution. Resourceful individuals with little income or wealth find other means toward fulfillment and health. The zero-sum fallacy is that the benefits enjoyed disproportionately by some individuals ultimately must come from others who have been deprived of those benefits. In the zero-sum view, the prosperity, well-being, and health enjoyed by better-educated individuals must somehow create the distress, impairment, disease, and early death disproportionately suffered by the poorly educated. That view has little basis in fact. The historical improvements in life expectancy show that all social strata can rise together, and typically do.

In the end, we argue that education is the solution to the problem of social disadvantage, not the source of it. In the long run, formal education provides the most likely solution to the health problems later in life associated with being from a disadvantaged family. A person's own educational attainment overcomes the harmful effects of disadvantaged origins. Education improves health because it makes individuals more effective, increasing personal control over their own lives. Formal schooling develops real skills and abilities that make individuals resourceful and capable of achieving many things, including health. It produces desirable outcomes partly by developing intellectual skills, but also by developing other effective traits. Formal education cultivates and promotes awareness, openness, creativity, and self-discipline. It instills habits of exploration, reflection, judgment, practice, and design. Such traits and habits constitute much of the resourcefulness behind the phenomenon of resource substitution. The lifelong improvements in health associated with higher educational attainment are greatest for individuals from low-status backgrounds. Unfortunately, this also means that the same students most inclined to drop out of school will suffer the most harm from living with little education. Individuals from lower-status backgrounds depend more on their own educational attainments for control over their own lives. The knowledge, skill, and resourcefulness developed through formal schooling give them independence, well-being, and health they otherwise would find extremely difficult to achieve. Any solution to the problem of disadvantaged origins lies in the direction of raising the levels of education in successive generations, particularly for low-status families.

| 1 |

Education As Learned Effectiveness

A great deal of evidence suggests that educational attainment leads to better health. Education increases physical functioning and subjective health among adults of all ages, and decreases morbidity, impairment, and mortality. Few social scientists studying health would find reason to doubt that educational attainment improves health. The question is how.

How does education foster health? The concept of human capital implies that education improves health because it increases effective agency on the part of individuals. According to the theory we develop in this book, education develops habits, skills, resources, and abilities that enable people to achieve a better life. To the extent that people want health, education develops the means toward creating that end through a lifestyle that promotes health. Thus health is not just a lucky but unintended consequence of the economic prosperity that is contingent on education. In this book we extend human capital theory beyond the economic concerns of productivity and wages to individual health. We develop and test our theory of "education as learned effectiveness." We propose that education enables people to coalesce health-producing behaviors into a coherent lifestyle, and that a sense of control over outcomes in one's own life encourages a healthy lifestyle and conveys much of education's effect.

Some research on socioeconomic status and health uses education and income as interchangeable indicators of socioeconomic status. In contrast, we argue that education and income indicate different underlying concepts. Schooling means something apart from socioeconomic status. According to a human-capital perspective of learned effectiveness, education indicates the accumulated knowledge, skills, and resources acquired in school. Income indicates economic resources available to people. Both likely affect health, but for different reasons. Further, education and income are not on the same causal level, so combining them obscures processes. Education is the key to people's position in the stratification system; it decreases the likelihood of being unemployed and gives people access to good jobs with high incomes. Part of education's effect on health may be mediated by economic resources, but most is not. Some researchers think that education as important to health mostly because it provides high incomes. We present a different view.

EDUCATION, LEARNED EFFECTIVENESS, AND HEALTH

Education is a root cause of good health. Education gives people the resources to control and shape their own lives in a way that protects and fosters health. The more years of schooling people have, the greater their stock of human capital—the productive capacity developed, embodied, and stocked in human beings themselves. Schooling builds skills and abilities that people can use to achieve a better life. To the extent that people want good health, education develops the means toward creating that end through a lifestyle that promotes health. A large part of the reason the well-educated experience good health is that they engage in a lifestyle that includes walking, exercising, drinking moderately, and avoiding over-weight and smoking. High levels of personal control among the well-educated account for much of the reason they engage in a healthy lifestyle.

The skills learned in school increase effective agency. In this book we will develop our ideas about "education as learned effectiveness." Learned effectiveness is the opposite of learned helplessness. People who feel helpless see little connection between their actions and important outcomes in their lives, they think there is not much they can do to improve their situation, so they lack motivation and persistence and are likely to give up. Education helps people avoid feelings of helplessness by providing resources that reduce actual helplessness and increase effectiveness. These resources are not mostly external to people, like money; instead they are resources that inhere in the people themselves. Education gives people a sense of control over their lives that increases the motivation to attempt to solve problems and increases their success in doing so. Good health is important to most people. Education helps people achieve the goal of good health. Education is associated with physical well-being—with feeling healthy, energetic, and fit, avoiding physical impairment and chronic diseases, and escaping frequent backaches, headaches, being in pain, or feeling run-down and tired.

According to our view of "education as learned effectiveness," schooling builds real skills, abilities, and resources that ultimately shape health and well-being. Education develops general cognitive skills. On the most general level, education teaches people to learn. Education develops the habits and skills of communication: reading, writing, inquiring, discussing, looking things up, and figuring things out. It develops analytic skills of broad use such as mathematics, logic, and, on a more basic level, observing, experimenting, summarizing, synthesizing, interpreting, classifying, and so on. Because education develops the ability to gather and interpret information and to solve problems on many levels, it increases control over events and outcomes in life. Moreover, in education, one encounters and solves problems that are progressively more difficult, complex, and subtle. The process of learning builds problem-solving skills and confidence in the ability to solve problems. Education instills the habit of meeting problems with attention, thought, action, and persistence. In school people learn to work hard, to plan, to be self-motivated, responsible, and not to give up. Even if the knowledge learned in school had no practical value, the process of learning builds the confidence, motivation, and self-assurance needed to attempt to solve problems. Thus, education increases effort and ability, the fundamental components of problem-solving effectiveness. The process of learning builds the confidence and self-assurance needed to *attempt* to solve problems, and it builds general cognitive skills such as thinking, analyzing, and communicating needed to *successfully* solve problems. These skills increase effectiveness in all aspects of life. In higher education, people also learn specific skills like chemistry, foreign languages, engineering, social work, geology, psychology, business, and nursing. This is where the general means of solving problems are tailored to a specific set of problems. Education develops the ability to solve problems on all these levels. The ability to solve problems increases one's control over life.

Education is a resource that inheres in the person. The ability to learn, to be persistent, to communicate successfully, to search out and use information, or to figure out the cause of a problem and solve it are things that nobody can take away. No one can take away your ability to make a better life for yourself. Education puts control in the hands of people themselves. Control does not rest in the hands of others. A paycheck, a welfare check, or a social security check is not a resource that is part of you. Somebody gives it to you, and someone can take it away. As the developmental psychologist Alan Ross wrote about the time he and his family were fleeing Nazi Germany with no material possessions, "All we had with us were the things we had learned, and our ability to learn more" (Ross 1991:191).

Because education is a resource that inheres in the person, it can substitute when other resources are absent. For instance, individuals who are well-educated need less money to fend off economic hardship than those with less education. The principle of resource substitution implies that education will be most valuable to those with few other resources. Of course, the well-educated are more likely to have those other types of resources, like jobs and money, thereby amplifying the health advantages of the well-educated and disadvantages of the poorly educated.

Individual responsibility and structured disadvantage often get contrasted as rival explanations of differences in health. Contemporary health science and popular culture alike put heavy emphasis on behaviors and lifestyles. Researchers who see health as a function of a social structure that allocates resources unequally (Crawford 1986) sometimes criticize the view that health is determined by lifestyle characteristics such as exercise and smoking (Knowles 1977). Such critics rightly argue that emphasizing insight and choice while ignoring means and circumstance blames individuals for their own health problems while ignoring the systematic limitations and disadvantages that endlessly generate suffering. In our view neither individual choice nor structured limitation can be ignored. An effective theory of health must recognize that many essential elements of health require the personal knowledge, insight, and will of the individual. No one can decide for another whether or not to smoke cigarettes, exercise, or eat a proper diet. Many health scientists view free will as a quaint but misleading concept. None of them has yet invented the drug or written the law that will make individuals do what those individuals must choose to do themselves. In our theory of education as learned effectiveness we argue that a low sense of personal control, smoking, overweight, and a sedentary lifestyle are the means by which the disadvantages faced by persons with little schooling create poor health. Personal control and healthy lifestyle connect educational attainment to health.

EDUCATION AND SOCIOECONOMIC STATUS

Socioeconomic status has four main components that can affect health: education, employment, work, and economic status. The first component, education, includes years of schooling and degrees. It indicates the knowledge, skills, values, and behaviors learned at school, as well as the credentials that structure job opportunities. The second, employment status, differentiates categories of labor, distinguishing among being employed full-time, employed part-time, laid off or unemployed, in school full-time, retired, or keeping house. The third, work characteristics or status, corresponds to various aspects of productive activity. It includes occupational prestige, rank and social class for employed persons, and the conditions and qualities of activity for employed persons and for others. The fourth component, economic status, includes aspects of economic well-being such as personal earnings, household income, and material or economic hardship.

Each element of socioeconomic status should be viewed as distinct, rather than as interchangeable with the others. Socioeconomic status represents general social standing in the relative distribution of opportunities and quality of life. Sometimes researchers measure general social standing by averaging together rank on a number of dimensions such as education, occupational prestige, and household income. That practice obscures two things needed for understanding the relationship of social status to health.

First, the practice of averaging different elements together obscures the differences among aspects of status in their effects on health. More is gained by understanding which aspect of status produces an effect on health. For example some research on socieoconomic status and health uses education and income as interchangeable indicators of socioeconomic status (Williams and Collins 1995). In contrast, we argue that education and income indicate different underlying concepts. Schooling means something apart from socioeconomic status. According to a human-capital perspective of learned effectiveness, education indicates the accumulated knowledge, skills, and resources acquired in school. Education also structures job opportunities (probably because employers prefer workers who can write, analyze, synthesize, plan, communicate, and so on, although some think employers just use college degrees as a social class marker). Income is money. Lack of money could affect health because of the worry or stress associated with not having enough money to pay the bills or buy food, clothes, and other necessities, or it could indicate an inability to get medical services and treatments. If education and income both affect health, it is probably for very different reasons.

Second, the practice of combining indicators obscures the causal relationships among the different aspects of social status. Education, employment, work status, and economic resources occupy ordered positions in a causal chain. To best understand how social differences in health evolve, research should represent the connections among aspects of status, not hide them. Part of education's effect may be mediated by employment and economic status. Higher education gives people access to good jobs with high pay. According to our theory of learned effectiveness, however, education's value to health goes beyond good jobs and economic resources. To understand the processes by which socioeconomic status affects health, education, work, and income must be distinguished and ordered sequentially: education affects the likelihood of being employed and the kind of job a person can get, and employment status and jobs in turn influence income.

Education, employment status, and income are applicable to everybody, but occupational prestige, rank, or status is not. Research that measures socioeconomic status as occupational prestige, status, or rank typically excludes people who are not employed. British researchers first recognized the consequences of social class for health, yet they almost always measured social class with reference to one's occupation. Research that measures socioeconomic status as occupation studies people with paid jobs. Studying people with paid jobs eliminates the most disadvantaged members of society. The exclusion of people not employed for pay severely truncates variation in socioeconomic status and attenuates the effects of educational and economic inequality on health. It can obscure the extent of social differences in health. People who have been fired or laid off, the chronically unemployed, homemakers engaged in unpaid domestic labor, the nonemployed elderly, and so on, are likely the most disadvantaged in valued resources such as health. Furthermore, many of these people are women: almost all homemakers are women, and because women live longer than men, the majority of nonemployed elderly are women. By one estimate 42 percent of British women aged sixteen to sixty-four were excluded from British studies of health and social class (operationalized as occupational rank) because they had no occupation (Carstairs and Morris 1989). Finally, when all three indicators of socioeconomic status are included in predictions of health and mortality, education has the largest effect, followed by income; occupational status is typically insignificant (Kitagawa and Hauser 1973; Williams 1990; Winkleby et al. 1992).

Research on socioeconomic status and health must consider persons outside the paid labor force, as well as paid workers. Almost everyone is doing some kind of work, even if it is not paid: work like cleaning the house, cooking, shopping, doing the dishes, taking care of children or elderly family members, budgeting, making appointments, gardening, or doing volunteer work. We assess the qualities of people's primary daily "work" or activity, paid or not: the amount of autonomy, freedom, fulfillment, enjoyment, opportunity to learn, positive social interaction, routinization, creativity, and so on.

Education is the key to one's place in the stratification system. It shapes employment opportunities and income. Some of the reason the well-educated experience better health than the poorly educated is that they are more likely to be employed full-time rather than part-time or not at all, they have jobs that provide autonomy and the chance to do fulfilling, creative, nonroutine work, and their incomes are higher. Their higher incomes mean that they face less economic hardship in the household, that is, less difficulty paying the bills and paying for food, clothes, and other necessities for their families. Because full-time employment, fulfilling, autonomous, nonroutine work, and the absence of economic hardship are associated with good health, these paths form part of the link between education and health. Part of the reason education is associated with good health is higher socioeconomic status, but most is not.

EDUCATION AS A ROOT CAUSE OF GOOD HEALTH

Educational attainment is a root cause of good health. Education gives people the resources to control and shape their own lives in a way that protects and fosters health. Education boosts people's sense of personal control over their lives, which improves health in large part because it encourages a healthy lifestyle consisting of exercising, walking, drinking moderately, and avoiding smoking and overweight. We propose that a sense of personal control and a healthy lifestyle are the primary links between education and health, but they are not the only links. Education also gives people access to full-time, fulfilling work and high incomes, which help stave off economic hardship. Education further helps people build and maintain supportive relationships and avoid divorce. Socioeconomic advantages and supportive relationships also link education to good health. Thus, all pathways between education and health are positive. If there are consequences of having a college education that negatively impact health we have yet to find them. Because all the pathways between education and health are positive, we could eliminate any one mediator of the relationship between education and health, and the association would still be a positive one.

Yet, health policymakers typically do not view improved access to education as a way to improve the health of the American population. Instead they usually view improved access to medical care as the way to decrease inequality in health (Davis and Rowland 1983), despite the fact that countries with universal access to medical care have large social inequalities in health (Hollingsworth 1981; Marmot, Kogevinas, and Elston 1987). We suggest that policymakers should invest in educators and schools, not just doctors and hospitals, for better health. Unfortunately, money for health (which goes to hospitals, physicians, pharmaceutical companies, and so on) often competes directly with money for schools, especially at the state level. In addition to the obvious benefits of education to knowledge, skills, jobs, wages, economic well-being, and living conditions, broadening educational opportunities for all Americans could also improve health.

To improve the health of the American population by way of education, policymakers must take a long view. Education is a long-term strategy for improving health. If we give young people today opportunities for more and better education, the effect on their health may not be evident until they are in their fifties, sixties, and seventies, when people start to experience serious health problems. The health benefits will likely be great in the long term.

Good health and a long life are unintended consequences of schooling. Universal schooling was implemented in democracies like the United States based on the principle that the public must be informed in order to vote. Literacy is the foundation of democracy. In the United States much of the function of higher education is the development and training of employees with knowledge and skills needed by employers in industrial and postindustrial societies. Proponents of education likely understood the benefits to democracy and the political order; and to employment levels, wages, productivity, and the economic order. It is unlikely that even the proponents of education understood the tremendous health benefits of education.

| 2 |

The Association between
Education and Health

Health, by any definition and by any measure, increases with the level of education. The better-educated generally feel more hale, well, sound, robust, and able. They ail and suffer less often and less severely. Their medical histories show fewer and lesser signs of dysfunction in critical organ systems, and they live longer. In this chapter we define the words "health" and "healthy" as used in common English and in health surveys. We describe the measures of health we use in our surveys, and show how each correlates with level of education. In later chapters we examine a variety of possible reasons for the correlation.

DEFINING HEALTH

The words "health" and "healthy" appear in writings that are among the earliest in the English language, being used much the same a thousand years ago as they are today. Summarizing that long history of usage, the *Oxford English Dictionary* (OED) defines health as

> 1. Soundness of body; that condition in which its functions are duly and efficiently discharged. . . . 2a. By extension, The general condition of the body with respect to the efficient or inefficient discharge of functions: usually qualified as good, bad, weak, delicate, etc. (OED 2000)

The *American Heritage Dictionary* concurs and elaborates, defining health in contemporary American usage as

> 1. The overall condition of an organism at a given time; 2. Soundness, especially of body or mind; 3. Freedom from disease or abnormality; 4. A condition of optimal well-being. (American Heritage Dictionary of the English Language 1992)

The World Health Organization (WHO) states an idealistic definition that goes beyond the traditional English and American usage, defining health as

a state of complete physical, mental, and social well-being and not merely the absence of disease or infirmity. (WHO 2001)

Stedman's Medical Dictionary (SMD) notes that the ambitious WHO definition

was . . . criticized as unquantifiable. In 1984, WHO advanced a revised statement that any measure of health must take into account "the extent to which an individual or a group is able to realize aspirations and satisfy needs, and to change or cope with the environment." Health in this sense is seen as a "resource for everyday life." (SMD 2000)

Stedman's itself defines health as

1. The state of the organism when it functions optimally without evidence of disease or abnormality. 2. A state of dynamic balance in which an individual's or a group's capacity to cope with all the circumstances of living is at an optimum level. 3. A state characterized by anatomical, physiological, and psychological integrity, ability to perform personally valued family, work, and community roles; ability to deal with physical, biological, psychological and social stress; a feeling of well-being; and freedom from the risk of disease and untimely death. (ibid.)

For our purposes we define health as feeling sound, well, vigorous, and physically able to do things that most people ordinarily can do. Freedom from debilitating or threatening disease contributes to health, and those who are healthy reasonably can expect a life not likely to end prematurely. Nevertheless, health means something apart from the absence of disease or the extension of life (Evans and Stoddart 1994). We continue the tradition of using the word "health" variously to mean three things: a dimension graded from very negative (unhealthy) to ideally positive (very healthy); an individual's current status or place on that dimension; or the apex of that dimension—the ideal state of health. We recognize that the health dimension has distinct aspects or elements, particularly the sense of being healthy (or unhealthy) and the experience of being able (or unable) to perform common physical activities or functions. We use health as a general term encompassing those elements.

MEASURING HEALTH

A good measure of health must suit its purpose. Social surveys of health have goals that differ from those of clinical practice and research. As a consequence the measures of health that serve best for our purposes differ from those that a clinician or clinical researcher might favor. A sociologist studying health needs to compare its general level across contrasting social categories or across social strata such as defined by years of education. A clinician needs a detailed description of an individual's biological status that reveals the distinctive nature of that person's problems. A clinical researcher needs a set of measures relevant to a specific diagnostic category that reveals average differences across treatment groups in the progress of the disease or condition. These different purposes lead to different measurement ideals. In particular, social surveys favor generality and simplicity whereas clinical practice and research favors specificity and detail.

Social surveys of health require measures that are plain, comparable, concise, general, and common. Typically most or all of the information comes from answers that individuals give to questions asked by the researchers. A plain question uses simple, common terms to ask about things that most individuals can readily perceive. If we asked, "Do you suffer from claudication?" few individuals would know what we mean because the term is obscure. If we instead ask, "Do you get pains in the leg that make you limp?" most people will understand what we want to know and will be able to report accurately whether they have the problem. The same properties that make a question plain make the answers comparable across social groups.

The questionnaires for social health surveys also must be concise. More people will give an interview and complete it if it is short. That makes the sample larger and more representative of the whole population. It also cuts cost, which increase with the average length of the interview and the difficulty of getting people to participate. Asking general questions about relatively common problems allows brevity and enhances comparability. For example, asking about difficulty climbing stairs gets at a problem with many causes and wide-ranging consequences. It can be caused by arthritis, asthma, clogging or hardening of the arteries, emphysema, neurological disease, heart disease, injury, or obesity. One question about a problem common to all these diseases or disorders can do the work of many questions about the symptoms and signs unique to each. In the terms of medical epidemiology, that one question is highly sensitive but not very specific. It reveals the presence of a health problem but tells little about which one. It measures health in terms that apply across a broad range of diseases and disorders, and that have significance in everyday life. Such questions may have little use in clinical diagnosis, but they are ideal for comparing the health of various segments of the population.

In the remainder of this chapter we describe several direct or indirect measures of health and show how the average amount of each differs across levels of education. The first two are the core measures of health we use in our surveys and analyses: subjective health and physical impairment. The next set is physical symptoms that indicate emotional as well as physical health: vitality and vigor in contrast to lethargy and malaise, and physical aches and pains. The next set directly assesses emotional well-being: feelings of depression and anxiety. The final set represents awareness of morbidity and risks to life: diagnoses of serious chronic diseases and personal longevity expectations.

EDUCATION'S CORRELATION WITH HEALTH MEASURES

Subjective Health

The best all-round survey measure of health comes from the answer to one simple question: "In general, would you say your health is very good, good, satisfactory, poor, or very poor?" If a survey researcher could ask only one question about health, this would be the best one. It asks in direct terms for a global judgment of personal health. In this book we call the resulting measure subjective health, but it is at times also called perceived health, self-reported health, and the like. It is subjective in the medical sense of being a state perceptible to the individual and not to those who observe or examine the individual. It is *not* subjective in the psychological sense of being moodily introspective or illusory. It reports something real, but directly observable only by the individual reporting.

Survey researchers have asked about subjective health for decades. They have found that responses to the question reflect many aspects of health, including acute and chronic disease, fatal and nonfatal disease, functional ability or impairment, and general well-being such as indicated by feeling energetic and fit rather than rundown and tired and being free of discomforts such as backaches and headaches. Thus responses to the question measure health as defined by the World Health Organization: a state of well-being and not simply the absence of disease.

Subjective health measurements show many signs of validity. They correlate highly with more objective measures such as physician diagnoses or ratings of overall health, and they predict mortality risk over and above measures of chronic and acute disease, physician assessment made by clinical exam, physical disability, and health behaviors like smoking (Idler and Kasl 1991; Kaplan 1987; Romelsjo et al. 1992). In fact, subjective health predicts mortality more strongly than does physician-assessed health (Mossey and Shapiro 1982; Maddox and Douglas 1973).

Reports of subjective health have remarkably high reliability for responses to a single question. A measure's reliability is the amount of information it contains relative to the amount of random noise. Theoretically, reliability ranges from 0 for a measure with no information to 1.0 for one with perfect information. When viewed as a measure of an individual's actual state, the answer to a typical survey question has a reliability of around .3. To get a more reliable measure of an individual's state the surveyor must ask a number of different questions all getting at the same thing and then average together the responses, with diminishing returns to each additional question. In our data we estimate the reliability of answers to the subjective health question as .58. To put that value in perspective, a psychometric equation called the Spearman-Brown Prophecy Formula tells us that it would take three questions with item-reliability of .3 to make an index as reliable as responses to the one question about subjective health. That one item's unusually high information content suggests that individuals have a clear sense of their own health and can characterize it broadly with relatively little random error.

Subjective health differs substantially across levels of education. Figure 2.1 shows the fraction of persons at each level of education reporting very good, good, satisfactory, poor, or very poor health. Most American adults report good or very good health at all levels of education. However the fraction increases greatly with level of education, from a little more than half at the elementary school level to around 90 percent for persons with bachelor's or advanced degrees. At the other end of the health scale, about 17 percent of persons with an elementary school education report poor or very poor health. That is about one person in six. It is over six times the prevalence of poor or very poor health reported by persons with bachelor's degrees, which is about 2.5 percent. Among persons who went to high school but did not finish, the prevalence of poor or very poor health drops to about 11 percent, or one in nine, which is still quadruple the prevalence among the college graduates. Among persons who finished high school the prevalence drops to 6 percent, or one in 17, which is double the prevalence among college graduates. Reports of very poor health effectively vanish at the level of some college, and reports of poor health effectively vanish at the level of the masters degree. If American adults with less than a bachelor's degree had the same low prevalence of poor or very poor health as those with bachelor's or advanced degrees, there would be 63 percent fewer individuals reporting poor or very poor health.

Average levels of education have risen steadily in successive generations of Americans. As a consequence the adults with lower levels of education also tend to be older. That raises a question. Are the differences in subjective health across levels of education really just the result of differ-

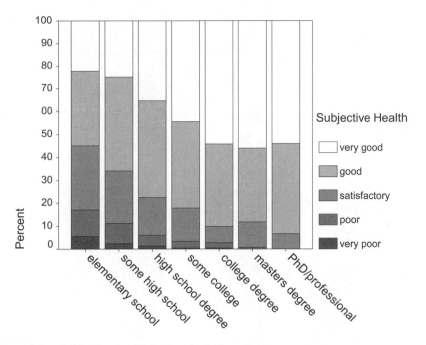

Figure 2.1.   Subjective health by level of education.

ences in average age? Figure 2.2 shows that they are not. It shows the average subjective health score within each ten-year age group for persons with no degree, a high school degree, or a college degree (bachelor's or higher). To calculate the means, we assign to the reports of very poor, poor, satisfactory, good, or very good health the scores of –2, –1, 0, 1, and 2, respectively. Figure 2.2 shows that the average score increases with the level of education within each ten-year age group. The differences across levels of education in average subjective heath score are statistically significant within each ten-year age group. (In other words, the differences are larger than the margin of error in estimating the means.) Figure 2.2 also shows that the differences in average subjective health between the higher and lower levels of education are as great as those between the oldest and youngest age groups. This means that education may be as important as age in determining subjective health.

Physical Impairment

Our second core measure of health represents the ability to do things that individuals normally can do: physical functioning in contrast to physical impairment. Such ability clearly influences subjective health, but the

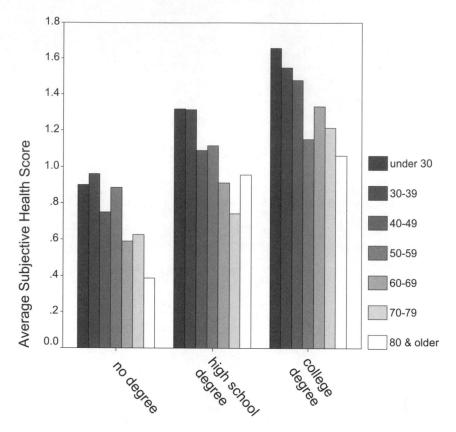

Figure 2.2.   Subjective health by age and education.

two aspects of health are not entirely the same. Physically impaired individuals can feel healthy because they exercise, eat right, sleep regularly, and have no chronic diseases, whereas unimpaired individuals can feel unhealthy because infection, disease, stress, or inactivity produces malaise and discomfort. Nevertheless, physical impairment and poor subjective health often go together because of common origins in lifestyle and disease, and because impairment increases the difficulty of maintaining subjective health (Johnson and Wolinsky 1993). Likewise, good physical functioning and good subjective health typically go together because of common origins and the impact of the former on the latter.

The questions that we ask about physical impairment have their beginning in research on workers done around 1970 (e.g., Nagi 1976). Researchers at that time wanted to measure physical impairment that might interfere with paid employment, and that also might result from prolonged occupational exposures. They discovered that among older workers impairment strongly influences the decision to retire. Since then researchers have elaborated and refined the measures in order to study the needs of older Americans for care and assistance. Researchers in gerontology typically distinguish between two types of assessments (Johnson and Wolinsky 1993). One set records problems with basic functions such as reaching, grasping, lifting, bending, walking, hearing, or seeing and the other records difficulties with routine activities such as talking on the telephone, reading a newspaper, shopping, preparing meals, driving a car, bathing, or dressing. Gerontologists generally want detail that highlights each individual's specific needs and that allows providers to know the amount of specific forms of therapy or assistance needed in a service population. Our research does not need that level of detail. Our questions about physical impairment ask about seven of the most general and common difficulties with basic functions or routine activities. Together the answers to those questions provide an efficient means of comparing the overall level of impairment across segments of the general population. They also do a reasonably good job of measuring an individual's overall level of physical impairment, even though they do not go into detail on the specifics.

To measure physical impairment we ask, "How much difficulty do you have climbing stairs? Kneeling or stooping? Lifting or carrying objects under 10 pounds like a bag of groceries? Preparing meals, cleaning or doing other household work? Shopping or getting around town? Seeing, even with glasses? Hearing?" For each item we ask "Would you say no difficulty, some difficulty, or a great deal of difficulty?" Figure 2.3 shows the percentage reporting a great deal of difficulty by level of education for each type of problem. Every one of the seven problems is most common among persons who did not go to or finish high school and least common among those who went to college. The seeming increase at the master's or doctoral level relative to the bachelor's level for some difficulties is not statistically significant. (In other words, it is within the margin of error and probably just the result of random noise in the data.) The pattern is essentially the same for some difficulty (rather than a great deal), except that the percentages are higher.

The seven impairments that we ask about all decrease in prevalence with increasing level of education. Figure 2.4 shows one measure of the strength of that association. It shows the percentage of the cases reporting a great deal of difficulty that would not have the problem if persons with a high school degree or less had the same low prevalence of the impairment as persons with a bachelor's degree or higher. Those figures range from a high of 72 percent fewer cases of great difficulty with household

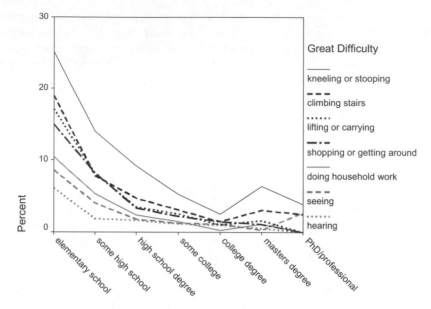

Figure 2.3. Prevalence of great difficulty with seven basic functions or ordinary
   activities, by level of education.

work to a low of 50 percent fewer cases of great difficulty with kneeling or
stooping and with seeing. Other measures of association tell the same
story. For example, the odds of reporting a great deal of difficulty with
household work is five times greater among persons with no degree or
only a high school degree than among those with a bachelor's degree or
higher. The odds also are higher for those with less than a bachelor's
degree by ratios respectively of 4.0, 3.7, 2.7, 2.5, 2.5, and 2.2 for a great deal
of difficulty lifting or carrying, shopping or getting around, climbing
stairs, hearing, kneeling or stooping, and seeing. These correlations suggest that education may have consequences that substantially influence
the risk of impairment.

   Although older American adults tend to have lower education, differences in age across levels of education do not account for the differences in
levels of impairment. Figure 2.5 shows substantial differences in amounts
of physical impairment across levels of education within each ten-year age
group. We calculated the impairment scores by assigning a value of 0 for
no difficulty, 1 for some difficulty, and 2 for a great deal of difficulty, and
then taking the mean across the seven items. The resulting index has a reliability of .78. Within each age group the differences across levels of education in the average impairment scores are statistically significant and quite

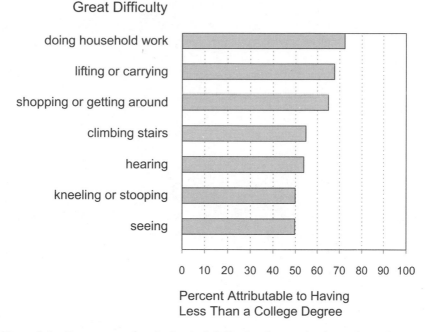

Figure 2.4. Percentage of each physical difficulty that can be due to low education.

substantial. For example, individuals under the age of thirty with no degree report levels of impairment equal to those of individuals in their fifties with college degrees. That same pattern holds for older age categories. The persons with no degree in each ten-year age group have about the same level of impairment as the ones with college degrees who are thirty years older. Likewise, the persons with high school degrees in each age group have about the same level of impairment as the ones with college degrees who are twenty years older. In terms of physical impairment, having a college degree is like being twenty or thirty years younger.

Vitality and Well-Being

The World Health Organization's definition of health emphasizes an ideal state of physical and mental well-being, not simply the absence of disease and disability. That definition can seem radical and overreaching to someone steeped in medical science, with its emphasis on correcting specific disorders. Popular concepts of health nevertheless include vitality and well-being, which vary along a continuum (Mirowsky and Ross 1989).

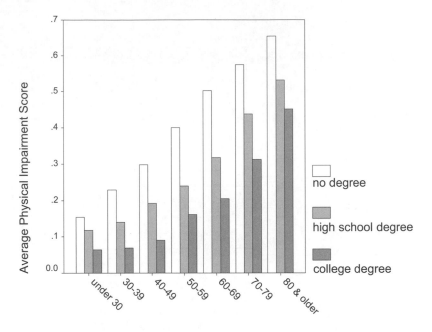

Figure 2.5.   Average physical impairment scores by age and education.

Individuals at one extreme feel tired, sick, and rundown. They find it difficult or impossible to do ordinary things, suffer many short-term illnesses like colds or the flu, have chronic aches and pains, and feel depressed, anxious, and demoralized. Individuals at the other extreme feel healthy and energetic, rarely spend a day sick in bed, and feel happy and hopeful about the future. Most people fall somewhere between these two extremes. To ordinary Americans being healthy in part means being on the good side of this dimension.

In our surveys we ask a number of questions about physical vitality and emotional well-being. The desirable states all become more prevalent at higher levels of education and the undesirable ones all become less prevalent. Figure 2.6 shows the pattern for signs of vitality and Figure 2.7 shows the pattern for signs of its absence. For all of the items we asked, "How many days in the past week did you feel . . . ?" The graphs show the average days per week. As the level of education increases, people generally report more days per week of feeling physically fit, having lots of energy, enjoying life, being happy, and feeling hopeful about the future. They report fewer days per week of trouble sleeping, finding everything an

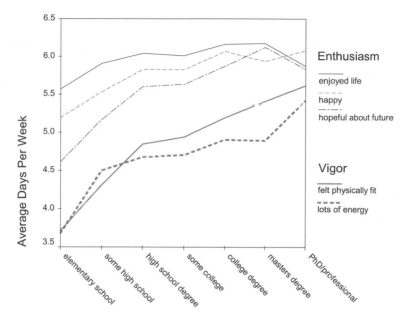

Figure 2.6. Average frequency of vigor and enthusiasm by level of education.

effort, being unable to get going, having trouble keeping their minds on things, and suffering from backaches, headaches, and other aches and pains. Differences in prevalence between the college-educated and others accounts for about 25 percent of all symptom days recorded for these items (counted as each day of the past week for which someone reported the presence of an undesirable state or the absence of a desirable one).

The presence of malaise and discomfort and the absence of vigor and enthusiasm reflect emotional well-being more directly than they do the presence of disease or disability. Our language and our cultural traditions distinguish between mental and physical. The distinction seems self-evident when comparing the pain of a broken leg with the pain of a lost love. Even so, a clear natural boundary between mental and physical cannot be found. Many symptoms that can seem completely physical to individuals coincide in their presence or absence more with emotional states than with physical diseases. Every state that one feels as an emotion has a corresponding physiological process that also creates physical symptoms. Feeling sad, lonely, and blue typically corresponds with lacking energy, feeling everything is an effort, and having trouble sleeping, concentrating, and getting going. Feeling worried, tense, and restless typically corre-

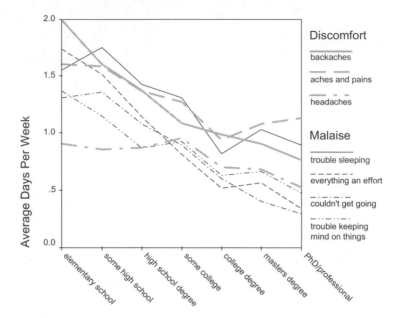

Figure 2.7. Average frequency of malaise and discomfort by level of education.

sponds with aches, pains, and signs of autonomic arousal such as shortness of breath, heart palpitations, faintness, or sweaty palms. The physical
symptoms are not imaginary, and many can be observed objectively by
others. These emotional states with mental and physical manifestations
can be caused by essentially behavioral or essentially physiological disturbances. Whatever the origin, they afflict individuals more frequently
the lower the level of education. Figure 2.8 shows by level of education the
percentage that felt sad, lonely, or blue most days of the previous week
and the percentage that felt worried, tense, or restless. Differences in
prevalence between the college-educated and others accounts for about 48
percent of the cases of feeling depressed most days (one in two) and about
18 percent of the cases of feeling anxious most days (one in five or six).

Diagnoses of Serious Chronic Disease

Having a diagnosis of a threatening or debilitating chronic disease suggests that an individual is in poor health, but it reflects selection and labeling processes too. People often think of a diagnosis as synonymous with
the inferred pathology implied by the label. In reality the diagnosis is the
label itself, acquired as the result of a behavioral and social process influenced by the individual's symptoms, signs, beliefs, motivations, and

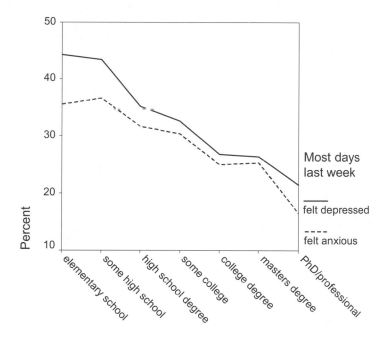

Figure 2.8. Prevalence of feeling depressed or anxious most days by level of education.

resources and by the theory, technology, standards, and organization of medical practice in the individual's time and place. Individuals have diagnoses in part because they sought medical explanations and treatments for their ailments and had access to medical doctors inclined to grant the diagnoses. That complicates the interpretation of differences across social groups in the prevalence of diagnoses. Nevertheless, diagnoses imply that the diagnosed individuals at some time had problems that seemed worthy of medical attention to themselves or their close associates, and that at least one physician saw in the symptoms and signs the likely operation of a pathological process with serious implications for function or survival.

We asked respondents, "Have you ever been diagnosed or told by a doctor that you have heart disease? High blood pressure? Lung disease like emphysema or lung cancer? Breast cancer? Any other type of cancer? Diabetes? Arthritis or rheumatism? Osteoporosis (brittle bones)?" These diagnoses cover threatening or debilitating chronic diseases that are most common among American adults. Figure 2.9 shows the percentage reporting each diagnosis at three levels of education: no degree, high school degree only, and college degree at the bachelor's level or higher. It also lists

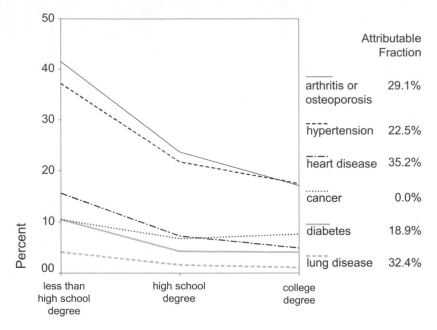

Figure 2.9. Prevalence of six serious chronic-disease diagnoses by level of education, with attributable fractions.

the percentage of the individuals with a diagnosis who would not have it if adults without a college degree had the same prevalence of the diagnosis as adults with a college degree. Because of small numbers we combined breast cancer with other cancers and osteoporosis with arthritis or rheumatism. With the exception of cancer, all of the diagnoses are most common among individuals with no degree and least common among those with college degrees. The probability of reporting at least one of the diagnoses rises from 35.7 percent among those with college degrees to 41.6 percent among those with high school degrees to 64.7 percent among those with no degrees. The fraction of each diagnosis potentially attributable to having less than a college education ranges from one in five for diabetes and high blood pressure to one in three for heart disease and lung disease, except for cancer, which is not related to level of education in these data.

Expected Longevity

People value health because it contributes to a long life, as well as valuing it for itself. Humans generally want to live, and they fear death even if

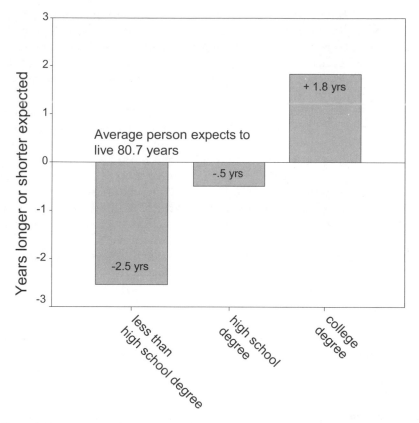

Figure 2.10. Average longevity expected by level of education, with longevity measured as a deviation from the overall mean.

suffering makes oblivion seem a refuge. Expecting a long life means expecting to have that which makes all other gratifications possible, the essential property—existence itself. Individuals who expect an early death implicitly project poor future health based on past and current health problems and on a heightened sense of future risk.

The end may not seem near to most individuals with low education, but it seems noticeably nearer to them than it does to others. In our survey we asked, "To what age do you expect to live?" On average the individuals in the survey expect to live until about age 80.7. Figure 2.10 shows how the average longevity expected at each level of education differs from the average in the sample as a whole. People with less than a high school degree expect to live an average of 2.5 years less than that, to about age 78.2. Those with only a high school degree expect to live an average of 0.5

years less, to about 80.2. Those with a college degree expect to live an average of 1.8 years longer, to about age 82.5. That makes the spread between no degree and a college degree 4.3 years. Given the fraction of persons at each level of education, the spreads imply that the average longevity expected would increase by 1.7 years, to 82.4, if everyone expected the same length of life as the college-educated do.

Viewed in actuarial terms, a life expectancy 4.3 or even 2.5 years shorter is substantial. To put the subjective life expectancy spreads in perspective, actuarial projections indicate that 35-year-old cigarette smokers can expect to gain an average of around 3 years of life by quitting (Grover et al. 1994; Tsevat et al. 1991; Tsevat 1992). People that age who never have smoked and never take up the habit can expect to live an average of about 7 years longer than smokers that age who persist in the habit (Basavaraj 1993). The shorter lives expected by persons with high school degrees or no degrees imply double or more the rate of mortality throughout adulthood.

Statistics on mortality and actuarial life expectancy suggest that individuals with lower levels of education are being realistic when they expect shorter lives, but may underestimate how much shorter. Actuarial estimates put the life expectancy spread across levels of education in the range of 5 to 6 years (Rogot, Sorlie, and Johnson 1992). The actuarial life expectancy spreads reflect substantial differences in mortality rates across levels of education. Compared to individuals with 17 or more years of education, those with 16 years of schooling are 25 percent more likely to die, high school graduates are 60 percent more likely, and those with less than 9 years are 100 percent more likely to die (Rogers, Hummer, and Nam 1999). Because level of education is a stable trait with many long-term consequences, ratios like these exist across the life cycle, adding up to substantial differences in average longevity.

The subjective estimates of longevity suggest some awareness of the mortality risks, but differences across levels of education tend to be smaller for subjective estimates than for actuarial ones. Several things may account for the implicit subjective underestimate of the mortality risks associated with low education. For one thing, lifestyle may account for much of the difference in mortality rates across levels of education. Individuals who see less risk to a habit like smoking are more likely to take it up, thus diluting the sense of risk among those most at risk. Once someone is overweight or out of shape or addicted to cigarettes they may downplay the risk as a psychological defense. As an example, the smokers in our sample expect only 1.2-year shorter lives on average than the nonsmokers. That represents a gross underestimate according to the actuarial statistics above. Another reason for the underestimates may be a realization lag. The differences in mortality rates across levels of education have been growing since around 1960 (Elo and Preston 1996; Feldman et al. 1989). Intuitions about longevity may draw heavily on the ages at death of family members and acquaintances, many of whom died when the education differentials in mortality rates were not as great.

Health in Sum

By every measure American adults with college educations enjoy better health than those with lower levels of education. The better-educated feel healthier, have less difficulty with common activities and tasks, more frequently feel vigorous and thriving, less often suffer aches, pains, and malaise, less often feel worried or depressed, carry fewer diagnoses of threatening or debilitating chronic disease, expect to live longer, and probably will live longer. Many health problems would be substantially less common if everyone had the same rate of those problems as among the college-educated. According to our data there would be 63 percent fewer American adults who feel their health is poor or very poor; around 50 percent fewer experiencing great difficulty seeing, hearing, climbing stairs, kneeling, or stooping; 60 to 70 percent fewer experiencing great difficulty shopping or getting around, lifting or carrying, and doing household work; 25 percent fewer suffering from malaise or aches and pains on any given day; 18 percent fewer feeling anxious most days of the week; 48 percent fewer feeling depressed most days of the week; 20 percent fewer with diagnoses of hypertension or diabetes; 30 percent fewer with diagnoses of lung disease and arthritis or osteoporosis; and 35 percent fewer with diagnoses of heart disease. Average subjective life expectancy would increase by 1.4 years, an amount on a par with the actuarial gains predicted if everyone who smokes quits and no one else takes it up.

Higher levels of education and better health generally go together. The rest of the chapters of this book look at the reasons why. We argue that control over one's own life and the healthy lifestyle that goes with that control account for most of the association between education and health. We review a number of other things associated with higher education that also may contribute to its association with health, including employment and the qualities of one's occupation and work, income and economic well-being, access to formal care, social support, marital quality, work-family accommodation, and older age at first marriage and first birth. We describe the phenomenon of cumulative advantage by which the beneficial effects of education accumulate and compound over the lifetime. We critique a number of views of education that would disparage its value as a means to health, including education viewed as mere credential, as false satisfier, as reproducer of inequality, and as spurious stand-in for IQ or social inheritance. We end with a recap of our findings and what we think they mean: education makes people effective, which helps them achieve something everyone desires—health.

| 3 |

Education, Personal Control, Lifestyle, and Health

Why does education improve health? In this chapter we present our view of the main reasons—but not the only reasons—why education affects health. Education improves health because it increases effective agency. Through education individuals gain the resources necessary to be effective agents in their own lives, which ultimately affects physical well-being. We propose that education improves physical functioning and self-reported health because it enhances a sense of personal control that encourages and enables a healthy lifestyle (walking, exercising, drinking moderately, and avoiding overweight and smoking). According to our human capital theory of learned effectiveness, education enables people to coalesce health-producing behaviors into a coherent lifestyle. It does so by enhancing the sense of control over outcomes in one's own life. Together the sense of personal control and its consequences for a healthy lifestyle convey much of education's positive effect on health. These ideas are supported in a number of data sets. We will illustrate them using our Aging, Status and the Sense of Control (ASOC) data, described in Chapter 9.

How does education foster health? The concept of human capital implies that education improves health because it increases effective agency on the part of individuals. According to the theory, education develops habits, skills, resources, and abilities that enable people to achieve a better life. To the extent that people value health, education develops the means toward creating that end through a lifestyle that promotes health. Thus health is not just a lucky but unintended consequence of the prosperity that is contingent on education. In this chapter we extend human capital theory beyond the economic concerns of productivity, wages, and jobs to individual health.

A great deal of evidence beyond ours shows that educational attainment leads to better health. Education increases physical functioning and subjective health among adults of all ages, and decreases the age-specific rates of morbidity, disability, and mortality (Feldman et al. 1989; Fox,

Goldblatt, and Jones 1985; Guralnik et al. 1993; Gutzwiller et al. 1989; Kita-gawa and Hauser 1973; Kunst and Mackenbach 1994; Pappas, Queen, Hadden, and Fisher 1993; Ross and Wu 1995, 1996; Williams 1990; Win-kleby et al. 1992). The positive association between educational attainment and health is largely due to the effects of education on health, not vice versa (Doornbos and Kronhout 1990; Wilkinson 1986). In this chapter we go beyond the established association between educational attainment and good health to see why education is associated with health.

EDUCATION AND HUMAN CAPITAL

Formal education indicates investment in "human capital"—the produc-tive capacity developed, embodied, and stocked in human beings them-selves (Schultz 1962; Becker 1962, 1964). According to theory, formal education develops skills and abilities of general value rather than "firm-specific" ones of value to a particular employer (Becker 1962; Schultz 1962). An individual who acquires an education can use it to solve a wide range of problems. Some are the problems of productivity that concern employ-ers and economists. Some are problems in which economic prosperity is one of several means toward a more basic end. Health is one of those basic ends.

Schooling builds the real skills, abilities, and resources called human capital on several levels of generality. On the most general level education teaches people to learn (Hyman, Wright, and Reed 1975). It develops the ability to write, communicate, solve problems, analyze data, develop ideas, and implement plans (Hyman et al. 1976; Hyman and Wright 1979; Kohn and Schooler 1982; Nunn, Crockett, and Williams 1978; Spaeth 1976). It develops broadly useful analytic skills such as mathematics, logic, and, on a more basic level, observing, experimenting, summarizing, synthesizing, interpreting, classifying, and so on. In school one encounters and solves problems that are progressively more difficult, complex, and subtle. The more years of schooling the greater the cognitive development, character-ized by flexible, rational, complex strategies of thinking (Hyman et al. 1976; Kohn and Slomczynski 1993; Nunn et al. 1978; Pascarella and Terenzini 1991; Spaeth 1976). Higher education teaches people to think logically and rationally, see many sides of an issue, and analyze problems and solve them (Pascarella and Terenzini 1991). In addition, the occupational skills learned in school have generic value. People learn journalism, biology, engineering, social work, geology, psychology, business, nursing, and so on. In school students learn to tailor the general means of solving problems to a specific set of problems commonly encountered in an occupation.

Education also develops broadly effective habits and attitudes such as dependability, good judgment, motivation, effort, trust, and confidence

(Kohn and Slomczynski 1993), as well as skills and abilities. In particular the process of learning creates confidence in the ability to solve problems. Education instills the habit of meeting problems with attention, thought, action, and perseverance. Thus education increases effort, which like ability is a fundamental component of problem-solving (Wheaton 1980). Apart from the value of the skills and abilities learned in school, the process of learning builds the confidence, motivation, and self-assurance needed to *attempt* to solve problems. Because education develops competence on many levels it gives people the ability and motivation to shape and control their lives (Ross and Mirowsky 1989; Wheaton 1980).

The more years of schooling, the greater is one's stock of human capital. Years of schooling captures an individual's exposure to increasingly complex environments, which produce better cognitive skills (Spaeth 1976). A number of empirical studies support the exposure model. Years of schooling has enduring effects on knowledge, receptivity to knowledge, cognitive flexibility, and cognitive ability (Hyman et al. 1975; Kohn and Schooler 1982; Pascarella and Terenzini 1991). Among adults, more years of schooling significantly increase intellectual ability, measured by the Armed Forces Qualification Test, even adjusting for earlier IQ score (Herrnstein and Murray 1994:Table, p. 591). (Herrnstein and Murray bury this finding in an appendix, and do not acknowledge it in their text.) Even among children of the same age, small differences in the amount, or quantity, of schooling significantly increase ability. Quantity of schooling, assessed by the number of hours per day for which school meets, the number of days in the school year, and the average daily attendance, has large effects on verbal, reading, and math scores (Wiley 1976). The more time children spend in school, the higher are their abilities. The strength and significance of the association is striking, given small variations in the quantity of schooling among children of the same age, as compared to large variations in the quantity of schooling among adults [and given the critique that school quality has little effect (Coleman et al. 1966)].

The skills gained in school give people access to good jobs with high earnings, but education's positive effects extend beyond jobs and earnings. The same skills help people shape their own lives. To the extent that good health is a goal most people hold, education enables people to coalesce health-producing behaviors into a coherent lifestyle that improves health. A sense of control over outcomes in one's own life encourages a healthy lifestyle and conveys much of education's effect. The following sections detail these propositions and facts relevant to them.

DESIGNING A HEALTHY LIFESTYLE

The human capital theory of learned effectiveness states that educated, instrumental people merge otherwise unrelated habits and ways into a healthy lifestyle that consequently behaves as a coherent trait. In theory education makes individuals more effective users of information. Education encourages individuals to acquire information with intent to use it. Thus the more educated may assemble a set of habits and ways that are not necessarily related except as effective means toward health.

Purposeful individuals may coalesce a healthy lifestyle from otherwise incoherent or diametric practices allocated by subcultural forces. Individuals tend to do whatever others like them do, particularly if it distinguishes the people they identify with from the ones they do not. Some of those things make health better and some make it worse. For example, men exercise more frequently than women; women restrict body weight more closely than men (Hayes and Ross 1987; Ross and Bird 1994). Likewise young adults smoke more than older adults, but also exercise more (Hayes and Ross 1987; Ross and Bird 1994; Ross and Wu 1995). Individuals putting together a healthy lifestyle must adopt the healthy habits of men and women, young and old. In doing so they create positive correlations among traits that otherwise are uncorrelated or even negatively correlated.

Education encourages healthy behaviors and pulls together the healthy elements from the lifestyles of various subpopulations. Compared to those with little schooling the well-educated are more likely to exercise, are more likely to drink moderately rather than abstain or drink heavily, and are less likely to smoke or be overweight (Ross and Bird 1994; Ross and Wu 1995), all of which improve health as we detail next. Education encourages and enables people to create a healthy lifestyle from diverse sources. The health behaviors associated with higher education show little consistent relationship to other sociodemographic traits. Only education correlates positively and consistently with healthy behaviors.

Smoking

The well-educated are less likely to smoke than the poorly educated because they are more likely to have never smoked or because they are more likely to have quit (Helmert et al. 1989; Jacobsen and Thelle 1988; Liu et al. 1982; Matthews et al. 1989; Millar and Wigle 1986; Shea et al. 1991; Wagenknecht et al. 1990; Winkleby et al. 1992). Figure 3.1 shows that as education increases the likelihood of smoking decreases, with the sole exception that people with an elementary school education are less likely to smoke than people who have gone to high school. In the United States this is an unusual group of older immigrants. Nonetheless even with adjustment for age and immigrant status, this group smokes less than people who have been to high school. Apart from this uncommon group, as education increases, the likelihood of having never smoked or having quit smoking increases, and the likelihood of currently smoking decreases.

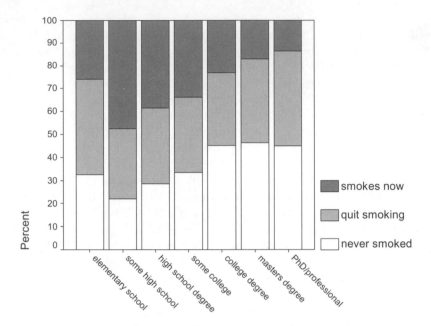

Figure 3.1.   Education and smoking status.

Smoking negatively affects health. Of all the practices that affect health, smoking has the most consequences (Rogers and Powell-Griner 1991). It increases the risk of coronary heart disease, stroke, atherosclerosis, aneurysms; lung and other cancers, including esophagus, pancreas, bladder, larynx, and cervix; emphysema, bronchitis, pneumonia, and other respiratory infections; liver disease; and burns. Smoking is also associated with poor self-reported health (Abbott, Yin, Reed, and Yano 1986; NCHS 1989; Segovia, Bartlett, and Edwards 1989; Surgeon General 1982; U.S. Preventive Services Task Force 1989). Heart disease, cancer, stroke, and emphysema alone account for about 65 percent of all deaths (NCHS 1992).

Walking and Strenuous Exercise

High levels of educational attainment are positively associated with physical activity (Ford et al. 1991; Helmert et al. 1989; Jacobsen and Thelle 1988; Leigh 1983; Shea et al. 1991). As education increases, people walk more often, as shown in Figure 3.2. Strenuous exercise like running, tennis, swimming, biking, basketball, and aerobics, is not as common as walking, but it also becomes more common with higher levels of education up through the master's level. (It drops off among Ph.D.s, M.D.s, lawyers,

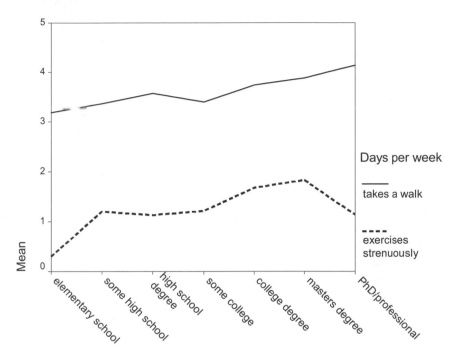

Figure 3.2.   Education and exercise.

and others with professional degrees, but with only fifty people, or less
than 2 percent of the ASOC sample in this category, there may be error in
this estimate).

People who are physically active experience better health than those
who are more sedentary. Compared to inactivity, any physical activity, aerobic or nonaerobic, reduces mortality (Berkman and Breslow 1983). Exercise reduces cardiovascular risk, back pain, osteoporosis, atherosclerosis,
colon cancer, obesity, high blood pressure, constipation, varicose veins,
adult onset diabetes, and improves subjective health reports (Berlin and
Colditz 1990; Caspersen et al. 1992; Duncan, Gordon, and Scott 1991; Leon,
Connett, Jacobs, and Rauramaa 1987; Magnus, Matroos, and Strackee
1979; Paffenbarger et al. 1993; Sandvik et al. 1993; Segovia et al. 1989; U.S.
Preventive Services Task Force 1989).

Overweight

Well-educated women are less likely to be overweight than those with
less education, but men do not show the same pattern. Well-educated men

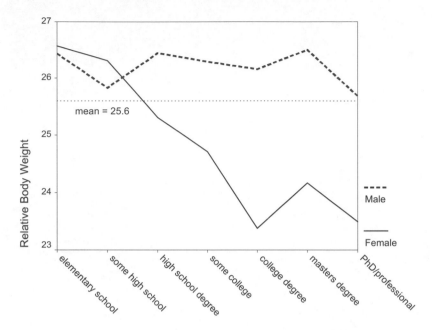

Figure 3.3.   Education and relative body weight among men and women.

are as overweight as men with fewer years of schooling. In the 1970s college-educated men were actually somewhat more overweight than those with high school educations, probably because the latter had physi-cally active jobs (Ross and Mirowsky 1983). Now the null association could be due to a trade-off in which working-class men get more exercise on their jobs, but college-educated men engage in more leisure-time physical activ-ity and restrict their calorie intake more. Figure 3.3 shows a steep decline in overweight for women as they advance in educational attainment from not having finished high school through having a college degree. [The small group of women with master's degrees (*n* = 31) shows an upturn in rela-tive body weight, which declines again at the Ph.D./professional level (n = 15).] Men show much higher levels of overweight than women, with almost no change in relative body weight with educational attainment. Figure 3.4 shows the same pattern for obesity. To be considered obese, a person must score 27 or higher on the relative body weight index. To understand what this means, the average women in the ASOC sample is 5 feet 4 inches and weighs 146 pounds. To be considered obese, she would need to weigh more than 165 pounds at that height. Women with college degrees are much less likely to be obese than their counterparts with less education.

Being overweight is a risk factor for a number of health problems, including high blood pressure, heart disease, adult-onset diabetes, lower-

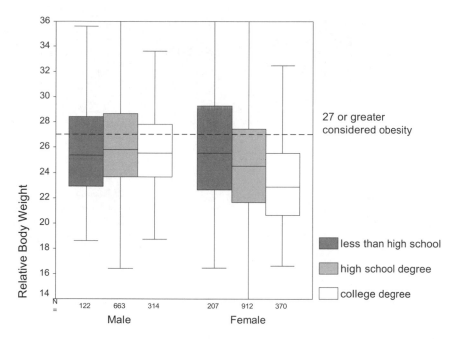

Figure 3.4. Education and obesity among men and women.

back pain, gallstones, limited physical functioning, and overall mortality; and the overweight report that they feel worse physically (U.S. Preventive Task Force 1989; Manson et al. 1995; Feinleib 1985; Segovia et al. 1989; Van Itallie 1985).

Drinking

The well-educated are more likely to drink moderately than the poorly educated. In contrast, people with lower levels of education are more likely to be abstainers and alcohol abusers (Darrow et al. 1992; Midanik, Klatsky, and Armstrong 1990; Romelsjo and Diderichsen 1989). Figure 3.5 distinguishes abstainers from moderate drinkers (who drink four or less drinks a day) and heavy drinkers (who drink more than four drinks a day). Our data only measure the quantity and frequency of drinking, not the problems associated with very heavy drinking, like losing one's job or getting arrested, which are more common among the poorly educated. Figure 3.5 shows that as educational attainment increases, moderate drinking increases and abstaining from drinking decreases. Heavy drinking is very rare in all groups.

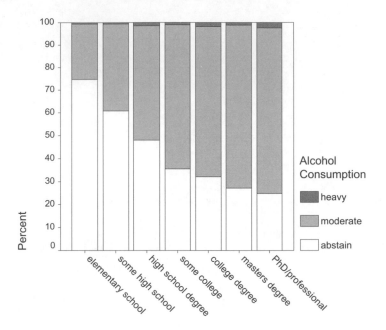

Figure 3.5.   Education and alcohol consumption.

Drinking is far less ubiquitous in its health consequences than are smoking or inadequate physical activity. Compared to smoking and sedentary lifestyle, very heavy drinking as a risk factor is implicated in only four of the leading fifteen causes of death—car accidents, cirrhosis of the liver, suicide, and homicide. Of these, only cirrhosis and injuries from car accidents affect self-reported health or physical functioning. Further-more, research indicates a U-shaped relationship between drinking and illness. Both abstainers and very heavy drinkers have higher mortality and morbidity than do those who drink moderately (Berkman and Breslow 1983; Guralnik and Kaplan 1989; Midanik et al. 1990). Moderate drinking, as compared to abstinence, is associated with lower risk of coronary heart disease, stroke, and hypertension, whereas very heavy drinking is associ-ated with higher risk (Gaziano et al. 1993; Gill et al. 1986; Stampfer et al. 1988). Moderate drinking appears good for health.

Education, Healthy Lifestyle, and Health

Smoking and overweight worsen health, and physical activity and moderate drinking improve it. Do all these practices really influence health, or are some apparent effects really due to their associations with other practices? For instance, people who do not exercise are more likely to be overweight than people who do exercise. We want to know whether—at the same level of relative body weight—people who exercise experience better health than those who do not. To see if each aspect of a healthy lifestyle independently affects health, we statistically adjust, or hold constant, the others. The multivariate analyses show independent effects of each aspect of a healthy lifestyle on subjective health and on physical functioning. Smoking and overweight correlate negatively with subjective health and physical functioning, and walking, strenuous exercise, and moderate drinking correlate positively. Each significantly affects health, holding the others constant. For example, smokers are less likely to exercise strenuously than are nonsmokers, and smokers have worse health, so without adjustment for smoking, we might spuriously attribute smoking effects to lack of exercise. With adjustment, we know that if we compare two people who both smoke, the one who exercises will feel healthier and function better than the one who is more sedentary. In fact, multivariate analyses show that each aspect of a healthy lifestyle influences health, even at the same level of background characteristics, like family origins, age, sex, race, and marital status; at the same level of employment, economic resources, and work fulfillment; and at the same level of social support and a sense of personal control. For example, older people are less likely to exercise strenuously than are younger people, and older people have worse health, so without adjustment for age, we might spuriously attribute age effects to lack of exercise. With adjustment, we know that if we compare two people who are both 65 years old, the one who exercises will feel healthier and have better physical functioning than the person who is more sedentary.

The well-educated consistently engage in healthy behaviors—those that positively impact health. Compared to people with less schooling, they are less likely to smoke or to be overweight, and they are more likely to walk, exercise strenuously, and drink moderately. All of their practices have positive, independent effects on health. This is in sharp contrast to any other social characteristic. The health behaviors associated with higher education show little consistent relationship to other sociodemographic traits. For instance, men exercise more than women, but men also smoke more than women. Men have some healthy behaviors and some unhealthy ones. Married people are less likely to smoke than people who are not married, but married people also exercise less and weigh more. Married people have some healthy behaviors and some unhealthy ones. Only education correlates positively and consistently with healthy behaviors.

THE SENSE OF CONTROL LINKS EDUCATION TO
HEALTHY LIFESTYLE

The better-educated may enjoy better health in part because education increases the agency and personal control that motivates people to design a healthy lifestyle. The theory of human capital converges with the theory of personal control. Through formal education people learn to solve problems and to be active and effective agents in their own lives (Mirowsky and Ross 1989; Wheaton 1980). People who feel in control of their own lives seek information by which to guide their lives and improve their outcomes. Logically then people who feel in control of their own lives tend to adopt a lifestyle that produces health. By developing personal control and effectiveness education develops individuals who seek and discover a healthy lifestyle.

The Sense of Personal Control

The sense of personal control is a learned, generalized expectation that outcomes are contingent on one's own choices and actions (Mirowsky and Ross 1989; Rotter 1966; Ross, Mirowsky, and Cockerham 1983; Seeman 1983). People with a high sense of control report being effective agents in their own lives; they believe that they can master, control, and effectively alter the environment. Perceived control is the cognitive awareness of a link between efforts and outcomes. On the other end of the continuum, perceived powerlessness is the belief that one's actions do not affect outcomes. It is the belief that outcomes of situations are determined by forces external to one's self such as powerful others, luck, fate, or chance. People with a sense of powerlessness think that they have little control over meaningful events and circumstances in their lives. As such, perceived powerlessness is the cognitive awareness of a discrepancy between one's goals and the means to achieve them. Perceived control and powerlessness represent two ends of a continuum, with the belief that one can shape conditions and events in one's life at one end of the continuum, and the belief that one's actions cannot influence events and circumstances at the other (Mirowsky and Ross 1989).

The importance of a sense of personal control is recognized in a number of social and behavioral sciences. The sense of personal control appears in a number of related forms with various names, including internal locus of control (Rotter 1966), mastery (Pearlin et al. 1981), instrumentalism (Wheaton 1980), self-efficacy (Bandura 1986; Gecas 1989), and personal autonomy (Seeman and Seeman 1983), and at the other end of the continuum, fatalism (Wheaton 1980), helplessness (Seligman 1975), perceived helplessness (Elder and Liker 1982), and perceived powerlessness (Seeman 1959, 1983).

Table 3.1.   Mirowsky-Ross Measure of the Sense of Personal Control vs. Powerlessness

---

Control over good

(1) "I am responsible for my own successes"
(2) "I can do just about anything I really set my mind to"

Control over bad

(3) "My misfortunes are the result of mistakes I have made"
(4) "I am responsible for my failures"

Powerless over good

(5) "The really good things that happen to me are mostly luck"
(6) "There's no sense planning a lot—if something good is going to happen it will"

Powerless over bad

(7) "Most of my problems are due to bad breaks"
(8) "I have little control over the bad things that happen to me"

To create a mean score perceived-control scale, responses to perceived control questions (1 through 4) are coded: -2 = strongly disagree, -1 = disagree, 0 = neutral, 1 = agree, 2 = strongly agree, and responses to perceived powerlessness questions (5 through 8) are coded -2 = strongly agree, -1 = agree, 0 = neutral, 1 = disagree, 2 = strongly disagree.

Source: Mirowsky and Ross (1991).

Personal Control

Personal control is the sense of directing one's own life. Our measure of personal control is shown In Table 3.1. The sense of personal control refers to oneself, not others. It is also general, not specific to any one realm of life, like work or politics. Our measure balances statements claiming and denying personal control, and balances statements in which the outcome is positive and negative. This eliminates defense, self-blame, and agreement bias from the measure. Defense is the tendency to claim control over good outcomes but deny control over bad outcomes. Self-blame, the opposite, is the tendency to claim control over bad outcomes but not good. Agreement is the tendency to simply say "yes" to survey questions, irrespective of content. Because of our balanced 2×2 design, none of these tendencies biases our measure of personal control.

Locus of Control

In cognitive psychology, perceived control appears as locus of control (Rotter 1966). Belief in an external locus of control is a *learned*, generalized expectation that outcomes of situations are determined by forces external to oneself such as powerful others, luck, fate, or chance. The individual believes that he or she is powerless and at the mercy of the environment. Belief in an internal locus of control (the opposite) is a learned, generalized expectation that outcomes are contingent on one's own choices and actions. Compared to persons with an external locus of control, those with an internal locus of control attribute outcomes to themselves rather than to forces outside themselves.

Our concept of personal control corresponds closely to the personal control component of Rotter's locus of control scale, which includes items like "When I make plans I can make them work" or "I have little influence over the things that happen to me." However, Rotter's locus of control scale also includes items that refer to other people in addition to oneself, and it includes items that are realm-specific in addition to general questions. In contrast our concept of personal control refers to *oneself*, not others, and it is *general*, not realm-specific (Mirowsky and Ross 1989). For instance, we do not consider questions from the Rotter scale like "The average citizen can have an influence in government decisions" or "There will always be wars" to be measures of the sense of personal control for two reasons: they do not refer to oneself, and they are specific to the political realm. Rotter included some realm-specific questions relating to politics, school, personal relationships, and so on. He also included perceptions about the amount of control *others* have over their lives, but we consider these beliefs are conceptually distinct from personal control. Belief about the amount of control that other people have has been termed ideological control (Gurin, Gurin, and Morrison 1978), universal control, and American instrumentalism (Mirowsky, Ross, and Van Willigen 1996). Ideological, or universal, control refers to the degree one feels that others' successes or failures are their own doing; personal control refers to one's own life outcomes.

Self-Efficacy

The sense of personal control overlaps to a large extent with self-efficacy despite Bandura's (1986) claim that sense of control and self-efficacy are distinct (although related) concepts. Bandura collectively refers to concepts of locus of control, or sense of control, as outcome-expectancy theories. Self-efficacy, according to Bandura, focuses upon the individual's belief that he or she can (or can not) effectively perform a specific action, whereas control focuses on the belief that certain actions will achieve ultimately desired goals. According to Bandura, self-efficacy is specific to particular contexts. The sense of control is a more parsimonious concept than self-efficacy, with more universal application. The degree to which people think they can or cannot achieve their goals, despite the specific nature of the actions required, has applicability to almost all circumstances. Hence, control is a more attractive measurable concept for health research. More importantly, the sense of personal control may be the root of self-efficacy. Persons with a high sense of personal control will likely try other actions if their current repertoire of behaviors is not working. New behaviors may successfully obtain desired goals, which may in turn increase the perceived ability to shape other events and circumstances in life. Therefore, for all intents and purposes, the sense of control may be measuring the same underlying factor as self-efficacy. The conceptual distinction Bandura outlines may well be a purely academic one.

Helplessness

Another related concept appears in behavioral psychology as learned helplessness. The behavior of learned helplessness results from exposure to inescapable, uncontrollable negative stimuli and is characterized by a low rate of voluntary response and low ability to learn successful behaviors (Seligman 1975). Although intended as an analog of human depression, it is important to remember that learned helplessness refers to the behavior, not to any cognitive attribution that reinforcements are outside one's control, and not to the imputed emotion of depression. Seligman studied animals. In humans, however, there is a link between an external locus of control (a cognitive orientation) and learned helplessness (a conditioned response): the perception that reinforcement is not contingent on action. Hiroto (1974) found that, compared to subjects with an internal locus of control, those with an external locus of control were less likely to see a connection between behavior and reinforcement, and as a result, learned more slowly. Humans may understand when their actions do not affect outcomes, producing the awareness of helplessness.

Subjective Alienation

In sociology, the concept of perceived powerlessness versus control can be traced to subjective alienation. Seeman (1959) defined alienation as any form of detachment or separation from oneself or from others. He further elaborated specific forms of alienation, defining powerlessness as the primary type of alienation (the others are self-estrangement, isolation, meaninglessness, and normlessness). He defined it as "the expectancy or probability, held by the individual, that his own behavior cannot determine the occurrence of the outcomes, or reinforcements, he seeks" (ibid.:784). Powerlessness is the separation from important outcomes in one's own life, or an inability to achieve desired ends. Perceived powerlessness is the cognitive awareness of this reality. Both Rotter (1966) and Seeman (1959) recognized that perceived powerlessness—the major form of subjective alienation—and external locus of control were related concepts. In fact, Rotter derived the concept of locus of control from the sociological concept of alienation, stating "the alienated individual feels unable to control his own destiny" (1966:263).

Other sociological concepts build on themes of perceived powerlessness versus control, and unlike some psychologists who focus on differences among related concepts, sociologists appear more likely to look for these common themes. As a result, many of the constructs used by sociologists overlap and often are conceptually indistinct. In sociology, concepts related to personal control appear under a number of different names in addition to powerlessness, notably mastery (Pearlin et al. 1981), personal autonomy (Seeman 1983), the sense of personal efficacy (Downey and Moen 1987; Gecas 1989), and instrumentalism (Mirowsky et al. 1996; Wheaton, 1980).

Education Boosts Personal Control

Through the accumulated experience of success or failure, a person learns his or her own behaviors can or cannot achieve outcomes. Continued experience of failure in the face of effort leads to a sense of powerlessness and helplessness, characterized by passivity and giving up (Ross et al. 1983; Seligman 1975; Wheaton 1980). Through continued experience with objective conditions of little control, individuals come to learn that their own actions cannot produce desired outcomes. In contrast, experiences of success lead to a sense of personal control, characterized by instrumentalism and an active approach to life.

Education raises the sense of personal control because it helps people successfully prevent problems, or solve them if prevention fails, to achieve their goals, and shape their own lives (Mirowsky and Ross 1989; Pearlin et al. 1981; Ross and Mirowsky 1992; Wheaton 1980). Through education, one develops capacities on many levels that increase one's sense of personal control. Schooling builds human capital—skills, abilities, and resources—that ultimately shape health and well-being because the human capital acquired in school increases a person's real and perceived control over life. Education develops the habits and skills of communication: reading, writing, inquiring, discussing, looking things up, and figuring things out. It develops basic analytic skills such as observing, experimenting, summarizing, synthesizing, interpreting, and classifying. Because education develops the ability to gather and interpret information and to solve problems on many levels, it increases control over events and outcomes in life (Ross and Mirowsky 1989). Moreover, in education, one encounters and solves problems that are progressively more difficult, complex, and subtle. The process of learning builds problem-solving skills and confidence in the ability to solve problems. Education instills the habit of meeting problems with attention, thought, action, and persistence. Thus, education

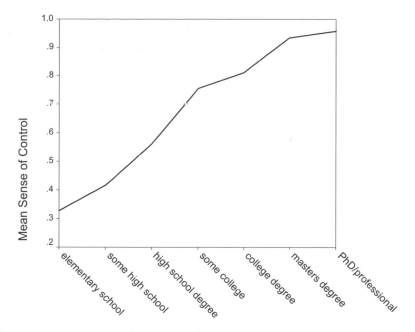

Figure 3.6. Education and the sense of control.

increases effort and ability, the fundamental components of problem-solving (Wheaton 1980). For this reason, high levels of education are associated with a sense of personal control (Pearlin et al. 1981; Ross and Mirowsky 1992; Wheaton 1980). The strong association between education and the sense of control is shown in Figure 3.6.

Personal Control Shapes a Healthy Lifestyle

People with high levels of personal control are effective forces in their own lives. According to the theory of personal control, control's benefit lies in effectiveness (Mirowsky and Ross 1986, 1989; Ross and Sastry 1999). The sense of not being in control of the good or bad outcomes in one's life can diminish the will and motivation to solve problems. Belief in the efficacy of external rather than personal forces makes active attempts to solve problems seem pointless (Wheaton 1980). The result is less motivation and less persistence in coping, and thus less success in solving problems and adapting. People who feel in control of their lives are more likely to attempt to solve problems; those who feel powerless are more likely to try to forget about problems and hope they go away (Ross and Mirowsky

1989). People with little perceived control over their lives have a reactive, passive orientation, whereas those with high perceived control have a proactive outlook. Instrumental persons are likely to accumulate resources and to develop skills and habits that prevent avoidable problems and reduce the impact of unavoidable problems. Thus, over time instrumental persons improve their positions even more, producing a self-amplifying reciprocal effect between achievements and perceived control.

The firm sense of personal control held by persons with higher levels of education improves health in large part by way of health-enhancing behaviors. Compared to people who feel powerless to control their lives, people with a sense of personal control know more about health, they are more likely to initiate preventive behaviors like quitting smoking, exercising, or maintaining a normal weight, and, in consequence, they have better self-rated health, fewer illnesses, and lower rates of mortality (Mirowsky and Ross 1998; Seeman and Lewis 1995; Seeman and Seeman 1983; Seeman, Seeman, and Budros 1988). In contrast, lack of personal control makes efforts seem useless; if outcomes are beyond one's control, what is the point of exercising, quitting smoking, or avoiding overweight? The higher a person's sense of personal control the greater their count of healthy behaviors, as shown in Figure 3.7.

Putting It All Together

Personal control and a healthy lifestyle link education to health. Figure 3.8 shows a path model that puts together all the links in the causal chain. This chain has the following links: education increases the sense of personal control, which shapes a healthy lifestyle, which improves health; and control and lifestyle largely (but not entirely) explain why education is associated with good health.

The path model shows relationships between constructs. Lines with arrows illustrate associations. (These associations can also be described by equations, so technically this is called a structural equation model). Education tends to increase (+.321) the sense of personal control, the sense of personal control tends to increase (+.354) healthy lifestyle, and healthy lifestyle tends to improve (+.810) health. A path is formed by tracing arrows between constructs, following the normal rules for multiplying signs. To see the total effect of education on a healthy lifestyle that is mediated by a high sense of personal control, multiply the paths. A positive path times another positive path produces a total positive effect (+.321 × +.354 = +.114). The path diagram also shows that education is associated with a healthy lifestyle, apart from its association with a sense of control. This is illustrated by the path from education to lifestyle, which does not go through control (+.140). The total effect of education on a healthy

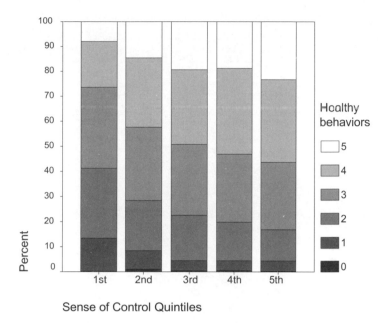

Figure 3.7. Sense of control and healthy behaviors.

lifestyle contains two paths: one in which control links education to lifestyle and one in which education directly shapes lifestyle, apart from its association with high personal control. Thus, education is associated with good health in large part because the well-educated have high levels of personal control, which shapes a healthy lifestyle, yet education also affects health apart from its links to control and lifestyle.

The path model also contains another type of relationship: that between the measure and the concept it indicates. For example, healthy lifestyle is measured by exercising, walking, and drinking moderately (which are positive signs of a healthy lifestyle) and by smoking and being overweight (which are negative signs). These healthy practices form a coherent lifestyle, as illustrated in Figure 3.9. Health is indicated by subjective, or self-reported health, and two types of physical impairment: sensory, which includes trouble seeing and hearing, and musculoskeletal, which includes difficulty climbing stairs, kneeling, stooping, lifting, carrying, preparing meals, cleaning the house, and getting around. Self-reported good health is a positive sign of health, and impairments are negative signs.

The detail of the measurement model shown in Figure 3.9 also shows that once impaired, a person is less likely to walk and exercise and more

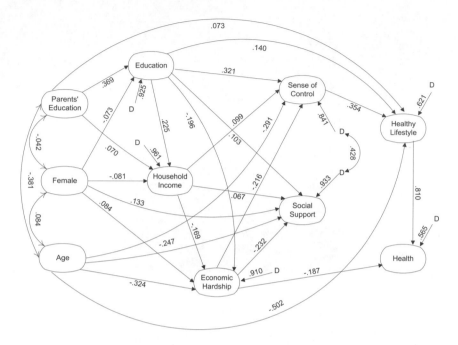

Figure 3.8.   Path diagram of structural equation model showing that the sense of control and healthy lifestyle link education to heath.

likely to be overweight. Thus, a sedentary lifestyle and physical impairment reinforce each other, each making the other worse. Persons who are not physically active experience more impairments, which in turn decrease their physical activity and fitness in a feedback loop that produces increasing impairment levels and decreasing activity levels as sedentary adults age.

The path model illustrated in Figure 3.8 also shows that relationships described are not spuriously due to economic factors like household income or economic hardship, or to background characteristics, like age, sex, or one's parents' education levels, or to supportive relationships with other people. These factors are statistically adjusted, or held constant. For example, if we compare two people with equal levels of economic hardship, the person with the higher sense of personal control or a healthier lifestyle will have better health. In the chapters that follow we will discuss whether education affects health partly because of the economic prosperity that high educational attainment brings and whether education affects health partly because it helps people build supportive relationships with others. As Figure 3.8 shows, and as we will discuss in the next chapter, eco-

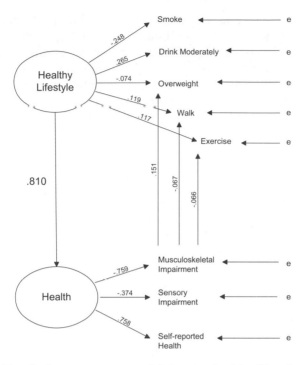

Figure 3.9. Detail of measurement model showing healthy lifestyle and health.

nomic hardship has a negative impact on health. Here the important fact is that a sense of control over one's own life encourages a healthy lifestyle and transmits much of education's effect on health, and that this process cannot be attributed to background characteristics, to economic resources, or to social support.

Education, Human Capital, Learned Effectiveness, and Health

A large part of the reason the well-educated experience good health is that they engage in a lifestyle that includes walking, exercising, drinking moderately, and avoiding overweight and smoking. High levels of personal control among the well-educated account for much of the reason they engage in a healthy lifestyle. The data support the view of education as learned effectiveness. This does not mean that education's effects on income and economic hardship are irrelevant. The path model indicates that economic hardship accounts for some of the association between low education and poor health. Full-time employment and creative work account for some, too, as shown in chapter 4. Education is a mark of socioeconomic status and a mechanism of its inheritance. But it is also schooling. As people learn they become effective agents. That effectiveness yields benefits that include prosperity but also transcend it. Education-based resources go beyond good jobs that provide high incomes to a sense of personal control and a lifestyle that protects and fosters health. Education makes individuals more effective agents in their own lives. It enables individuals to gain control of their lives, including their health.

| 4 |

Education, Socioeconomic Status, and Health

Socioeconomic status refers to the gradation of opportunity, prosperity, and standing in human populations. Sociologists try to understand how that gradation comes to exist and what consequences it has. Socioeconomic status has three main components among adults in the United States. Education itself acts as the primary and core status dimension. It influences standing on other status dimensions throughout the lifetime, and forms the main link between the adulthood status of one generation and another in the same family. Economic resources and work-based statuses constitute the other two main components. Some research emphasizes one component of status while ignoring or downplaying the others. Other research blurs the distinctions among aspects of status by averaging ranks on various dimensions. Both approaches can be useful. Nevertheless, a complete and precise understanding of the relationship between health and socioeconomic status requires a careful distinction among its aspects. What specifics of social standing improve health? Is it money and wealth? Prestige and prominence? Knowledge and ability? Power and authority? Freedom and independence? How do gradations of opportunity, prosperity, and standing translate into gradations of physical health and functioning?

To answer that question we define the various dimensions of adult socioeconomic status in the United States, describe their relationships to education and to each other, and analyze their relationships to health. We divide the chapter into two broad sections. The first, on economic resources, looks at education's relationship to income and economic prosperity, and explores the roles of privation, hardship, and access to medical care as possible links to health. The second section looks at education's relationship to work-related statuses such as categories of employment, occupations, and their attributes, and the autonomy, creativity, and authority of the work. It analyzes the correlations between health and these work-related statuses, looking for the specific links that reveal the nature of the connection.

ECONOMIC RESOURCES

Education and Household Income

Economic well-being comes to mind immediately when thinking of the benefits education provides that may protect and promote health. Higher educational attainment corresponds with substantial economic advantage, as illustrated in Figure 4.1. The graph shows the mean and median levels of household income across levels of education in our 1995 U.S. survey. At the low end, respondents with elementary-school educations report incomes in the previous year with a mean of $16,800. At the high end, respondents with doctoral or professional degrees report incomes with a mean 5.4 times higher, or $91,000 per household. That is 1.6 times greater than the $58,500 mean reported by persons with four-year college degrees, and 2.6 times greater than the $35,200 mean reported by persons with high school degrees.

Education's Compounding Relationship with Income

Overall, the mean level of household income increases by an average of about $4,500 for each additional year of formal education. However the size of the increment also increases with the level of education. For example, the respondents with high school degrees average about five years of schooling more than those who did not go to high school. The mean household incomes of the two groups differ by $18,400, or $3,680 per additional year of school. Individuals with four-year college degrees average about $23,300 more than those with high school degrees but no college, or about $5,825 per additional year of school. Individuals with doctoral or professional degrees average about $32,500 more than those with four-year college degrees only, or about $6,500 more per additional year of schooling (assuming the doctoral work takes about five years).

With respect to education, the mean and median levels of income follow a pattern similar to that of compounding interest. The mean and median incomes go up an additional 14 or 15 percent with each additional year of schooling. About 75 percent of that represents the impact of education on income through various mediators discussed later. That part, called the total effect in causal analysis, represents the 11 percent compounding increase in household income resulting from each additional year of education. The rest represents the impact of background traits or statuses that influence educational attainment and also directly influence income apart from their effect through education (mostly age and sex, but also partly parents' education). The 11 percent compounding total effect adds up to about 52 percent for an additional four years of school and 230 percent for an additional eight years.

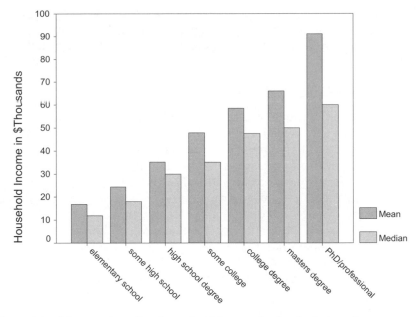

Figure 4.1. Mean and median household income by level of education.

Income's Skewed Distribution

The growing dollar income increments associated with added years of education illustrate one of the most important facts about differences in income and their causes and consequences. Progressive increments in income tend to be percentages or multiples rather than fixed amounts. The multiplicative nature of the income distribution has many important repercussions. One is that most people get less than the average amount of income. In fact, a household with the mean income would be getting as much or more than about two-thirds of all households. A household right in the middle at the median, with half of the other households getting more income and half getting less, has an income about 30 percent below the mean. These relationships hold within levels of education too. Income follows what statisticians call a skewed distribution. It takes much larger increments in income to move up to the top ranks than to move up from the bottom ranks. For example, in our data only $2,000 separates the household at the bottom of reported income from the one at the first percentile, where 99 percent of the sample gets more. At the other end, $574,000 separates the household at the ninety-ninth percentile (where only 1 percent get more) from the household at the very top. It takes twice as much additional income to move up *from* the median to the eightieth percentile as it does to move up *to* the median from the twentieth percentile.

Reasons for Education's Compounding Effect

Theorists often attribute the skewed, multiplicative distribution of income to the diminishing subjective utility of additional money. The perceived value of additional money depends on the base amount someone already has or normally gets. One thousand dollars would be a powerful inducement to someone who earns $10,000 a year, a sweetener to someone who earns $100,000, and insignificant to someone who earns $1,000,000. As a result, businesses and other organizations generally must give monetary rewards and inducements in percentages rather than fixed amounts. There is little doubt that the subjective value of additional income decreases as the base to which it is added increases. However, this phenomenon probably does not explain the compounding increase in household income with each additional year of education.

Theoretically it can appear that the reward for additional education must increase because it is added to an ever larger base of expectation. Although theoretically elegant, the explanation seems distant from reality as people experience it. Employers generally do not contract with students, negotiating higher future salaries with those who will sign up for additional years of education. Students generally have only vague ideas about the relationship between education and income. While most Americans probably expect income to go up with education, there is no reason to think most would know the compounding form of the relationship. Educational aspirations take shape in family and friendship networks that only rarely calculate the expected incremental gains from the additional years of schooling. Fewer still submit the estimates to the student so that he or she can judge the utility of continuing. The student might be inclined to discount severely the uncertain and far-off benefits relative to the certain and immediate demands of school. Better to point out that the student's friends are going to college, which is a place where one may continue to live at parental expense without incessant parental oversight. The short-run consequences of staying in or dropping out probably influence student decisions far more than does the subjective utility of the expected increment to future income.

Perhaps education's compounding effect on average household income results from something inherent in the nature of education itself: the compounding effectiveness of added intellectual skill. Productivity may multiply with each new ability. An avid reader who then becomes a clear and persuasive writer or speaker may in so doing raise the impact of the reading to a new power. Each intellectual skill multiplies the scope of the others. Problems in mathematics provide the clearest illustration of the principle. The rules of logarithms solve some problems. The rules of derivatives solve others. The two sets of rules combined solve problems that neither alone can. Learning a new intellectual skill does not simply incorporate additional material in the manner of a city growing into the surrounding farmland. It does not simply cover more territory within the existing dimensions, it adds a new dimension. Many learned intellectual abilities also produce self-developing effects. If a student learns to articulate an issue, summarize the range of opinions on it, probe and abstract the assumptions and interests behind each, seek information that might validate or invalidate the assumptions, judge the quality and relevance of the information found, and consider the issue logically based on the best available information, then the student creates a self-sharpening intellect. Each part of the procedure improves the quality of judgment and enhances the value of the other elements. Perhaps the impact on income of additional education grows with the amount of education to which it is added because each new intellectual skill multiplies the effectiveness of the others to which it is added.

Employment, Earnings, and Marriage Linking Education with Income

Whatever the theoretical reason for the relationship between education and household income, the empirical links are straightforward. Household income in the United States overwhelmingly comes from current wages and salaries or from pensions, social security, and savings based on past wages and salaries. Education increases the probability and consistency of employment during the earning years, and increases the current and past wage or salary rates. Education also increases the probability of being married, which increases the probable household income because two people generally can earn more than one. In addition, higher education increases the likely current or past earnings of one's partner because people generally marry someone with a similar level of education.

Income and Health

The relationship of health to household income has two important characteristics. The first is that lower income and poorer health tend to go together. The average subjective health scores go up and the average impairment scores and number of serious diagnoses go down as the level of income rises from its lowest values, as illustrated in Figures 4.2 through 4.4. The graphs show the average subjective health scores, physical

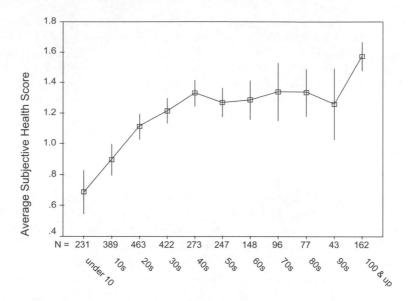

Family Income in 1994 in $ Thousands

Figure 4.2. Subjective health scores: mean and 95 percent confidence interval, by
level of household income (in thousands of dollars).

impairment scores, and numbers of serious diagnoses in ten-thousand
dollar ranges of household income from all sources. Each square represents the arithmetic mean for a segment of the sample. The lines bracket-
ing it represent the 95 percent confidence interval likely to contain the
mean for the corresponding segment of the entire population (i.e., the sample's margin of error.)

Income's Diminishing Incremental Association with Health

The second important fact about the relationship is that the size of the
improvement in health with each additional step up in level of income gets
smaller and smaller. The biggest improvements in health are on the low
end, moving up from the bottom of the economic ladder to the middle.
Beyond the $40,000 level the differences in average health with increased
level of income get considerably smaller than the margins of error. That is
somewhere around the sixty-fifth percentile of the income distribution.
Roughly two-thirds of the population gets that income or less and roughly
one-third gets more. It is a little above the average household income
reported by persons with high school degrees but no college. Beyond that

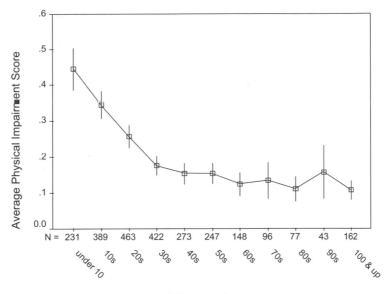

Figure 4.3. Physical impairment scores: mean and 95 percent confidence interval, by level of household income (in thousands of dollars).

level of income the correlation of higher income with better health becomes tenuous. Some researchers argue that it disappears entirely. Others argue that it just gets so small that it often becomes undetectable given the margin of error in typical samples.

The shape of the relationship between income and health turns out to be as important as the fact that the relationship exists. For one thing, it has apparent implications for economic policy. It suggests that a nation's overall level of health might improve more by raising income at the bottom end than by raising it across the board. Indeed, when nations are compared to others with similar per capita gross national product, the countries with greater equality of income tend to have higher life expectancy and lower infant mortality (Evans 1994; Hertzman, Frank, and Evans 1994). Theorists suspect this happens because a smaller fraction of the population is down at the low end of income, where even modest increases would improve health substantially. Likewise, a smaller fraction is up at the high end, where even large increases in income would have little or no impact on health. Some policy analysts take these observations and interpretations as a sign that governments should seek to improve the health and well-being of their populations by moving incomes toward the middle, taxing the

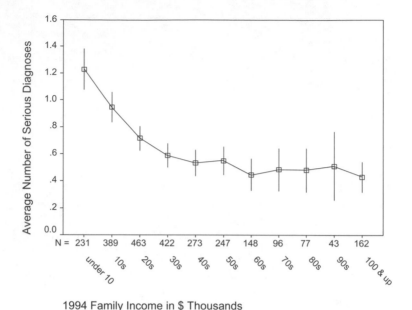

1994 Family Income in $ Thousands

Figure 4.4. Number of serious diagnoses: mean and 95 percent confidence interval, by level of household income (in thousands of dollars).

wealthiest to provide benefits and subsidies to the poorest. The trouble with doing so, others argue, is that it discourages investment and reduces the incentives for diligence and ingenuity, thereby slowing and perhaps reversing the growth in national prosperity. This dilemma produces the counterpoint of much political debate. However, education's role in forming the association suggests a solution to the apparent dilemma, as we will show.

Education as Moderator of Income's Association with Health

The shape of the relationship between income and health is important for a second reason. It provides a clue to the forces that connect the two. Comparing the association of health with income across levels of education reveals education's extra benefit. The differences in health across levels of income get smaller at higher levels of education. Figures 4.5 through 4.7 show the mean subjective health scores, impairment scores, and counts of serious diagnoses by level of income for persons with no high school degree, a high school degree but not a four-year college degree, and a four-year college degree or higher. All three health measures show roughly the same pattern: (1) at any given level of income, health tends to be better at

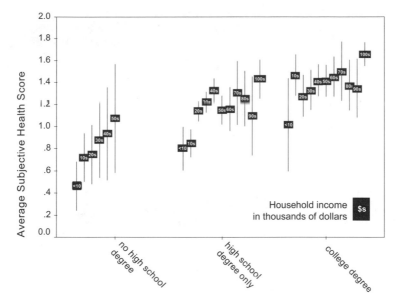

Figure 4.5. Subjective health scores: mean and 95 percent confidence interval by level of income and education.

higher levels of education, (2) within each level of education health tends to be worst at the lowest levels of income, but (3) the differences in health across levels of income are smaller at higher levels of education.

Education improves health by reducing the health problems associated with low income, as well as by increasing the average level of household income This is an instance of what we call resource substitution. Resource substitution exists when having more of one resource makes the lack of another less damaging. In the present case the effect on health of low income tends to diminish as the level of education increases.

Education, Economic Hardship, and Health

Several things about higher income might improve health. The most obvious is that household income helps individuals meet human needs (Williams 1990). Indeed, poverty can be defined as lacking the means necessary for physical well-being—as the inability to meet basic needs for food, shelter, clothes, and care. The higher one's income is, the more likely these needs will be met. Education plays a major part in shaping the relationship. Education not only increases income, it also decreases the association of lower income with poorer health. It does so in large part by

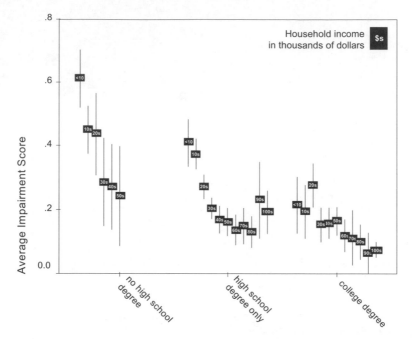

Figure 4.6. Impairment scores: mean and 95 percent confidence interval by level of income and education.

reducing the association of lower income with greater difficulty paying the bills and meeting household needs for food, clothing, housing, and medical care.

Education as an Effective Substitute for Income

One of the most important resource substitutions occurs between education and household income in their effects on economic hardship, which in turn shapes the association between income and health. At any given level of income, people with higher levels of education are more successful at avoiding trouble paying the bills or buying things the household needs such as food, clothing, housing, and medical care (Mirowsky and Hu 1996; Mirowsky and Ross 1999; Ross and Huber 1985). A poorly educated person needs more money to fend off economic hardship than does a well-educated person. Education does two things. It reduces the risk of economic hardship at every level of income. It also reduces the amount that the risk of economic hardship increases at successively lower levels of household income. Persons with low education are doubly disadvantaged. Low education restrains income and also increases the difficulty of

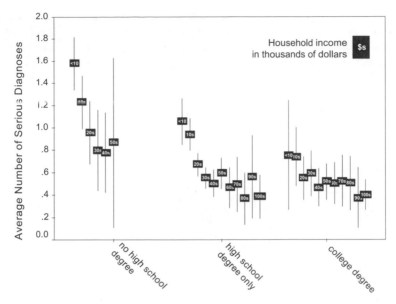

Figure 4.7. Number of serious diagnoses: mean and 95 percent confidence interval by level of income and education.

managing with low income. Education provides information and develops skills and habits of thought and action that help individuals use income efficiently. As a consequence it helps individuals avoid situations that greatly elevate the risk of economic hardship.

Children and Economic Hardship

Our research finds that two aspects of household composition heavily influence the risk of economic hardship: having dependent children in the household, and not being married. It should come as no surprise that dependent children in the household greatly increase the prevalence and severity of economic hardship. Partly that is because they create work-family strains that tend to reduce the earnings of at least one parent, which is typically the mother. Interrupted employment, part-time employment, and hampered job performance reduce current earnings and slow the rate at which pay increases. More importantly, though, dependent children increase economic hardship because they *are* dependent. Children need food, clothes, shelter, transportation, school supplies, and medical care, not to mention toys, entertainment, and minding. As a consequence, dependent children greatly increase the risk and severity of economic hardship at any given level of household income, while tending to reduce the amount of household income. People with higher levels of education more often avoid these problems by having fewer children and starting their families later in adulthood when jobs are more secure, careers better established, and earnings more ample.

Partners and Economic Hardship

The presence of a spouse or other adult partner in the household also greatly influences the level of economic hardship. Again this happens by influencing average household income and by altering the risk of hardship at every level of income. Each partner's earnings can enhance the other's or fill gaps in the other's, or one partner can help the other maximize earnings. In addition, the presence of a partner reduces economic hardship at any given level of household income. To put that another way, a household with an income of, say, $30,000 has a *lower* risk of economic hardship if there are two adult partners rather than one lone adult. This is true even though two adults cost more to support than one. Apparently households headed by two adults use income more efficiently than those with a lone householder.

The presence of a partner seems especially valuable when the household has dependent children. Persons with dependent children but no partners have by far the highest levels of economic hardship net of income (and consequently the highest levels of depression and malaise). Those with partners but no children in the household have the lowest levels of economic hardship. Our statistical models allow us to estimate the income ratios needed to keep the risk of economic hardship the same between households with different compositions (partner present or absent and children present or absent)(Mirowsky and Ross 1999). Compared to married people with no children in the household, the married with children need 1.5 times more income to have the same low levels of economic hardship. Persons who have no children but also no partners likewise need 1.5 times more income than the married with no children. Individuals with children but no partners need 3.5 times more income than the married without children to have the same low level of economic hardship. That is about 2.3 times more than needed by the married with children or the nonmarried without children. The probability of having a partner but no children in the household increases with the level of education, and the probability of having children but no partner decreases.

Economic Hardship, Privation, and Health

Why does economic hardship undermine health? Material privation may be part of the answer. Privation is lack of the basic necessities or comforts of life. In wealthy countries such as the United States few families go without the basic minimum of food, clothing, and shelter needed to stay alive and functioning, even when experiencing economic hardship (Evans 1994; Evans, Hodge, and Pless 1994; Mayer 1997). When extreme privation does occur it generally comes and goes as an episode rather than forming a persistent damaging and lethal status. More commonly low income and economic hardship limit housing options to dilapidated buildings, frequently in squalid and threatening neighborhoods. The dwellings are plagued by a host of problems that increase exposure to infection, injury, toxins, carcinogens, and physical stress from excessive heat or cold. The problems include infestation with insects and rodents that can carry infectious diseases, plumbing that fails to work or leaks, leaky roofs, damp basements or other interior areas growing mold and mildew, heating systems that break down or cannot keep up or release allergens and dusts and hazardous gases such as carbon monoxide, hot water that does not get hot enough to clean and disinfect well or that suddenly and unexpectedly gets scalding hot, uninviting bathtubs or showers, poor ventilation, little or no natural light, no air conditioning, no washer and dryer, no electric dishwasher or garbage disposal, electrical wiring that is frayed or overburdened, stairs and banisters in bad repair, lights in halls and stairways that are burned out or do not work, poorly maintained or filthy stoves and ovens, disgusting refrigerators that cannot keep food sufficiently cold, broken furniture, broken windows or doors, torn or nonexistent screens, poor insulation to keep heat in and noise out, and decaying surfaces shedding paint and other chemicals.

Dilapidated apartments and homes often are located in neighborhoods that add biophysical exposures such as heavy traffic, abandoned vehicles and buildings, sanitary sewers that leak or back up into storm sewers that back up into streets, garbage and trash left on the streets or dumped in abandoned lots, excrement from pets and sometimes from humans, stray dogs and cats, the nests and guano of pigeons or other birds that harbor parasites, poorly controlled populations of rats and other scavengers that can carry disease, uncontrolled populations of mosquitoes, soil under abandoned gas stations saturated with carcinogenic hydrocarbons leaching into local groundwater, abandoned industrial facilities with old spills and dumps of hazardous chemicals or materials, active facilities of moribund industries that cut costs by violating environmental regulations in places where the authorities rarely look closely and the locals rarely interfere, and in rural areas exposure to fertilizers and herbicides and pesticides during application or as residue in the dust raised by farming operations. Such neighborhoods may add social risks to health such as unhealthy lifestyles among the neighbors that may draw a person in or that create risks to others in physical or social proximity. These might include widespread abuse of alcohol and other psychoactive drugs or addiction to tobacco, prostitution, risky acts of abandon such as sharing dirty needles, driving while intoxicated, or having unprotected sex or multiple sexual partners, diets that rely on packaged or prepared foods high in fat and sugar and poorly balanced in other nutrients, passive recreations with little or no exercise, frequent outbursts of violence among family members and acquaintances, and male subcultures glorifying violence, domination, risk-taking, and lawlessness.

The litany of risky exposures that are more common in low-cost housing and poor neighborhoods paints a grim picture. The material privations and risky exposures resulting from low income and economic hardship can get as extreme as the full list implies. Usually, though, individual households face some of the privations and risks but not most. The material wealth of the United States is so great that even households at the bottom of the economic ladder often have amenities once considered luxuries of the well-to-do. In her outstanding study of childhood poverty, Mayer (1997) reports the percentage of children living in homes with various design or maintenance problems and various amenities or durable goods. In households at the bottom 10 percent in terms of income, only 31.3 percent had any of the eight problems on her list: incomplete bathroom, no central heat, no electrical outlets in one or more rooms, exposed wires, holes in the floor, open cracks in the wall or ceiling, leaky roof, and signs of rats or mice (ibid.:Table 6.2). Only 14.1 percent had at least two of the problems, and only 5.8 percent had at least four of them. On the other hand, in those same households at the bottom 10 percent of income, 13.9 percent had at least two bathrooms, 16.5 percent had a dishwasher, 17.3 percent had two or more motor vehicles, 37.5 percent had a clothes dryer, 52.3 percent had air conditioning, 57.3 percent had a motor vehicle, 57.8 percent had a clothes washer, and 68.7 percent had a telephone (ibid.:Table 6.3).

Clearly, some households suffer from material privations that a wealthy society need not accept. Nevertheless, material privation probably does not account for most of the impact on health of low income and economic hardship in the United States. There are good reasons to suspect that relegation to substandard housing or a bad neighborhood may degrade health for reasons that go beyond the exposures and physical stress of material privation. Perhaps more to the point, economic hardship typically means something other than a leaky roof and rats in the walls. Even for the great majority of adults in their comfortable homes and decent neighborhoods, economic hardship is a taste of inadequacy and failure, laced with a threat that what one has may be lost.

Economic Hardship, Stress, and Health

Biomedical research shows that threatening situations produce physiological responses that may impair health in several ways: by creating symptoms experienced as illness, by increasing susceptibility to pathogens and pathological conditions, and by accelerating the degradation of critical physiological systems (Fremont and Bird 2000). Perceived threats trigger a primitive, biological, fight-or-flight response (detailed below) that we humans share with other mammals. To some extent, low income and economic hardship degrade health by limiting housing options to squalid and threatening neighborhoods with filthy streets, decaying and abandoned buildings, graffiti and vandalism, noise, crowding, crime, people hanging out on the streets drinking or taking drugs, and mutual hostility more than mutual aid between neighbors. Those conditions probably do arouse the fight-or-flight response frequently and intensely, as well as exposing individuals to pathogens. Nevertheless, our statistical analyses suggest that they account for only about 5 to 10 percent of the effects of low income and economic hardship on health.

Being in an economically strained household has a far greater negative correlation with health than does living in a neighborhood rife with signs of disorder and decay. We estimated and compared the effects of economic hardship in the household and of disorder and decay in the neighborhood on a health measure that combines the indexes of subjective health, physical functioning, and freedom from serious chronic conditions, using data from our 1995 Survey of Community, Crime and Health, which interviewed 2,482 randomly selected adult household residents of Illinois, many of whom live in Chicago and its suburbs. The survey measured neighborhood disorder and decay by asking respondents to rate the strength of agreement with statements describing the neighborhood. The statements describe physical signs of disorder such as graffiti, vandalism, noise, and abandoned buildings, and social signs such as crime, people hanging out on the street, too much drinking and drug taking, and trouble with the neighbors. It includes reverse-coded signs of neighborhood order, such as people taking care of their houses or apartments and watching out for each other, and the neighborhood seeming clean and safe.

We estimated the effects on health of household economic hardship and neighborhood disorder and decay adjusting for each other and for age, sex, race, urban residence, education, income, employment, and having children and/or a partner in the household. The standardized regression coefficients for household economic hardship and neighborhood disorder and decay are −.198 and −.076, respectively. (For comparison, the standardized effect of age is −.372.) Economic hardship's standardized effect is 2.6 times greater than that of disorder and decay in the neighborhood. Roughly speaking, these numbers suggest that moving up several ranks in level of economic hardship while remaining in the same neighborhood is much worse for health than moving up the same number of ranks in neighborhood disorder and decay while keeping the household's frequency of economic hardship steady. It is better for health to live within your means in a poor neighborhood than to live beyond your means in a prosperous one. The problem is that individuals with low income and little education find it very difficult to make ends meet, particularly with children in the household.

Economic hardship poses a direct threat to the well-being of oneself and one's family. As a result, people exposed to economic hardship probably experience frequent, intense, and prolonged activation of the physiological stress response, with consequences for their health. According to current biomedical theory, threats stimulate a two-phase response (Evans et al. 1994; Memmler, Cohen, and Wood 1996; Sapolsky 1998; Thibodeau and Patton 1997). In the initial alarm stage, sympathetic nerve fibers and the adrenal medulla release the hormone epinephrine and the neurotransmitter norepinephrine. This increases heart rate, blood pressure, and respiration rate, dilates the blood vessels of the heart, lungs, and skeletal muscles, constricts the vessels of the digestive tract, and releases glucose from the liver into the blood. The activation of the sympathetic nerves also stimulates the sweat glands and suppresses the salivary glands. These physiological responses may be experienced as illness, particularly if the response becomes frequent or generalized and thus seemingly detached from specific stimuli. Individuals exposed to chronic psychosocial strains develop heightened reactivity (Pike et al. 1997; Pruessner et al. 1997). They enter the stage of alarm more readily, quickly, and intensely, and take longer to recover from it.

In a follow-up resistance stage of the "fight or flight" response, an endocrine gland in the brain called the anterior pituitary releases adrenocorticotropic stimulating hormone (ACTH), which stimulates the release of cortisol (hydrocortisone) from the adrenal cortex. This hormone suppresses pain, inflammation, allergy, and immunity. It raises blood glucose levels by decreasing glucose metabolism and accelerating the conversion of fats and proteins (including muscle) to glucose. While cortisol relieves inflammation, it appears to create other symptoms—notably fatigue and sleep disturbance (Glaser and Kielcolt-Glaser 1998; Brunner 1997). Excess cortisol produces central obesity, hypertension, and hyperglycemia (Sapolsky 1998; Thibodeau and Patton 1997).

The hormones released in both phases of the stress response may reduce resistance to infections and cancers (Glaser et al. 1999; Herbert and Cohen 1993; Irwin et al. 1997). Chronic stress appears to inhibit innate, nonspecific immunity, in which natural killer lymphocytes detect and destroy cells that show signs of viral infection or other abnormalities. It also appears to suppress the production of antibodies and T-lymphocytes keyed to detect and destroy specific invaders. As a result, social and psychological stress undermines the immune system's ability to suppress an infection before it produces unpleasant or incapacitating symptoms. Psychosocial stress correlates positively with the likelihood of developing symptoms after exposure to cold viruses, and with antibody concentrations that suggest widespread viral proliferation (Cohen, Tyrrell, and Smith 1991).

Stress also may reactivate latent viral infections such as varicella zoster, herpes simplex, and Epstein Barr (F. Cohen et al. 1999; Cohen and Herbert 1996; Glaser and Kielcolt-Glaser 1998; Irwin et al. 1998). The late-adulthood disease called shingles provides a good example of how stress may activate latent infections. Almost all Americans over the age of forty harbor the herpes zoster virus, which produces childhood chickenpox. The virus lies dormant in sensory nerves. The immune system's lymphocytes cannot attack it until it moves out of the nerves into surrounding tissue. As people age the immune system becomes less effective at producing the T-lymphocytes keyed to detecting and destroying cells infected with the virus. As a consequence the virus can proliferate in tissue surrounding the nerves, causing the inflammation and itching of shingles (Irwin et al. 1998). Prolonged or intense psychosocial stress may increase the likelihood of reactivating latent infections by slowing the production of the lymphocytes specialized in finding and destroying cells infected with the virus. Observations such as these suggest that chronic exposure to a threatening environment may undermine the body's natural defenses.

Stress hormones also can exacerbate chronic health conditions (Fremont and Bird 2000; Marmot and Mustard 1994). An acute stressor can precipitate heart problems such as irregular beat (arrhythmia), platelet clotting that can produce inadequate blood flow (ischemia), perhaps resulting in death of heart tissue (infarction). The alarm phase of the fight-or-flight response thus may stimulate a heart attack. It also can damage the lining of coronary arteries, instigating the formation of plaque that eventually occludes the arteries or bursts open to create a clot (thrombus) that clogs a downstream artery. The cortisol released in the resistance phase apparently accelerates the progressive thickening and hardening of arteries through the buildup of fatty plaque (atherosclerosis) and perhaps also the buildup of calcium salts and scar tissue (arteriosclerosis) throughout the body, including arteries supplying the heart, brain, and other vital organs.

An endless and sometimes losing struggle to pay the bills and feed and clothe the family exacts both alarm and exhaustion. Anxious arousal alternates with depressed collapse. Gnawing worries make sleep restless and drain the joy from life. Tense, restless dread partners with listless, prostrate hopelessness. Susceptibility to disease increases when life becomes a relentless, unending struggle to get by.

Income, Access to Formal Care, and Health

Money goes a long way toward buying relief from economic hardship. That protection improves health. Does income also improve health because it buys access to needed medical care? Many people, including many researchers, assume that a commodity—something that can be bought and sold—must form the bridge between household income and health. In fact, difficulty paying for medicine or medical care is one indication of the economic hardship that erodes health. Some may take that as a sign that people need medical care to stay healthy, and that money helps meet that need. However, a number of findings cast doubt on the effectiveness of medical access as a health-producing commodity that might explain the effects of income and economic hardship on health. In this section we review those findings. Money can indeed buy access to medical care, but it is questionable whether buying more access improves health (Evans 1994; Marmor, Barer, and Evans 1994). In particular, the differences in health across levels of income apparently do not result from differences in access to medical care.

Medicine and Population Health

Many people think that the health and longevity of modern populations came from the development and use of increasingly sophisticated medical treatments. Given that belief, it seems to make sense that wealthier individuals are healthier than others because they obtain more treatments, particularly the newest, best, and most expensive ones. This idea builds on the false premise that advances in medical treatments created the health and longevity enjoyed by modern, industrialized societies. Historical epidemiology finds that the rise of modern life expectancy cannot be attributed to the medical and surgical treatment of disease, because most of the declines in mortality rates preceded the advent of effective medical treatments for the declining causes of death (Evans 1994; McKinlay and McKinlay 1977; McKeown 1979; Sagan 1987).

Surprisingly few studies directly question and test the general proposition that consumption of medical services accounts for the better health of wealthier populations. However the existing studies show consistent results. Thirty years ago an econometric study questioned the contribution of medical expenditures to differences in mortality rates across American states (Auster, Leveson, and Sarachek 1969). It found that environmental factors such as levels of education and smoking make much larger contributions. Twenty years ago a sociological study questioned the contribution of medical resources such as physicians, specialists, and hospital beds per 1,000 population to differences in mortality and decreases in mortality across northern U.S. counties (Miller and Stokes 1978). It found no apparent beneficial effect of differences or increases in medical resources on mortality and infant mortality rates adjusting for factors such as education, with the exception of apparent benefits of increases in the number of nurses per 1,000 population. Even today, differences among countries in medical resources such as doctors and hospitals per capita explains little of the variance in infant mortality rates adjusting for social and economic resources such as education and gross domestic product per capita (Kim and Moody 1992; Lee and Paxman 1997).

National Health Care Systems and Socioeconomic Differences in Health

Based on the belief that medical treatments create healthy populations, many countries such as Great Britain instituted national health care systems, providing universal access to treatment. Doing so reversed the social gradient in the use of services. For example, prior to the National Health Service, Great Britain's lower socioeconomic strata used far fewer medical services, but since its institution they use more. Even so, the National Health Service did not reduce the socioeconomic gradient in health and survival (Angell 1993; Evans 1994; Hollingsworth 1981; Macintyre 1997; Marmot et al. 1987; Morris 1990; Wagstaff, Paci, and Van Doorslaer 1991). Indeed, socioeconomic status mortality differentials are stable or growing in countries with national health care systems, just as they are in the United States (Blaxter 1987; Diderichsen 1990; Evans 1994; Hertzman et al. 1994; Kunst and Mackenbach 1994; Kunst, Looman and Mackenbach 1990; Lagasse et al. 1990; Lahelma and Valkonen 1990; LaVecchia, Negri, Pagano, and Decarli 1987; Pamuk 1985, 1988; Pappas et al. 1993; Pearce, Davis, Smith, and Foster 1985; Siskind, Copeman, and Najman 1987; Townsend, Davidson, and Whitehead 1992). Stable or increasing economic inequality may be responsible (Kawachi and Kennedy 1997; Wilkinson 1986, 1997). Evidence that social inequalities in health have been stable or increasing since the advent of universal access to medical care implies that the causes of socioeconomic differentials in health lie outside the medical system.

Socioeconomic Status and Use of Medical Services

Despite the absence of universal medical coverage in the United States, the use of medical services now increases as social status decreases. Lower-status persons use more medical services because they have more health problems (Aday, Andersen, and Fleming 1980; Pincus 1998) and more favorable attitudes about the medical system and visiting the doctor (Sharp, Ross, and Cockerham 1983).

> Associations of good health with access to insurance and medical care lead some to believe that better health in people of high socioeconomic status is a result of more frequent interactions with the health care system and that improved access to care is the primary approach to improving the health of persons of low socioeconomic status. However, persons of low socioeconomic status currently use medical services more often than persons of high socioeconomic status. (Pincus 1998:407)

On the surface of it, the use of preventive services seems like it might account for some of the status differences in health. Higher socioeconomic status (particularly higher education) increases the likelihood of getting check-ups, or secondary prevention (catching and treating disease early) (Ross and Wu 1995). Yet the benefits to overall health of uncovering and treating disease early are uncertain (Bailar and Smith 1986; Roos and Roos 1994). Yearly checkups have little effect (Canadian Task Force on the Periodic Health Examination 1988; Kaiser Foundation Health Plan 1976; U.S. Preventive Services Task Force 1989). Screening often entails some risk, such as exposure to small amounts of radiation (Bailar 1976). The risks and side effects of treatment often outweigh the benefits for low-level disease, which may usually get better if left untreated (Deyo 1998; Deyo, Cherkin, Conrad, and Volinn 1991; Epstein 1996; Johansson et al. 1997; Roos and Roos 1994; Verrilli and Welch 1996; Wennberg et al. 1996.)

Screening programs can create epidemics of case finding with questionable net benefit for the patients and society. For example, mammography increased the rate of breast-cancer diagnosis without decreasing the rate of mortality from breast cancer (for an interesting perspective, see Lantz and Booth 1998). Because of finding earlier, smaller, and less certain cancers, the rate of death among women with breast cancer diagnoses declined, and the fraction of women surviving five years from the time of diagnosis increased. While none of this appreciably decreased women's risk of death from breast cancer overall, it did increase rates of medical and surgical morbidity in the form of the standard but nevertheless debilitating, nauseating, and disfiguring treatments. Presumably it also brought much fear into the lives of the diagnosed women and their families, and in some cases economic hardship, with likely adverse consequences.

Like mammography, most "preventive medicine" for adults is actually looking for signs of hidden or early pathology not currently producing obvious discomfort or disability but frightening enough in its implications to justify costly and dangerous treatment (Evans and Stoddart 1994). Higher-status individuals are more likely to present themselves for such scrutiny, thereby increasing the likelihood of getting the diagnosis given the qualifying signs of pathology. This may suppress the socioeconomic status differences in counts of serious chronic disease, to the extent that low-status individuals with the same obscure signs are less likely to get a label.

Socioeconomic Status and the Quality of Care

Clearly, differential access to medical care cannot explain the differences in health and survival across levels of education and income. Williams (1990) notes that variable quality of care might yet account for some of those differences. Some evidence exists that uninsured patients suffer higher rates of medical injuries in the hospital than other patients, are more frequently hospitalized for conditions that could have been treated on an outpatient basis, are more seriously ill upon hospitalization, and are more likely to die while hospitalized (Billings and Teicholz 1990; Burstin, Lipsitz, and Brennan 1992; Hadley, Steinberg, and Feder 1991; U.S. Congress, Office of Technology Assessment 1992; Yergan, Flood, Diehr, and LoGerfo 1988) (although others find insurance unrelated to early pre-natal care or outcomes following myocardial infarction (Kreindel et al. 1997; Parchment, Weiss, and Passannante 1996)). The poor and poorly educated may gain least from the services they receive and suffer the most iatrogenic (doctor-caused) disease.

Private and Public Medical Insurance and Health.

Like it or not, health is not something that can be bought. People cannot just buy medical services that make them and their families healthy. Businesses cannot just buy medical services that make their employees healthy. Governments cannot just buy medical services that make their citizens healthy. Some of the clearest evidence of this comes from research examining the effect of medical insurance on health.

Americans consider medical insurance so important that 78.6 percent of the households in our 1995 U.S. sample have private medical insurance, much of it provided as a benefit from current or past employment. The federal government's Medicaid and Medicare programs cover many of the rest, bringing the total with some kind of medical insurance up to 87.7 percent. Only 12.3 percent of the households in our sample go without any medical insurance, private or public. Not surprisingly, households with no private medical insurance tend to be near the bottom of the economic ladder. Among the households with incomes of less than $10,000 only 47.5 percent have private medical insurance. Public programs cover another 30.2 percent, leaving 22.3 percent without medical insurance of any kind. As income increases, the fraction privately insured rises toward a ceiling of about 95 percent for households with incomes above $80,000, and the fraction with no insurance falls toward a floor of about 3 percent, with public insurance covering the rest. Most of the increases in coverage occur at the low end of the income scale. For households with incomes in the $10, $20, $30, and $40 thousands the percentage privately insured is 63.1, 74.5, 82.9, and 86.6, respectively, and the percentage uninsured is 18.1, 17.5, 11.1, and 7.7, respectively.

The substantial association between income and medical insurance coverage gives the impression that lack of coverage accounts for much of the poor health in low-income households, and that government programs soften some of that deleterious effect. Our analyses show that this cannot be true, for two reasons: private medical insurance does not improve adult health, and public insurance seems to make it worse (Ross and Mirowsky 2000). This statement may seem shocking. Most people probably assume that the beneficial effect of medical insurance on health is so great that scientists stumble across it all the time. On the contrary, surprisingly few published studies have attempted to measure the effect of medical insurance on health. The existing studies compare individuals in three broad categories: those with private medical insurance provided as a benefit of current or past employment (including the spouse's) or purchased directly (including supplements to Medicare); those with public insurance from Medicaid (which goes primarily to the poor or medically indigent) or Medicare (available to seniors) with no private supplement; and no medical insurance. All of the studies find essentially the same thing. People with private medical insurance have the best health, those with only public medical insurance have the worst, and those with no medical insurance are in between but close to the privately insured. This pattern holds for the full range of health measures, from subjective health to mortality rates. What does it mean?

The belief that people need access to medicine is so strong that the research reports often try to explain away their own findings. They argue that the benefits of public medical insurance may be obscured by traits of those who must rely on it. Notably, only the poor or very unhealthy qualify for Medicaid and typically only the poorest retirees with Medicare rely on it alone. To take that into account the researchers use various statistical models to estimate the differences in health that would be observed across categories of insurance if the profiles of education, income, age, and traits such as sex and race were the same across categories. Those adjustments reduce the apparent negative effect of public insurance, but they also reduce the apparent positive effect of private insurance. In the end the reports typically say that perhaps more complete adjustments for background socioeconomic status and health care needs would reveal a clear beneficial effect of public medical insurance on health. Our analyses provide the most thorough set of adjustments yet, as described below.

People who believe that access to medicine improves health think that selection processes bias the estimated effects of medical insurance on health. Selection bias exists when the outcome under investigation influences the very thing that is supposedly its cause. In this case, one's health may influence whether one gets medical insurance and whether it is private or public. People who feel healthy and have no impairments or chronic conditions have less motivation to buy medical insurance or to find a job that provides it. Given similar resources and situations, it seems possible that poor health increases the likelihood of having private medical insurance. That would make the insurance seem less beneficial to health than it really is. Similarly, young or middle-aged adults generally must be poor, very sick, or seriously impaired to qualify for public medical insurance, and it helps to be all three. That could make public medical insurance seem unhealthy when actually it bolsters the health of sick and impaired people who would otherwise get worse. A fair test of the benefits of medical insurance needs to minimize the bias from selection.

Our analysis of the effect of medical insurance on health eliminates selection biases in several ways. First, it relates insurance status to subsequent changes in health. Those later changes cannot influence whether or not a person had medical insurance at the outset, or whether the insurance was private or public. Second, it adjusts for baseline health. In essence, the model compares the effect of insurance on the subsequent changes in health of individuals with similar initial levels of subjective health, physical impairment, and chronic conditions. Thus it tests the idea that medical insurance keeps healthy people from getting unhealthy and keeps unhealthy people from getting worse. Third, it adjusts for initial demographic and economic statuses that might influence medical insurance status and might also influence the rate of deterioration in health over time for reasons unrelated to medical insurance. These include age, sex, race, education, employment, marital status, income, and economic hardship at the beginning of the period. Finally, it adjusts for changes in the household that might be influenced by initial insurance status and produce changes in health for reasons that have little or nothing to do with the medical services provided. For example, among persons with health problems the ones with medical insurance might better avoid increases in economic hardship over time, thereby recovering faster for reasons that have nothing to do with the medical services used. The models adjust for changes in employment, marital status, household income, and economic hardship.

Our results find no differences between those with private medical insurance and those with no medical insurance in their changes in subjective health, physical impairment, and diagnosed chronic conditions over a three-year period. In other words, private medical insurance shows no sign of preserving or improving health. The better health seen among individuals with private medical insurance results entirely from their high levels of education, employment, marriage, and economic well-being, which preserve and improve health directly and also increase the likelihood of having private medical insurance. Our results find a more complicated pattern for public insurance compared to no insurance. Public insurance has no effect on subsequent changes in physical impairment, but it increases the accumulation of diagnosed chronic conditions and decreases subjective health over time.

The results summarized above clearly imply that lower rates of medical insurance cannot explain the high levels of health problems found among persons with low socioeconomic standing. Oddly, though, the tendency of those on public insurance to get more diagnoses and to feel less healthy might contribute to the socioeconomic gradient in those health indexes. We adapted our models to estimate the percentage of the socioeconomic differences in health that might result from differences in the prevalence of public, private, and no medical insurance. To do this we estimated the effects of education, income, and economic hardship on changes in the health measures without and then with adjustment for medical insurance. The adjustment makes almost no difference in the estimated effects of those variables (or others such as age, sex, and race). In some cases the estimated effects were a tiny bit smaller and in others a tiny bit larger, and all the differences were well within the margins of error. So, even though public insurance predicts worse changes in diagnosed chronic conditions and subjective health, this fact does not account for any appreciable part of the socioeconomic differences in those measures.

The one benefit of medical insurance that we could find is that it helps protect the household from economic hardship. Persons with private or public medical insurance have much less subsequent trouble paying medical bills than persons with no medical insurance who are otherwise similar in terms of age, sex, race, education, income, marital status, employment status, and health. This implies that medical insurance may have a small and indirect beneficial impact on health because it reduces the economic hardship that erodes health. That small and indirect beneficial effect probably is not what people have in mind when they spend or forgo hundreds or thousands of dollars in household income to have private medical insurance, or when they pay taxes toward public insurance. In any case, it is not large enough to make private medical insurance significantly improve health overall, not large enough to neutralize the detrimental effect of public medical insurance on the number of diagnosed conditions and subjective health, and not large enough to account for a significant share of the effects that education, income, and economic hardship have on health.

What should we make of the findings about medical insurance and health? Three possible interpretations come to mind. The first one is to go on assuming that medical insurance must be good for health despite mounting evidence to the contrary. To take that view we must assert that some powerful unmeasured factor creates the false impression that private medical insurance does not improve health and that public medical insurance does not improve physical functioning but increases the accumulation of chronic conditions and worsens subjective health. The imaginary factor must correlate more strongly with public medical insurance than private, and more strongly with chronic conditions and subjective health than with physical impairment. The imaginary force must *not* work by determining baseline health, education, income, economic hardship, marital status, or employment, or by creating changes in income, economic hardship, marital status or employment, because our models adjust for those. Perhaps means testing for public coverage taps some occult problem not captured by the adjusted variables. Researchers who want to endorse this interpretation must specify that imaginary factor, bring it into the light of observation by measuring it, and then demonstrate that when people are similar in terms of the factor, those with medical insurance of both kinds get healthier than those without medical insurance.

The two other interpretations both accept as fact that having medical insurance does not on the whole improve health. One interpretation is that neither type of medical insurance really affects health much one way or the other, but public insurance leads individuals to get more diagnoses and that makes them say they are less healthy. This labeling interpretation makes use of the fact that public medical insurance does not appear to accelerate the rise of physical impairment. That measure may be less susceptible to medical labeling bias. The other interpretation is that public medical insurance really does increase chronic disease and make people feel less healthy, and private medical insurance really does have no overall effect on health. These two interpretations may be hard to accept. They may seem frightening, or contrary to self-interest, or just too far removed from common belief to sound plausible (Lomas and Contandriopoulos 1994). Still, one of them may be true.

Income, the Sense of Control, and Health

Money cannot buy health, but it can reinforce a sense of control that encourages healthy behavior and makes things seem less threatening. Not surprisingly, greater household income increases the sense of directing and regulating one's own life. Low income reinforces a sense of fatalism, powerlessness, and helplessness in which individuals feel that random chance or powerful others determine the important events and outcomes in their lives, and that they have little ability to avoid bad things or to make good ones happen. Higher income reinforces a sense of mastery, instrumentalism, and self-efficacy, in which individuals feel responsible for the good and bad events and outcomes in their lives, able to correct mistakes and avoid them in the future, and able to do things they set their minds to.

Household income reinforces the sense of control developed through education. That sense gained through education then becomes relatively stable until old age, when it declines toward the end of life. Although an individual's sense of control can and often does rise and fall over time in response to events and changes, education's lifelong consequences tend to shape a characteristic sense of ability and efficacy. At successively higher level of education, two things happen with the average sense of control: it starts out higher in early adulthood, and it stays at that level longer into old age. To some extent that pattern reflects the trajectory of household income across the life course. At successively higher levels of education, income starts out higher and rises faster and longer to a higher peak. Income, and the jobs and earnings that contribute to it, reflect the real and present effectiveness built up over a lifetime. Higher income bolsters the sense of control by providing the economic means useful in achieving one's ends, and by indicating the effectiveness of past actions.

A sense of control over one's own life improves health in two ways. The most important is that it encourages efforts to find ways of staying healthy, as discussed in the previous chapter. When people see the important events and outcomes of their own lives as beyond their control, they see little connection between the things they do or the way they live and the prospect of a long and healthy life. In contrast, when people feel effective and able, they believe they can find things to do that will create a long and healthy life. That in turn encourages them to discover healthy ways of living and to change themselves and their lives to be healthier.

The second way a sense of control improves health is by making life seem less threatening. The fight-or-flight response described in a previous section is a natural, unconditioned response to threats. "Unconditioned" means that it is built into the organism, like salivating when hungry and smelling food. The fight-or-flight response evolved for quick response to predators and aggressors. In modern human life those natural reactions to physical attack become conditioned onto menacing, symbolic perils. In humans the perception of threatened economic well-being, status, self-esteem, marriage, friendship, and so on stimulates the body's response to flesh-and-blood attack (Evans et al. 1994; Sapolsky 1998). Individuals with little sense of control feel more exposed to such threats. Partly that results from the history of poor outcomes that left them feeling powerless, helpless, and fatalistic. Partly, though, it results from uncertainty about the causes of effects and the actions that shape outcomes.

Uncertainty about distinguishing the feasible from the unworkable creates a sense of risk. Likewise, uncertainty about distinguishing the genuine from the counterfeit or the candid from the deceitful creates a sense of danger. Individuals with a firm sense of control feel confident of their ability to judge risks accurately and deal with threats effectively. That self assurance reduces susceptibility to alarm. In the terms of psychoendocrinology, it makes them less reactive. Events and situations seem more benign to individuals who believe they can avoid most problems and correct or manage the rest. Other things being equal, that perception reduces the triggering of physiological alarm.

The relationship between health and the sense of control has one final, important quality. The relationship is what causal analysts call a deviation-amplifying reciprocal effect. A strong sense of control improves health and functioning, and good health and functioning strengthen the sense of control. Unfortunately this works both ways. A weak sense of control degrades health and functioning, which further weakens the sense of control. Over time these reciprocal effects push individuals in different directions. That has two consequences. It enlarges the differences among individuals in health and in the sense of control. It also increasingly combines poor health with a low sense of control in some individuals and good health with a high sense of control in others. The deviation-amplifying reciprocal effect enlarges the disparity among individuals while making some of them the beneficiaries of multiple advantages and others the bearers of multiple disadvantages. Similar feedback exists in health's relationship with income and economic hardship, but the strongest is with the sense of control. A later chapter on age and the cumulative advantage in health details these self-amplifying effects and their consequences.

Recap: The Economic Link

Economic well-being forms one of the most important links between education and health, but mostly not for the reasons many people think. Individuals and societies cannot get healthier by buying more or better medical interventions. They *can* get healthier by buying their way out of privation, but true destitution is unusual in modern industrial societies. Destitution is want of the means of subsistence—the means barely sufficient to maintain life. Few individuals suffer from prolonged and severe hunger or exposure in societies such as the United States. Charities, government programs, and excess production combine to assure that almost everyone gets the food, clothing, and shelter needed for survival. Health-damaging privation typically arises only when an economically disadvantaged and socially isolated individual also suffers from cognitive problems such as schizophrenia or dementia. Most of the poor health associated with low income results from other kinds of problems. Some of it comes from living in poor housing and poor neighborhoods where exposure to pathogens, toxins, and carcinogens is more common. Most of it, though, results directly from the stress of poverty and economic hardship and the attendant sense of powerlessness, helplessness, and failure. Low income and difficulty paying bills or buying necessities make individuals feel at the mercy of merciless forces. The sense of helplessness undermines the motivation to find and adopt healthy ways of living, while the sense of dread spawns cycles of agitation and depletion that feel like illness, compromise immune response, cultivate pathologies such as high blood pressure or atherosclerosis, and instigate crises such as heart attacks.

Economic well-being forms a major link between education and health, but the nature of that connection is not what it might seem. Ability and effectiveness create the link, more than money itself. Income enhances the ability to achieve ends, but the well-educated with low income can achieve the same outcomes through other means. Higher levels of education decrease the amount of health problems associated with low income. They do that in part by decreasing the amount of economic hardship associated with low income. Whatever the level of income, the better-educated individuals tend to avoid the circumstances most likely to generate intense or prolonged economic hardship. In particular, they get married and start families later in adulthood, have smaller families, stay married more consistently, and avoid single parenthood. The well-educated tend to avoid difficult circumstances, but they also manage difficult circumstances better when faced with them. Even among individuals with the same household composition, education reduces the economic hardship associated with low income. The well-educated achieve economic well-being and physical health through higher income, but they can and do achieve the same ends just as well through other means.

Our models consistently indicate that less trouble paying the bills and buying household necessities accounts for somewhere in the range of 40 to 60 percent of income's effect on health. Reduced exposure to neighborhood disorder and decay accounts for another 5 percent. Most of the rest results from income's impact on the sense of control, which improves health by encouraging a healthy lifestyle and by reducing stress. Of course, the reality does not separate into parts as neatly as these numbers suggest. Low income restricts housing options and undermines the sense of control, and these in turn may suppress the rise of household income over the long run. More importantly, these facts are like sentences in the paragraphs of a description that must be read as a whole for complete understanding. They are facets of a reality with adjoining sides. Economic resources and economic well-being constitute a major path from education to health. They in turn link to education through employment, occupation, and work, which influence health through additional pathways.

PRODUCTIVE ACTIVITIES

Professors who teach social and behavioral sciences quickly learn that students often come with strong preconceptions about how individuals and society function. The utility and near-truth of some misconceptions make them especially widespread and tenacious. The biggest misconception about social status and health is that money is what counts. It is easy to see where this idea comes from. Earnings and income do contribute to well-being and health, and the lucrative educations and jobs generally provide other benefits to well-being and health too. Individuals only discover the error in the assumption if they push it to the extreme, sacrificing those other benefits for the money alone. In this section we look at employment, occupation, and work as links between education and health. Paid work contributes to health in various ways, but at the sacrifice of some autonomy. Higher levels of education lead to jobs that are more rewarding in themselves, as well as better paid. Moreover, higher education changes the nature of pay from compensation for sacrificed autonomy to reward for productive creativity. Prosperity, autonomy, and creativity all contribute to health, and all characterize the work of the well-educated.

Employment, Occupation, and Work

Employment Status

Social scientists distinguish among employment, occupation, and work. Employment status refers to a set of categories that are exhaustive (everyone is in a category) and mutually exclusive (each person is in only one category): employed full-time, employed part-time, keeping house, retired, unable to work because of a disability, temporarily unemployed or laid off, in school, in the military, or in an institution (generally a prison or asylum). The categories embody several distinctions that can be seen best in outline:

In the labor force (subdivided by degree of employment)
   Currently working for pay (subdivided by hours per week)
     Full-time
     Part-time
   Not currently working for pay
     Unemployed: laid off or looking for work
Not in the labor force (subdivided by volition)
   Chosen (subdivided by reasons)
     Keeping house
     Retired
     In school full-time
     In the military
   Not chosen (subdivided by constraints)
     Unable to work because of sickness or disability
     Involuntarily in an institution

Figure 4.8 shows the percentage of the males and females of our sample in each employment status. For practical reasons our surveys exclude persons in the military or in institutions. A large majority of the men in our sample have jobs: 63.9 percent full-time and another 5.4 percent part-time, for a total of 69.3 percent with paid employment. Most of the male

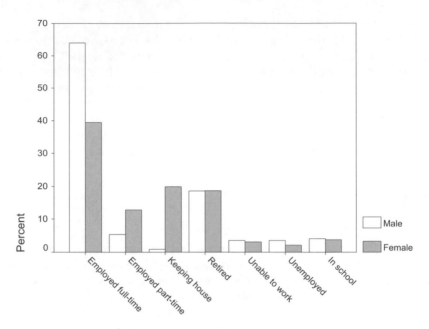

Figure 4.8.   Percentage in each employment status, by sex.

part-timers are older and easing into retirement and most of the rest are young and just starting out. Among the women, 39.5 percent have full-time jobs and another 12.9 percent have part-time ones, for a total of 52.4 percent with paying jobs. Among women, the part-time employees tend to be married mothers with young children.

Individuals with paid jobs or looking for paid jobs are considered in the labor force. The unemployment rates published by the government give the percentage of the labor force currently looking for jobs. In the United States the unemployment rate drops to around 4 percent in good economic times. That does not mean that 96 percent of American adults have jobs though. Around one-third of all U.S. adults are considered out of the labor force because they are in school, in the military, in prison, keeping house, retired, or unable to work. Some say that makes the unemployment rate seem worse than it really is, since only about 2.7 percent of adults are looking for jobs when the unemployment rate is 4 percent. Others say the opposite, that the official rate understates the true extent of unemployment because many discouraged workers opt for keeping house, retirement, the military, or school depending on their age and sex. On the other hand, keeping house and being in school or the military are considered

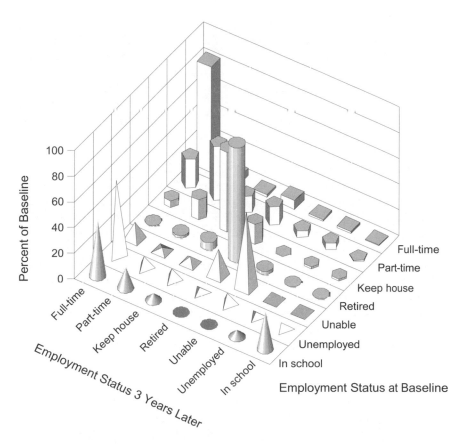

Figure 4.9. Percentage in each employment status three years later by employment status at the beginning of the study.

socially constructive activities. Together with retirement they are socially
legitimate statuses that many individuals choose freely.

Some employment statuses are stable over time, but others tend to be
transitional. Transition profiles show the stability of each employment status and also the relationships among categories in the set. Figure 4.9 illustrates the transition profiles. It shows the percentage of persons in each
employment status that stayed in it and the percentage that moved to each
of the other categories over the three-year period of the study. It shows that
full-time employment is highly stable, with 82.4 percent of the persons in
that category at the beginning of the period also in it at the end. Of course,
some people may move out of full-time employment temporarily and then
back in during the three years. Most moves out of full-time employment

are into retirement (6.6 percent) or part-time employment (5.9 percent). The rest of the moves out are mostly into keeping house, being unemployed, and being unable to work (about 1.5 percent each). Part-time employment is much less stable, with three years later 41.5 percent remaining in the category, 22.3 percent employed full-time, 13.8 percent retired, 12.3 percent keeping house, and 9.2 percent split evenly between being unemployed and being unable to work. Not surprisingly, unemployment is the least stable of the labor force categories: three years later, 60 percent are employed full-time; 10 percent each are working part time, keeping house, or unable to work; 5 percent each are retired or still unemployed. Retirement is the most stable category out of the labor force (89.3 percent), with some transition to keeping house (6 percent), disability (2.7 percent), and part-time employment (1.9 percent). Keeping house is moderately stable (62.0 percent), with most transitions to part-time employment and retirement (15.3 percent each) and most of the rest to full-time employment (4.9 percent). Disability is nearly as stable as keeping house (59 percent), with most transitions to retirement (20.5 percent), but some to full-time and part-time employment (12.8 and 2.6 percent, respectively) and some to keeping house (5.1 percent). Most people in school at the beginning of the period are employed at the end (43.2 percent full-time and 16.2 percent part-time).

Occupation

Social scientists classify paid work according to occupation. The U.S. Department of Labor and the Bureau of the Census have a system for classifying every paid job. Each category defines an occupation, distinguished from others by the requirements and demands of the work. The occupational titles are described in an outline that gets progressively more detailed and distinctive. For example: service>other than household or protective>food preparation and service>cook. The Department of Labor's Bureau of Labor Statistics publishes summary descriptions and detailed descriptions of each occupation at each outline level. For example, the brief description of Medical Assistants (fifth level) says they

> perform administrative and certain clinical duties under the direction of a physician. Administrative duties may include scheduling appointments, maintaining medical records, billing, and coding for insurance purposes. Clinical duties may include taking and recording vital signs and medical histories, preparing patients for examination, drawing blood, and administering medications as directed by a physician. Exclude "Physician Assistants."

The Department of Labor used to publish the descriptions and ratings of occupations in a printed volume called the *Dictionary of Occupational*

Titles. Now they provide the information as a searchable database called O*NET, which is available through their Internet web site.

Occupational Status

Some occupations carry greater status and prestige than others. Occupations can be graded by the level of respect and esteem ascribed to them. Social psychologists have asked randomly selected individuals to rate or rank the prestige of various occupations. Analyses of the ratings find that the average education and earnings in an occupation largely determine its average prestige rating (Blau and Duncan 1967). As a consequence, researchers often measure an individual's occupational status by reference to the average education and wage or salary in the person's occupation. The term "occupational status" should not be confused with "employment status." Occupational status is a graded dimension (similar to temperature or height) that represents the relative prestige, honor, standing, and esteem typically accorded a person's occupation. Employment status is a classification based on labor force participation, typical weekly hours of paid employment, or reasons for nonemployment, as described earlier. A worker's Socioeconomic Index (SEI) is a measure of occupational status based on the average education and income in the person's occupation (Nakao, Hodge, and Treas 1990).

Occupational Conditions and Demands

Notice that a worker's SEI treats a quality of that person's occupation (its prestige) as a quality of the person himself or herself. Probably most social scientists think doing this is logically questionable, but nevertheless often useful. Similarly, a scientist can assign to each person who is or has been employed the attributes that describe the typical conditions and demands in the person's occupational category. Information published by agencies or social scientists allows survey researchers to look up the extent of various demands or risks common in each person's occupation. Federal agencies regularly publish information on the occupations, including average wages, number of workers, growth or decline in number of workers, education levels of the workers, and rates and types of injuries or fatalities on the job. The Department of Labor also publishes tables that classify or quantify the typical demands of each occupation, such as the extent to which it involves physical labor, dangerous machinery, extremes of heat or cold, planning, directing the work of others, or complex work with people, data, or things. While handy, assigning an occupation's attributes to individuals in the occupation has two problems. First, the conditions in a person's own job may differ from what is normal or common in the occupation as a whole. Second, the codes often represent judgments made by outside observers, which may not correspond to the perceptions or experiences of the persons in an occupation.

Work

In the end, the qualities of a person's own work may be what really matter. Notice that we use the word "work" rather than "job" here. A job is something performed in return for pay. Work is an activity directed toward production or accomplishment. The work a person does may pay well, poorly, or not at all. It may be varied, engaging, and enjoyable, or repetitious, tedious, and oppressive. It can be high, low, or middling in a chain of command, or not in one at all. Most importantly, work can be self-expressing or self-suppressing. Some people see work as the things they would not do if they did not have to. Others see it as they way they create things of value.

Karl Marx and Friedrich Engels may have been the first social scientists to contrast oppressive work with an ideal of expressive work. Decades ago, in the depths of the cold war, students in the social sciences had to read the essays and monographs of Marx and Engels. History probably will remember them as the ideologists who inspired brutal and repressive political regimes tied closely to monopolistic and inefficient economic systems. Those of us who had to read their work also remember their serious scholarship, clever insights, and compassionate indignation about nineteenth-century industrial working conditions. They wrote of jobs that were "physically exhausting and mentally debasing," of humans used as replaceable and disposable parts in an inhuman productive apparatus, of life sold off by the hour until there was little of value left. In particular, they wrote about wage slavery—about turning over your own body and mind to be used as the instrument of someone else's will.

In order to illustrate the problem with nineteenth-century industrial labor, Marx and Engels contrasted it with an ideal typified in the craft work of earlier eras. A cobbler would own the tools, materials, and workshop, design and make the shoes, sell them, and get the profit. Each pair of shoes was the physical embodiment of the cobbler's skill. He found pleasure in making them, seeing them take shape, and thinking of them in service. Indeed, this may be the most important insight. By nature, human beings make things. Humans enjoy the things they create, and the process of creating them. Somehow, the joy of creation had been lost in the nineteenth-century industrial machine. It made food, clothing, shelter, transportation, and wealth, but crushed something at the core of human nature: productive self-expression.

Marx and Engels imagined an ideal world of the future that used industrial technology and organization but let workers again feel their own wills expressed in the process and product. They thought ownership of the means of production was the key. That was the big mistake. It led to communist states that owned all means of production and managed them centrally for the benefit of all citizens. The result was so dismal that the most powerful "workers' paradise" dismantled itself by near-universal consent of its supposed beneficiaries. The others are rapidly returning to private ownership of industry too.

Is the ideal of self-expressive labor a hopeless dream of the past? Not at all. It has become the reality for many workers here in the United States—the heart of the capitalist beast. Many, but not all. As American optimists, we think the workers who now enjoy productive self-expression are pioneering new occupational and industrial forms that will become standard for almost all paid workers. Colleagues with a more pessimistic view (they would say "realistic") might argue that productive self-expression is a prerogative of the elite that will never be available to the majority of paid workers. Either way, the current situation in the United States allows us to explore the effects on health of productive self-expression in contrast to alienated labor. As proponents of dialectical materialism, Marx and Engels might have savored the irony. By becoming a reality in advanced capitalist nations, the ideal self-expressive labor exists alongside the older alienated labor, providing the opportunity for scientific comparison of their effects on health.

The Employment Link

Education and Employment

Education greatly increases full-time employment and decreases both part-time employment and unemployment. Education does more than just move people up the labor force ladder from unemployed to part-time and from part-time to full-time. It brings more people into the labor force, and keeps more people in, at the highest level of participation: full-time employment. Figure 4.10 shows the proportion of persons in each employment status across levels of education. The proportion employed full-time increases sharply, from less than 20 percent among those with elementary school educations to almost 70 percent among persons with doctoral or professional degrees. Some of this difference reflects the fact that older generations now of retirement age had much lower levels of education than common among middle-aged and young adults. That is part of the reason why persons with elementary-school educations are twice as likely to be retired as employed full-time, and those with some high school but no degree are about equally likely to be retired and to be employed full-time. Even so, education greatly influences the likelihood of full-time

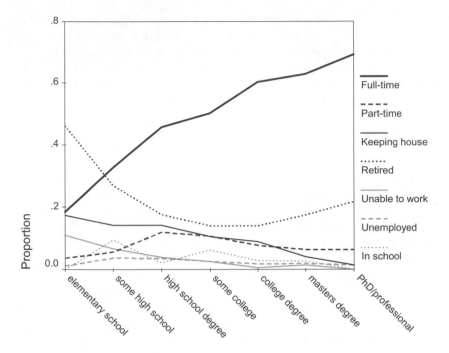

Figure 4.10. Employment status by level of education.

employment. Logistic regression models allow us to adjust for differences in age and sex across levels of education. The models allow us to estimate the effect of education on employment status among persons of the same sex and age. The results describe the effect of education on the odds of being in a particular category of employment. (The odds are the ratio of the probability of being in a category to the probability of not being in it. So, if 75 percent are in a category, the odds of being in it are 3 to 1.) On average, each additional year of education increases the odds of full-time employment by 11 percent. That adds up to a 51.6 percent increase in the odds for a four-year difference in education and 129.8 percent for an eight-year difference. That in turn drives corresponding increases in the odds of employment (9.5 percent per additional year of education) and of labor force participation (8.7 percent per additional year).

The increases in full-time employment across levels of education require corresponding decreases in the other categories. Three other categories account for most of those decreases: keeping house, unemployment, and inability to work. The odds of keeping house decrease an average of 10.8 percent for each additional year of education. Men almost never report keeping house, so that component applies almost entirely to women. The

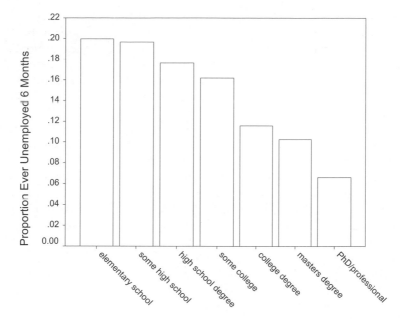

Figure 4.11. Proportion ever unemployed and looking for work six months or more, by education.

odds of being laid off or unemployed and looking for work decrease an average of 10.0 percent for each additional year of school. The odds of being unable to work because of a disability decrease by an average of 22.9 percent for each additional year of education.

Education's positive impact on full-time employment and negative impact on unemployment combine to reduce the unemployment rate, which is the fraction of persons in the labor market but not currently employed. Adjusting for age, each additional year of education decreases the odds of unemployment given labor force participation by 11.8 percent.

Education also improves the stability of labor force participation and employment by improving the stability of full-time employment. Higher levels of education decrease the probability of ever having been unemployed and looking for work for six months or more, as shown in Figure 4.11. Each additional year of education cuts the odds of ever having been unemployed 6 months or longer by an additional 10.7 percent. Higher levels of education also increase the stability of full-time employment over the three-year period of our study. For persons who were employed full-time at the beginning of our study, the odds of being employed full-time three years later increase 19.0 percent for each additional year of education. That adds up to a 100 percent increase in the odds of full-time employment remaining stable for an additional four years of education, and a 300 percent increase for an additional eight years of education. That positive impact on the odds of full-time employment remaining stable increases the odds of later participating in the labor force and of later having a job, even though education tends to decrease unemployment and part-time employment. Once again we see that education bolsters employment at the highest level of participation.

Education has an especially large impact on the odds of reporting inability to work due to a disability. As mentioned earlier, each additional year of education decreases those odds by an average of 22.9 percent. That adds up to a 64.7 percent decrease for an additional four years of school, and an 87.5 percent decrease for an additional eight years. Very few individuals with a college degree or higher report being unable to work because of a disability. Education has similarly large effects on the odds of transition into or out of inability to work. Among persons who were able to work at the beginning of our study, education decreased the odds of becoming unable to work three years later by an average of 17.9 percent for each additional year of schooling. The effect of education is especially strong for persons who were employed full-time at the beginning of the study. For them the odds of becoming unable to work three years later decreased an average of 27.0 percent per additional year of education. On the other side, among persons who were unable to work at the beginning education increases the odds of becoming able to work three years later by an average of 21.8 percent for each additional year of school. That education effect occurs through moves into full-time employment, rather than through moves into retirement, keeping house, and so on.

Employment and Health

The level of health differs considerably across employment statuses for several reasons. Figure 4.12 shows the overall pattern. It shows the percentage of persons in each employment status who feel their health is not good, who have much difficulty with at least one physical function, and who have at least one serious diagnosis. Persons employed full-time or in school full-time have the best health by all three measures. Higher proportions of persons who are unemployed, working part-time, or keeping house are unhealthy by each measure. Not surprisingly, people who are unable to work have by far the highest proportion impaired and feeling their health is not good. However the retired have a slightly higher percentage with at least one of the serious diagnoses on our list. By the other two measures the retired have considerably fewer health problems than persons unable to work but considerably more than persons in other categories. Three things account for the heath differences across employment

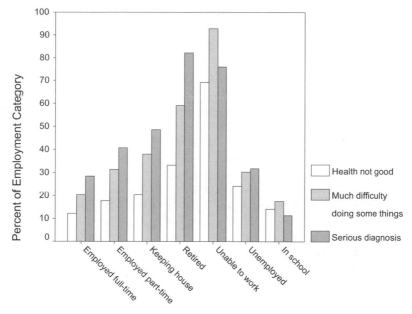

Figure 4.12. Percentage feeling their health is not good, having much difficulty with a physical function, and having at least one serious diagnosis, by employment status.

statuses: traits that influence both employment status and health, the effect of employment status on health, and the effect of health on employment status. We discuss each below.

Traits that heavily influence employment status also may affect health, creating some of the differences in health across categories. In particular, combinations of age, sex, marriage, and parenthood heavily influence the probability of being in school, in the labor force, keeping house, or retired. With the exception of parenthood, they all have substantial effects on health too. Younger adults tend to be healthier than older ones, men tend to be healthier than women until old age, when women become healthier, and married adults tend to be healthier than those who are not married. This complicates efforts to find out if some employment statuses are healthier than others. Retirement provides an obvious case. The retired have a lot more health problems than full-time paid workers, but some of that must be because they are older. Other issues arise with other comparisons. Persons keeping house are less healthy on average than those employed full-time. Both groups tend to be middle-aged, but 96.2 percent of persons keeping house are women, compared to 38.8 percent of persons employed full-time.

Education's effects also might complicate the comparisons. We know that education improves health and improves the odds of full-time employment. We want to know if education improves health partly *because* full-time employment improves health. The problem is that education might improve health for other reasons, making full-time employment look more beneficial than it really is. A similar problem arises with regard to status of origin. Persons who were raised in relatively advantaged and prosperous families are healthier in adulthood and more likely to hold full-time jobs.

Statistical adjustment allows researchers to make fair comparisons across employment statuses, adjusting for differences in the typical sex, age, race, marital status, education, and status of origin. Comparisons making those adjustments continue to show meaningful differences in health across categories of employment status. For example, persons employed full-time continue to have the lowest mean physical impairment score, as illustrated in Figure 4.13. The retired and the unemployed have the highest adjusted mean levels of impairment, except for persons unable to work because of a disability. We left them off the chart because being unable to work *requires* some degree of impairment. The part-time employed and students have higher adjusted mean levels of impairment than the full-time employed, but less than persons in other categories. Persons keeping house have adjusted mean levels of impairment between the part-time employed and the unemployed or retired.

Overall, full-time employment and better health go together. But why? There are two possibilities: causation and selection. In causation, something about employment status affects health. For example, full-time employment may promote health through economic well-being and independence, personal development, and healthier lifestyle. In selection, health affects the employment status individuals can be in or choose to be in. Being unable to work due to a disability provides the most obvious case of selection. Everyone in that status must have some impairment (although most people with impairments are in other categories). In general, good health may improve the chances of finding and holding full-time jobs, which is called the healthy-worker hypothesis. Employers may hesitate to hire individuals with impairments, chronic diseases, or histories of poor health, because of fear the individuals will perform poorly, raise insurance costs, or wind up getting workmen's compensation at the company's expense. On the other side, individuals who feel unhealthy or have physical limitations may be more inclined to opt out of the labor force when possible, by retiring or keeping house.

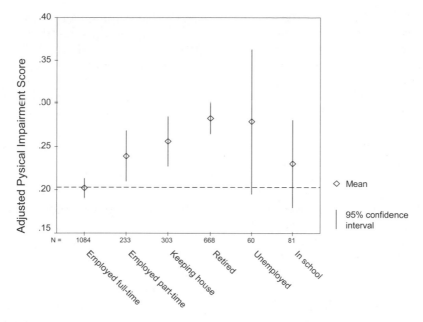

Figure 4.13. Mean physical impairment score by employment status, adjusted for sex, age, race, marital status, education, and parents' education.

In our research we find evidence of both causation and selection in the relationship between employment and health. We find that full-time employment helps to create and maintain the higher levels of health and functioning that make full-time employment more likely and more stable. Employment in the United States today typically does *not* act like a "meat grinder," taking in healthy young workers, wearing them out at an accelerated rate, and then ejecting them old and used-up before their time. Whatever the case may have been in the nineteenth century when Marx and Engels wrote their tracts, employment today seems generally good for health. Apparently better health also makes workers more valuable to employers, or makes employment more attractive to individuals with other options, or both. Employment and health have something like a symbiotic relationship: each helps create the conditions beneficial to the other.

Researchers correlate baseline conditions with subsequent changes in order to distinguish causation from selection. So, to find out if employment affects health, researchers compare the changes in health over a period among the persons who were in different employment statuses at the beginning, and adjust for the health differences at the beginning. The reasoning behind the method has two parts. First, subsequent changes in health cannot cause the initial employment status. Any correlation between the two cannot exist because the subsequent changes caused the initial status. That leaves only two other possibilities. Either the initial employment status caused the subsequent changes in health, or something else caused both the initial employment status and the subsequent changes in health. That something else might be a preexisting health problem. That leads to the second part of the reasoning behind the method. Adjusting for initial health takes into account the possibility that earlier health problems influenced both the initial employment status and the subsequent rate of decline in health. The adjustment in effect compares individuals with similar initial health but different initial employment status. The analyses also adjust for other things that might influence both the initial employment status and the subsequent changes in health, such as age, sex, race, marital status, education, and status of origin. Whenever causation and selection seem equally plausible theoretically, distinguishing one phenomenon from the other requires advanced statistical analyses using the logic above.

Our results indicate that persons who are employed full-time have better subsequent changes in subjective health and physical functioning than persons who are not employed (Ross and Mirowsky 1995). Persons employed part time have subsequent changes in health that are in between—not quite as good as among the full-time employed, not quite as bad as among the nonemployed. For employment aged adults (eighteen to sixty-five) as a whole, the average levels of health decline over time. Essentially all of that decline happens among the persons who are not employed full-time at the beginning of the period. Among those employed full-time some get healthier and some get unhealthier, but the average levels of health stay about the same from one year to the next. Average levels of health deteriorate significantly among working-aged adults who are not employed full-time at the beginning of the observation period. The nonemployed include persons unable to work because of a disability, but that category does not account for most of the overall decline in health. For men, most of the declines in health occur among the ones retired, unemployed, or working part-time at the start. For women, most of the declines occur among the ones keeping house. However, this difference between the sexes is diminishing as women's employment life cycles become more like men's and the fraction keeping house declines. Full-time students are in the only category of nonemployment that does not contribute to the overall declines in health, partly because they typically get full-time jobs after leaving school.

Just as full-time employment helps individuals to stay or become healthy, health helps them stay or become employed full-time. However, the importance of health for full-time employment depends on sex, and seems to have declined in recent decades. Combinations of age, sex, marital status, and parental status largely determine the obligation to be employed, and education heavily influences the availability and desirability of jobs. Together those sociodemographic statuses shape the likelihood of full-time employment, and leave little room for other contingencies to hold sway. Data from interviews recorded a few decades ago in 1979 and 1980 show that physical impairment reduced the likelihood of a working-aged adult of either sex remaining or becoming employed full-time, but poor subjective health reduced the likelihood for women only. Neither physical functioning nor subjective health influenced women's likelihood of remaining or becoming homemakers, which was influenced mostly by education, race, and marital status. Data from more recent interviews in 1995 and 1998 show a different pattern. Physical impairment no longer reduces men's likelihood of remaining or becoming employed full-time, which is influenced largely by their age and education. Physical impairment continues to reduce women's likelihood of remaining or becoming employed full-time, but poor subjective health no longer does. For women, being married and having children in the home reduce the likelihood of full-time employment. Physical impairment now increases the tendency of women to remain or become homemakers, but poor subjective health continues to have no effect on it.

The changes in the effects of health on employment status may reflect three trends over recent decades: the improved economy, the advent of the information age, and the waning differentiation of men's and women's roles. The improved economy increased employers need for workers, which may have made employers more willing to keep, hire, and accommodate workers with health problems. The shift to a service-oriented, information-age economy may have reduced the fraction of jobs that require physical labor and increased the fraction unaffected by common impairments. The increasing similarity of women's roles to men's may have had two consequences. Working for pay may be less optional for women than it once was, so that women who feel unhealthy now stay employed unless impairment interferes. Homemaking may be more optional for women now, in the sense that it is no longer required or even typical. Homemaking may now act as a catch basin for women finding employment difficult to maintain and having the option of being supported by a spouse. Although most homemakers these days are out of the labor force temporarily while their children are young, and some chose homemaking as a vocation, some now keep house because physical impairment makes paid employment difficult.

Although the relationship between employment status and health works both ways, selection for healthy workers seems to be on the decline. For men in particular, full-time employment improves health and functioning, but in recent years men between school and retirement generally keep or get full-time jobs regardless of their health and functioning. This situation may depend on the strong economy. Nevertheless, causation rather than selection seems dominant in the relationship of employment to health among men. For women the relationship still works both ways. Full-time employment improves women's subsequent physical functioning (although not as much as men's), which in turn increases women's subsequent likelihood of remaining or becoming employed full-time. This self-reinforcing feedback may sharpen the differences in physical functioning associated with employment status as women who entered adulthood at the same time go through life, with an increasing concentration of impairment found among the women not employed full-time. Of course, historical trends in the economy and in sex roles might eventually eliminate the feedback loop by eliminating the effect of physical impairment on women's employment.

Higher levels of education greatly increase the likelihood of full-time employment in the United States, particularly for women. Full-time employment helps individuals stay healthy, which explains some of education's beneficial effect on health. Employment, in and of itself, seems to be good for health, but it is not the whole story. Education also greatly influences the nature and qualities of jobs. Indeed, education increases the likelihood of full-time employment in part because it improves the intrinsic and extrinsic rewards typically provided by jobs. The following sections examine the qualities of occupations and work that contribute to the connection between education and health.

The Occupation Link

The more arduous, dangerous, and unpleasant an occupation is, the lower the average education of persons doing it for a living. Even so, differences in those qualities of occupations account for very little of the differences in health across levels of education. Partly that is because hazardous occupations often require physical activity that benefits health. Mostly, though, it reflects the success of occupational health and safety regulations and practices. Even though some occupations are much riskier than others, the overall levels of occupational risk are so low that differences in health associated with occupations generally vanish against the background of health differences created by other socioeconomic forces.

Education and Occupational Risks

The higher the level of education among the workers in an occupation is, the lower the occupational exposure to physical, chemical or biological hazards, physical exertion, and noxious environments. Figure 4.14 illustrates the relationship. It shows the mean and 95 percent confidence inter-

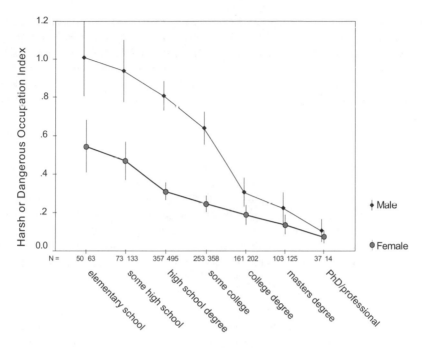

Figure 4.14. Harsh or dangerous occupational conditions, by education and sex.

val for an index representing occupational exposure to harsh or dangerous conditions by level of education and sex. The index counts the presence of six conditions: extreme cold, extreme heat, wetness or high humidity, noise or vibration, physical or chemical hazards, and atmospheres with fumes, odors, dusts, gases, or poor ventilation. The likelihood of occupational exposure to such conditions increases considerably at lower levels of education, particularly for men. A graph of demanding physical labor would show a similar pattern. Despite the clear pattern of association with level of education, these and other occupational attributes have little or no effect on health overall, and do not explain the differences in health across level of education. Part of the reason can be seen in the graph itself. Even at the lowest level of education the men's occupations average a score of one on the index, which corresponds to having only one of the six exposures.

Risky Occupations

Workplaces today are remarkably safe. While some of this reflects the shift from industrial to service occupations, much of it reflects the precautions taken in stable, indoor work sites such as factories, warehouses, stores, hospitals, and offices. In terms of fatalities, today's twenty riskiest occupations mostly involve outdoor work at changing locations using vehicles or power tools (Toscano and Windau 1994; Toscano 1997). The deadliest occupations include fishermen (21.3 times the overall fatality rate, typically from drowning), timber cutters (20.6 times), airplane pilots (19.9 times), structural metal workers (13.1), construction laborers (8.1), roofers (5.9), electric power installers (5.7), truckers (5.3), and farmers (5.1). Other high-risk occupations involve handling money while interacting with the public, or providing security. Taxi drivers dominate that part of the list, with 9.5 times the overall occupational fatality rate, mostly from homicides but also from accidents, followed by police (3.2) and guards (2.3). The fatalities in high-risk occupations mostly involve vehicles or weapons, with electricity and falls major factors too. Bad weather frequently contributes. The important thing to recognize about the occupations on this list is the absence of anything like the grim and deadly industrial environment of the nineteenth-century factory. Nonconstruction laborers do appear on the list, with 3.2 times the overall fatality rate. However those deaths typically involve vehicles rather than machines, tools, chemicals, fires, and the like. Today's factories and offices create so little risk to life that, for most occupations, the workers face greater risks to life at home, and much greater on the way to and from home.

Nonfatal injuries also reveal the relatively safe nature of today's occupations. A nonfatal injury or illness gets counted when it results from on-the-job exposure and requires time off for recovery or makes it impossible for the worker to continue in the occupation. About half of the ten riskiest occupations by that measure involve construction trades, laborers, and assemblers. Most of the injuries in those occupations involve "contact with an object." Injuries in the other half of the occupations on the list typically involve "overexertion." For example, nurses aids and orderlies are a shade above construction laborers in risk of nonfatal injury (1 in 13 compared to 1 in 12 in the most recent annual statistics), somewhat above truck drivers (1 in 15), and well above manufacturing assemblers (1 in 22). While the construction laborers and assemblers generally get hit, cut, or crushed by something, the nurses aids, orderlies, and truckers typically injure a muscle or joint when lifting, pushing, or pulling. Janitors, stock handlers, and cashiers have problems similar to those of nurses aids and orderlies, but at much lower rates (1 in 23, 30, and 74, respectively). Most of the nonfatal occupational injuries are not serious. Half require five days or less off from work. Individuals unable to work because of an illness or injury necessarily have worse health than average. However, most prolonged inability to work results from chronic problems like heart disease that reflect lifelong habits far more than occupational risks.

Unhealthy Attributes of Occupations

With one exception, the qualities of occupations measured by the federal government do not account for individual differences in subjective health and physical impairment after adjustment for individual qualities such as age, sex, education, earnings, household income, and history of unemployment and economic hardship. Many qualities of occupations such as physical demands and harsh or dangerous environments *seem* relevant to individual differences in health because they correlate with average levels of education, earnings, unemployment, and so on. A few occupational attributes, such as high noise levels, correlate with specific health problems, such as difficulty hearing, but not with health in general. However, one occupational attribute consistently predicts individual differences in health, because it measures the occupational constraints on individual productive creativity: the percentage of workers in an occupation who must perform repetitive work, doing the same thing according to a set procedure, sequence, or pace.

Some of the most restrictive and constraining occupations are quite safe in traditional terms. These include telephone operators, meter readers, payroll and timekeeping clerks, bank tellers, records clerks, elevator operators, messengers, maids, and personal service supervisors. Some of the least restrictive and constraining occupations are physically challenging or risky. These include roofers, duct installers, structural metal workers, elevator installers and repairers, insulation workers, plasterers, sailors and deck hands, marine engineers, explosives workers, mining engineers, and firefighters. Personal health problems, and the differences in health problems across levels of education, mostly reflect the constraints imposed by occupations, not their physical demands or their harsh or dangerous conditions.

The Work Link

Work is physical or mental effort or activity directed toward the production or accomplishment of something. Employment is paid work. Employment almost always trades some degree of freedom for income. In a market economy everyone needs money to get things they require or want, and most people must work for the money. The balance in that trade depends as much on the amount of freedom given up, and the burden of the work, as it does on the pay. Often when people think of the burden of work they think of time spent, physical and mental strain endured, risk taken, and harm suffered. The true burden lies in the denial of self-expression and the inhibition of autonomous action—the stifling of free will. Humans need to work, and not just because they need the money. Directing physical and mental effort toward production and accomplishment is to humans what running is to horses. Work is so deeply enmeshed in our species' mode of survival that humans do it in the absence of immediate need, like a riderless horse galloping for no reason except the desire to run and the joy of doing it. Humans take pleasure in work, and must do it to be whole, hale, and healthy.

So how is it that, for many, "work" means the things they would not do were it not for the money? The burden of employment results from the loss of independent choice and self-generated action (Evans 1994). Education lifts this burden. It minimizes the loss of independence, maximizes the opportunity for creative self-expression, and transforms pay from compensation for surrendered freedom to reward for productive accomplishment. Two qualities of work that affect health neatly illustrate the transformation: autonomy and creativity. We define each below, and show its relationship to employment and education.

Education and the Autonomy and Creativity of Work

Autonomy is the condition or state of being self-directed, self-governing, and not controlled by others. Almost all paying jobs require some loss of autonomy. However the average amount of autonomy sacrificed gets smaller at higher levels of education, as illustrated in Figure 4.15. To measure autonomy we asked everyone in our sample how they spend their time on a daily basis. We asked employed persons to tell about their paid jobs and asked others to tell about the work, tasks, or activities that they mostly do during the day. Three questions get at autonomy. The first asks, "Is there someone who supervises your work or to whom you report?" If the person is not employed the question substitutes "daily activities" for "work." Anyone with a supervisor is then asked, "How free are you to disagree with the person who supervises your [work/daily activities]? Not at all free, somewhat free, largely but not completely free, or completely free to disagree?" The second and third questions ask everyone with or without a supervisor, "Who usually decides *how* you will do your [work/daily activities]? Who usually decides *what* you will do in your [work/daily activities]?" For both questions the responses offered are "You, someone else, or you and someone else about equally?" We assign positive scores to responses that indicate personal autonomy, negative scores to ones that indicate control by others, and zeros to responses that indicate roughly equal control by oneself and others. The index scores run from −2 to +2. For example, someone with no supervisor who personally decides what to do and how to do it gets a score of +2. A person with a supervisor who allows no disagreement and makes all the decisions gets a score of −2. A person

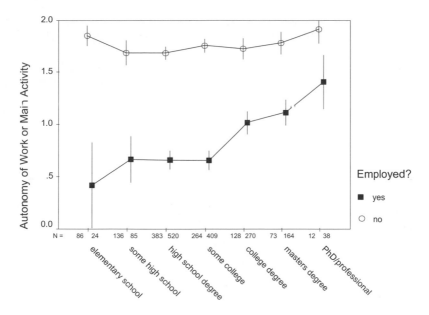

Figure 4.15. Autonomy of work or main activity by education and employment.

who is somewhat free to disagree with a supervisor and shares decisions about equally gets a score of zero.

The mean autonomy scores show three important patterns when compared across categories of employment and education. First, individuals with paid jobs have less autonomy than others with the same level of education. The differences are statistically significant at every level of education, in that there is no overlap of the 95 percent confidence intervals representing the sample's margin of error. The average levels of autonomy among persons who are not employed approach the maximum score on the index. This may seem obvious, but it is not trivial. Greater autonomy is one of the few benefits of not having a paying job. Second, the average autonomy among the employed generally rises with level of education. As a result, the difference in autonomy between the employed and others gets smaller at higher levels of education. Third, employees at all levels of education have positive mean autonomy scores. In fact, only about 20 percent of employed persons have negative autonomy scores, and almost all are workers with less than a college degree.

Creativity is the production of favorable or useful results in an original and expressive manner. The creativity of work generally increases with the

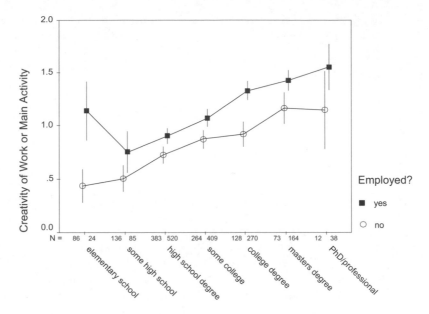

Figure 4.16. Creativity of work or main activity by education and employment.

level of education, as shown in Figure 4.16. To measure creativity the survey asks, "Does your [work/daily activity] usually involve doing the same thing in the same way repeatedly, the same kind of thing in a number of different ways, or a number of different kinds of things?" It then asks if the person strongly agrees, disagrees, or strongly disagrees with each of three statements: "My [work/daily activities] [gives/give] me a chance to do things I enjoy. My [work/daily activities] [gives/give] me a chance to develop and to learn new things. In my [work/daily activities] I have to figure out how to solve problems." Positive scores indicate task variety, opportunity for enjoyment and development, and the demand for ingenuity. Negative scores indicate their absence. As with autonomy, the creativity scores range from –2 to +2.

The mean creativity scores show several important patterns. First, paid work tends to be more creative than unpaid activity. This contrasts with the pattern for autonomy. On average, paid work provides more opportunity and stimulus for creative effort than unpaid daily activity does. Second, the creativity of work or daily activities generally increases at higher levels of education. While similar to the case for autonomy, education's association with creativity applies to persons without paid jobs as well as to the employed. Third, the mean creativity scores are positive at all levels of education for both the employed and the nonemployed. About 9 percent of employed persons have negative creativity scores, whereas 15 percent have maximum index scores of +2. In contrast, about 16 percent of persons without paying jobs have negative creativity scores, and only about 5 percent have the top scores of +2.

Taken together, the patterns described above illustrate the important difference between reward and compensation. People often speak of wages and salaries as compensation. The concept implies reparation for lost time, effort, or well-being. It is not clear where this view of wages and salaries came from originally, but it lies at the heart of many erroneous ideas about workers and pay. Those ideas begin with a commonsense assertion: employers must pay workers more money to get them to do the harsh, stressful, risky, or distasteful jobs. That may seem true, but it implies that the best-paid workers are doing the most onerous work. Nothing could be further from the truth. The reality is exactly the opposite. The best-paid jobs are more rewarding in a variety of ways. Desirable job characteristics such as security, safety, comfort, flexible scheduling, autonomy, and enjoyable, engaging tasks generally go along with higher earnings (Brown 1980; Jacobs and Steinberg 1990, 1995; Rosen 1986; Ross and Mirowsky 1996; Smith 1979). The same goes for symbolic rewards such as recognition, acknowledgment, honor, and prestige. Education helps individuals orchestrate this symphony of desirable outcomes. It helps them find ways to do things they enjoy doing, and want to do, that others reward.

The more creative a person's work or daily activities the better their health. Figure 4.17 illustrates the relationship. It shows the unadjusted mean subjective health scores within three broad categories of education (less than high school degree, high school degree, college degree) and three categories of work creativity (top score of +2, other positive score, negative or zero score). Using broad categories simplifies the graph, showing the general pattern. Within each level of education, subjective health improves progressively as the level of work creativity increases. In addition, the creativity of work and daily activities increases with the level of education. Among persons with less than a high school degree, 26.8 percent have negative or zero creativity scores, compared to only 6.1 percent of persons with college degrees. In contrast, 19.3 percent of persons with college degrees have top creativity scores, compared to only 5.5 percent of persons with less than a high school degree. Better-educated persons have better health partly because their work and activities are more creative.

Creative Work, Autonomous Work, and Health

Creative work correlates with significantly better subjective health, better physical functioning, and fewer serious chronic conditions, even after adjusting for age, race, sex, parental education, personal education, marital status, history of economic hardship, history of prolonged unemployment, occupational prestige and restrictiveness, current employment

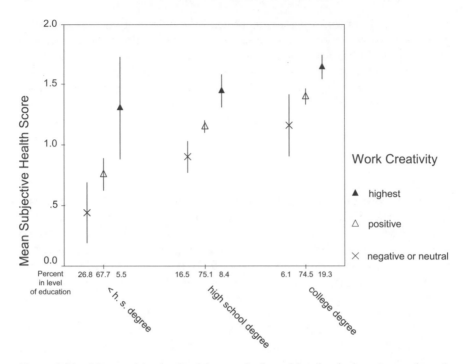

Figure 4.17. Mean subjective health score by broad levels of education and work creativity.

status, the amounts of personal and other household income in the previous year, and autonomy. Creativity scores increase an average of a quarter of a point between persons with high school degrees and those with college degrees, after adjustment for age, race, sex, and parental education. That translates into differences in subjective health and chronic conditions about equivalent to the ones expected from a doubling of household income. It translates into a difference in physical impairment about equivalent to the one expected from a 50 percent increase in household income. Keep in mind that those values measure the differences in health associated with creative work itself. They do not include the differences in health that might result indirectly from effects creative work might have by reducing prolonged unemployment, history of economic hardship, and so on.

The creativity of work and activities seems more directly important to health than does their autonomy. Subjective health and the number of serious chronic diseases have no significant association with the autonomy scores after adjustment for creativity scores and for age, race, sex, parental education, etc. Only the impairment scores have a significant net correlation with autonomy, but much smaller than the parallel correlation with creativity. To illustrate, the average difference in autonomy between persons with high school degrees and those with college degrees correlates with a net difference in physical impairment equivalent to the one associated with a 6.6 percent increase in household income. That is about 1/13th the size of the corresponding creativity effect. Autonomy accounts for less of the educational differences in health than does creativity in part because it increases with education only among the employed. For the employed, the increase in average autonomy going from high school to college degrees correlates with a net decrease in impairment equivalent to the one from a 25.5 percent increase in household income. While more substantial, that is still only about half the equivalent amount for creativity, and it applies to only one of the three health measures. Creativity is far more important to health than autonomy is, and paid work provides the greatest opportunity for creativity.

Authority: The Contradiction

Authority is the power to judge, decide, and command. Most paying jobs place workers in a pyramid of organizational power. Authority at work has two aspects that contradict each other's effect on health and well-being. On the positive side, having authority means getting to make decisions, or at least getting to have a vote or voice in the decisions. That tends to bolster autonomy and make room for creativity. In addition, higher pay generally comes with greater authority. On the negative side, having authority means being responsible for the actions and accomplishments of others. A person who supervises or manages others must get them to cooperate and produce. That invariably creates frustration and conflict. No amount of authority changes the fact that individuals themselves decide what they do, and may lack the ability to accomplish things they willingly try. Even so, a person who judges and decides what others *should* do bears responsibility for the success of their actions and efforts. In a hierarchy those responsibilities go in both directions, to persons higher up as well as to persons lower down. Decision-makers often feel apprehension about how things will turn out and tension about resolving the conflicting interests of others higher and lower in the organization. When things go poorly, guilt and shame, anger and resentment often mingle with disappointment and fear of consequences. Authority has costs as well as benefits. With respect to health, the positives and negatives balance each other out. Organizational authority has no effect on health overall.

Productive Self-Expression: A Reprise

We human beings deliberately transform the world around us. We meet our needs and pursue our wants through production. We design, devise, plan, practice, order, arrange, assemble, shape, frame, mold, mobilize, fashion, build, construct, contrive, and cultivate. We manufacture and enact the reality we live in. The connection between working and living turns out to be more than simply providing food and shelter. Like physical activity, productive self-expression enhances and sustains human health.

EDUCATION, SOCIOECONOMIC STATUS, AND HEALTH

What can we conclude about socioeconomic status and health? First, health does benefit from economic well-being, although not for the reasons many individuals might suppose. Increments in income have their greatest impact on health among persons at the bottom of the economic order, who have the lowest amounts of income. That can make it seem that economic well-being protects and advances health solely because it buys the most basic necessities of life, protecting the human organism from the ravages of hunger, thirst, and exposure. Destitution and privation certainly account for some of the health problems found near the bottom of the economic ladder. Wherever such extreme want occurs, it erodes and eventually destroys the health of those who suffer it. That kind of poverty is rare in an advanced and wealthy society such as the United States, even among those in the bottom 10 or 20 percent in terms of income and wealth. Most of the Americans that others of us would consider poor have access to the minimum food, water, clothing, shelter, and sanitary facilities needed for survival, yet still suffer the ill effect of poverty. Some of that ill effect comes from the exposures and strains of living in dilapidated, tumultuous, and frightening neighborhoods. Far more of it comes from repeated or prolonged difficulty paying bills or buying things the household needs. Economic hardships undermine health by evoking dread and hopelessness. Daunting and demoralizing experiences stimulate physiological responses felt as sickness that also reduce the effectiveness of the immune system and degrade other critical systems through a variety of mechanisms.

The second important conclusion is that education greatly moderates the association between economic resources and health. Sparse economic resources erode health more the lower a person's level of education. Partly that is because better-educated people more often avoid household situations, such as early or single parenthood, that greatly magnify the risk of economic hardship at any given level of income. Partly it is because better-educated persons use income more efficiently to meet household needs. The effectiveness learned through education, and the confidence based on that effectiveness, operate as an alternative resource that substitutes for money if money is in short supply. Higher levels of education make individuals less dependent on money for solutions to their problems while also reducing the likelihood of problems and increasing the reserves and flows of money available to address them. These interactions help create the diminishing impact on health of progressive steps up in income. Differences in income produce the largest differences in health at the bottom of the income scale because individuals at that end generally have low levels of education. Differences in income produce almost no differences in health in the top third of the income scale because almost everyone at that end has high levels of education.

The third important conclusion is that money cannot buy health. Some amount of money is necessary, but no amount is sufficient. Health is not a commodity. No product or service one can buy will provide it. Medical insurance does not buy health because medical services do not create health. Medical interventions sometimes keep alive individuals who otherwise would die, but sometimes do the opposite. They sometimes restore a measure of health and function, but often fail or make things worse. The overall balance of medical risks and benefits is not as favorable as many Americans want to believe. Perhaps more important, medical interventions attempt to correct problems rather than to avoid them. Individuals who deliberately try to prevent health problems generally will be healthier than those who let the problems develop and then rely on medical intervention for remedies. Clearly, some diseases cannot be avoided, and sometimes the generally avoidable ones happen through pure bad luck. Even then, the individuals who are healthy otherwise fare better than the ones who have let themselves go on the expectation that medicine would save them from whatever serious problems arose. We realize that some readers will find the conclusion that money cannot buy health difficult or impossible to accept. It is in the nature of bad habits that one wishes to continue them even knowing the risks. The belief that medicine will correct unwelcome consequences relieves the psychological tension. Much of the wealth and power of the medical industry relies on selling that palliative. Those who buy it buy treatments, not health.

The final important conclusion is that productive self-expression nourishes health. Work need not be drudgery. Creative work challenges the mind, exercising and developing it. Humans need to direct physical and mental effort toward production and accomplishment. In modern societies they also need income. The ideal is to find or design jobs that meet both these needs. Education helps individuals to do that. It makes workers better able to find engaging, enjoyable, and challenging things to do that others reward. In addition, a better-educated work force allows employers to design jobs that give employees greater autonomy and scope for creativity. Higher levels of education are transforming paid work from self-denying wage slavery to self-expressing productive creativity. That progressive unleashing of the human spirit improves health and functioning beyond the level that meeting economic needs alone can achieve.

| 5 |

Education, Interpersonal Relationships, and Health

EDUCATION, MARRIAGE, AND SOCIAL SUPPORT

The well-educated have more stable and supportive interpersonal relationships than do those with less schooling, which may also protect health. At any one point in time, the well-educated are more likely to be married, which confers social support, and apart from marriage people with higher levels of education report more social support than do those with less schooling.

People with high levels of education are more likely to be married than those with less education. In our data from the ASOC survey, 62 percent of those with a college degree or higher are currently married, compared with 56 percent of people who have a high school degree but not a college degree, and 40 percent of people with less than a high school degree. Much of the reason that the well-educated have a higher likelihood of being currently married is that their marriages are less likely to end in divorce or widowhood. The well-educated are less likely to divorce, probably due to the fact that they marry later and do so under more favorable economic conditions, and they have happier and more satisfying marriages (Glick 1984). Education is negatively associated with widowhood, too, since men and women choose partners with similar levels of education (Qian and Preston 1993) and well-educated people live longer than those with lower levels of education (Rogot et al. 1992). On the other hand, because the well-educated marry later, among young people those with less education are more likely to be married. Unfortunately many of these early marriages end in divorce. All told, well-educated men and women are more likely to be currently married than those without high school degrees.

Figures 5.1 through 5.3 illustrate these patterns. At almost every age, people with a college degree are most likely to be married and people who have not finished high school are least likely to be married (see Figure 5.1; the only exceptions are within the sample's margin of error and are probably random). Since marital status is so structured by age, with young per-

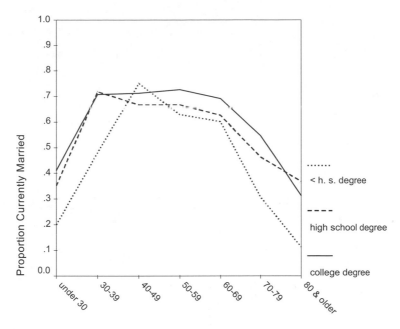

Figure 5.1. The association between education and marriage at various ages.

sons likely to be single and old persons likely to be widowed, each graph shows the association of education with marital status taking age into account. Figure 5.2 shows that the proportion divorced or separated is much lower among those with a college education, with one exception. Among people over age sixty-five, the college-educated are more likely to be divorced than are those with less education. This could be real or it could be a methodological artifact. If the latter, it could simply be that only married people are at risk of divorce, and among people with less than a college education, a higher proportion are widowed so they are not at risk of divorce. Or it could be that college-educated women from older cohorts were more likely to divorce. At every age under age sixty-five people with a college degree are less likely to be divorced than are people who finished high school but not college. People who have not finished high school are most likely to be divorced or separated, and they divorce young after marrying early. (The blip down in divorce and up in marriage among persons in their forties who have not finished high school is probably random.) Finally, Figure 5.3 shows that at every age, people with a college education have the lowest probability of being widowed. A large proportion of people over age sixty who did not finish high school are widowed.

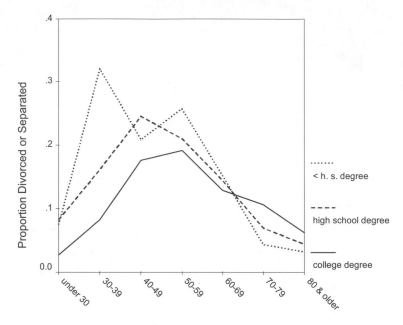

Figure 5.2.   The association between education and divorce at various ages.

The well-educated have more supportive and equitable relationships than those with less education because schooling helps partners understand and negotiate with each other, see more than one side of an issue, and respond flexibly with attempts to understand the other's position and to arrange something that is mutually satisfactory. Communication skills—the ability to talk things through rather than resort to violence, and the ability to compromise and solve problems—are part of the learned effectiveness discussed earlier. In addition, people with high levels of education experience less economic hardship because they are likely to be employed full-time and have higher incomes, and because education increases the value of each dollar, so that they avoid the economic troubles that strain relationships (Atkinson, Liem, and Liem 1986; Gore 1978). Hence, the human capital gained in school improves the ability to build and maintain supportive relationships, including but not limited to, good marriages.

The association between education and social support is illustrated in Figure 5.4. The higher one's level of education, the more likely a person is to agree that "I have someone I can turn to for support and understanding when things get rough," "I have someone I can really talk to," "I have

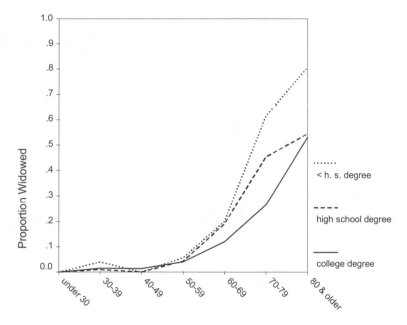

Figure 5.3. The association between education and widowhood at various ages.

someone who would help me out with things, like give me a ride, watch the kids or house, or fix something," and "I have someone who would take care of me if I were sick." The well-educated report more emotional support, as assessed by the first two questions, and more instrumental support, as assessed by the second two.

MARRIAGE AND HEALTH

Marriage protects health and decreases mortality (Waite 1995; Waite and Gallagher 2000). Compared to married people, the single, divorced, and widowed have more physical health problems, including more acute conditions, chronic conditions, days of disability, physical impairment, and poor subjective health (Tcheng-Laroche and Prince 1983; Berk and Taylor 1984; Riessman and Gerstel 1985; Anson 1989). Follow-up studies show that the nonmarried have higher mortality from all causes of death than the married [1.4 times higher among women ages thirty to sixty-nine, and three times higher among men, according to Berkman and Breslow (1983)]. Compared to married people, the divorced and widowed have higher

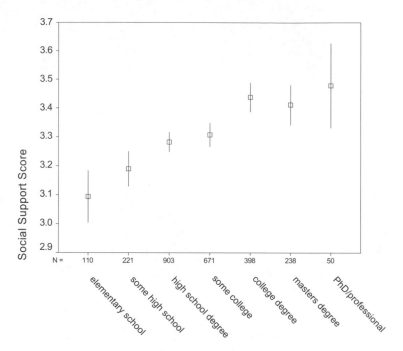

Figure 5.4. The association between education and social support.

death rates from coronary heart disease, stroke, pneumonia, many kinds of cancer, cirrhosis of the liver, automobile accidents, homicide, and suicide, all of which are leading causes of death (Tcheng-Laroche and Prince 1983; Kaprio, Koskenuo, and Rita 1987; Berkman and Breslow 1983). For causes of death that also kill young people, especially suicide, single people also have higher death rates than the married (Smith, Mercy, and Conn 1988). Widows, especially, have higher levels of depression and anxiety and higher death rates than the married. Death rates are greatest immediately after the death of one's spouse (Kaprio, Koskenuo, and Rita 1987), but stay higher than those of married people until the widowed remarry or die (Helsing, Moysen, and Comstock 1981; Bowling 1987). (In mortality studies most of the nonmarried are widowed or divorced; few are single, since single people tend to be young.)

Figures 5.5 and 5.6 show that married people report better subjective health and physical functioning at all ages. Because age structures health to a great extent, it must be accounted for. When we do so, we see that the marriage gap in physical functioning and, to a greater extent, subjective health appears to widen as people age.

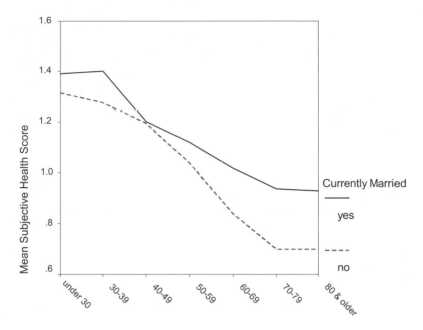

Figure 5.5.   The association between marriage and subjective health at various ages.

Some researchers claim that selection of healthy people into marriage accounts for some of the association, but the evidence is equivocal. For example, Brown and Giesy (1986) find that people with spinal cord injuries are less likely to be married. They interpret this as selection, arguing that people with severe health problems are less likely to marry or to remain married. However, it is more likely that marriage protects against spinal cord injuries because married people engage in fewer risky activities like drinking and driving or riding a motorcycle without a helmet than do unmarried people (Umberson 1987). Although there may be some selection effect keeping or taking the unhealthy out of marriage, the causal effect of marriage on health probably accounts for more of the association (Ross, Mirowsky, and Goldsteen 1990).

Overall, the well-educated are more likely to be married, and married people are healthier than those who are single, divorced, or widowed (Waite 1995; Waite and Gallagher 2000). Furthermore, education brings the benefits of marriage with few of the stressors. If marriage has any negative effects on well-being, they are due to the stressors children create, especially having many children, having children early in life, the economic strains children generate, heavy child care responsibilities, and difficulties

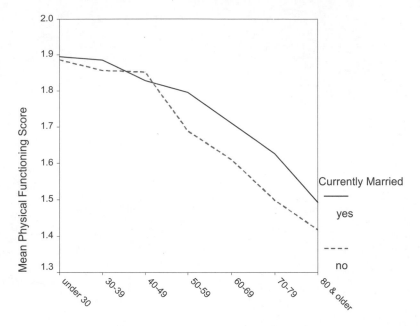

Figure 5.6.   The association between marriage and physical functioning at various ages.

arranging child care while parents are at work (Ross and Huber 1985; Ross and Mirowsky 1988). Since children often accompany marriage, the effect of marriage on well-being may not be uniformly positive. However, the well-educated may get the benefits of marriage, without the stress associated with children, since well-educated women have fewer children, and they have their first child later in life when they are more prepared. Women with high levels of education are more likely to remain childless, to postpone having children, and to have fewer children than are those with lower levels of education (Bloom and Trussel 1984; Rindfuss, Morgan, and Swicegood 1984; Veevers 1979). Since men and women tend to choose partners with similar levels of education, well-educated men have fewer children, too.

Why does marriage improve health? Married persons experience less economic hardship, have more social support, and have a more orderly lifestyle than the nonmarried, which benefits their health. Given the same health problems, married people also visit the doctor more than the nonmarried, but there is no evidence that this accounts for the benefits of marriage to health.

Economic Resources

Marriage raises people out of poverty, which improves health largely by way of reducing the stress associated with economic hardship. Married people have higher household incomes than the nonmarried. In our 1995 data, married people reported average annual household incomes of $50,543. Nonmarried females had average household incomes of $28,196 and nonmarried males, $40,797. The economic benefits of marriage hold for both women and men, even adjusting for age, minority status, employment status, and education (Ross 1989), although the economic benefits of marriage (and losses from divorce) are much greater for women than for men (Gerstel, Riessman, and Rosenfield 1985; Cherlin 1981). Especially for women, income drops precipitously after divorce and remains close to the new low for up to five years (the period of observation)(Weiss 1984). Nonmarried women fall far below the level at which income makes a big difference to health and nonmarried men hover at the edge, around $40,000. Furthermore, even at the same income level, married people experience fewer economic strains—they have fewer difficulties paying the bills and paying for food, clothes, shelter, and other necessities for their household—than do people who are not married (Mirowsky and Ross 1999).

Social Support

Marriage also provides social support, which is associated with physical health largely indirectly because of its strong impact on psychological well-being. Stated another way, social support improves psychological well-being, and because psychological well-being correlates with physical health, social support is also associated with physical health. Still, the impact of social support on health is not that large. Figure 3.8 shows that social support does not directly impact physical functioning, once the sense of personal control is held constant. Social support has little impact on physical functioning—problems with going up and down stairs, kneeling and stooping, using one's hands and fingers, lifting and carrying, seeing, and so on. Social support does improve self-reported health, which has a large subjective component and is correlated with emotional health.

Most marriages provide emotional support, which is a sense of being cared about, loved, esteemed, and valued as a person. Married people are more likely than people who are not married to report that they have someone they can turn to for support and understanding when things get rough, are more likely to have someone they can really talk to, and are more likely to report having a confidant. [A good marriage provides emotional support, although the small group that reports being unhappy with their marriage reports less support and more distress than those who are not married (Gove, Hughes, and Style 1983; Ross 1995).] Social support, especially emotional support, decreases depression, anxiety, anger, and other psychological problems, which indirectly improves health (Kessler and McLeod 1985; Thoits 1982; Wheaton 1985; LaRocco, House, and French, 1980; Kaplan, Robbins, and Martin 1983; Cohen and Syme 1985; Mirowsky and Ross 1989; Ross and Van Willigen 1997; Umberson and Williams 2000). Over time, psychological well-being improves subsequent physical well-being (Aneshensel, Frerichs, and Huba 1984; Mechanic and Hansell 1987), and in a fifteen-month follow-up of people age fifty and over, the severely depressed were four times more likely to die than others, adjusting for history of hypertension, heart attack, stroke, cancer, or limitation of physical functioning (Bruce and Leaf 1989).

Marriage provides emotional support, which is crucial to psychological well-being and thus indirectly improves health. But the benefits of marriage to physical health are not mostly explained by social support. In fact, social support itself has less of an effect on physical health than previously thought because most studies of social support and health did not adjust for the sense of personal control, which correlates with social support. People with high levels of personal control are typically the same people who have high levels of social support, but it is the sense of control more than the social support that improves physical health. The sense of personal control has large effects on health in part because it shapes a healthy lifestyle. Social support has less of an impact on health lifestyle.

Emotional support—the sense of being cared about and loved and of having someone you can really talk to and share your problems with—does not shape a healthy lifestyle. People who have someone who cares about them that they can talk to are no more (or less) likely to exercise, walk, drink moderately, or avoid overweight and smoking than are people with less supportive relationships with friends and family. Talking to others about how hard it is to quit smoking could substitute for actually quitting, especially if these confidants commiserate; supportive friends could drink too much together; and supporters could actually sabotage efforts to adopt a healthier lifestyle (Ross and Mirowsky 1989; Thoits 1995). Personal control is effective because it shapes healthy behavior, but social support does not appear to.

An Orderly Life

Marriage may shape health behaviors through mechanisms other than emotional support, however. Marriage's effect on lifestyle may be explained more by regulation and orderliness than by supportiveness. Having a spouse who nags you may be more important to a healthy lifestyle than having a spouse who dotes on you. Marriage provides a stable, coherent, regulated environment, and compared to single, divorced, and widowed people, the married experience more social control and regulation of behavior (Anson 1989; Hughes and Gove 1981; Umberson 1987). Married men are less likely than single and divorced men to go out to bars, get in fights, drive drunk, drive too fast, take illegal drugs, engage in risky sports, get in trouble with the law, be sexually promiscuous, and they are generally less likely to take risks that increase the likelihood of accidents and injuries, probably because their wives discourage it (Waite and Gallagher 2000; Umberson 1987, 1992). Married men and women are less likely to smoke and to drink heavily, possibly because their spouse persuaded them not to: Heavy drinking can be disruptive, smoking is noxious to others in the house, and secondhand smoke is especially dangerous for children (Venters 1986; Umberson 1987). Marriage provides a more orderly and controlled, less chaotic, less unpredictable, and less risky lifestyle than ones associated with being single or divorced. Much, but not all, of this lifestyle is associated with good health. A few healthy behaviors are less common among the married. Married people are more likely to be overweight, and they are less likely to engage in physical activity and exercise than the nonmarried (Hayes and Ross 1986; Ross and Mirowsky 1983; Venters 1986).

The fact that married people are less likely to exercise and more likely to be overweight than the nonmarried fits the regulation hypothesis of why marriage improves health more than it does the supportiveness hypothesis. If married people quit smoking because someone really cared about them, then why would they not also exercise and maintain a normal weight? Smoking has the largest overall impact on health of any health behavior, but overweight and a sedentary lifestyle rank second. Yet married people are more sedentary and overweight than the nonmarried, probably because their orderly, home-oriented lifestyle means they have more family dinners, skip fewer meals, sit around more with the family watching television and eating snacks, go to the gym less, or are less concerned about staying trim to attract a partner. It is probably marriage alone, not supportive relationships with other family members or friends, that decreases risky behaviors and largely (but not entirely) increases healthy behaviors.

Use of Medical Care

Married people are healthier than those who are not married, so they visit the doctor less because they have less of a need to; but at the same level of health, married people are more likely to see the doctor for checkups, screening, and other early detection than the nonmarried (Berkman and Syme 1979; Neale, Tilley, and Vernon 1986). Yet, the benefits to overall health of uncovering and treating disease early are uncertain. Yearly checkups appear to have no effect on maintaining health (Canadian Task Force on the Periodic Health Examination 1988; Ross and Wu 1995). Screening often entails some risk, like exposure to small amounts of radiation with x-rays and even with mammography (Bailar 1976). Also, the risks and side effects of treatment often outweigh the benefits for low-level disease, which might not get worse and may even get better if left untreated. In many instances the benefits of screening people with no symptoms are questionable. Although married persons are more likely to get checkups than people who are not married, having regular checkups cannot explain any of the association between education and health because checkups do not significantly affect health (Ross and Wu 1995).

Why do check-ups and screening not improve health? Annual checkups are secondary prevention. The goal of *secondary* prevention is to *catch disease early* to limit the consequences. In comparison, the goal of *primary* prevention is to *prevent the onset of disease* by reducing risks (through exercise, not smoking, or drinking in moderation). Almost all prevention in our medical care system is secondary, not primary, despite much better evidence for the health benefits of primary prevention. In fact, there is little evidence that checkups protect *adults'* health (U.S. Preventive Services Task Force 1989). The rationale behind annual physical exams makes four potentially false assumptions: (1) checkups catch disease early, (2) detecting disease early makes a difference in outcome, (3) checkups do no harm, and (4) the people who might benefit from checkups get them (Canadian Task Force on the Periodic Health Examination 1979, 1988). First, annual physical exams are not targeted to an individual's risk, so they are unlikely to find undetected disease. Second, early detection is not useful unless the treatment that follows is effective in slowing the course of illness, or ideally in curing it; this is rare for many chronic diseases. Third, screening that is not targeted at high-risk groups produces a certain percentage of false positives that can lead to dangerous and unnecessary treatments for nonexistent diseases, distress caused by the false diagnosis, and risks from the actual screening tests, which can expose people to risk of infection from invasive procedures, small amounts of radiation, and so on (Bailar and Smith 1986; Canadian Task Force 1988). Fourth, the people who need checkups the least are the most likely to get them, and vice versa. Married people—who need secondary preventive care less because they are at lower risk of illness—are most likely to receive it. We illustrate some of these principles with cancer, the second leading cause of death in the United States (heart disease is first).

Many believe that early detection and treatment of cancer decrease mortality. Despite great improvement in early detection and increased early treatment, cancer deaths in the United States have been stable over the past forty years (NCHS 2002). In the past forty years, *age-adjusted* cancer mortality rates per 100,000 in the United States remained about 200. According to Bailar and Smith (1986) and Cairns (1985), early detection and treatment of cancer, including breast cancer, is largely ineffective. (Hodgkin's disease and leukemia are exceptions.)

Lung cancer causes more deaths than any other type of cancer (30 percent of all cancer deaths). X-rays can detect lung cancer before symptoms or signs appear. However, finding the cancer does little good because the treatments do not work (Cairns 1985). Screening creates an illusion of improved survival because many of the small cancers detected by X-ray would not be fatal even if untreated (Bailar and Smith 1986). Mortality due to lung cancer decreased from 75.2 to 65.4 per 100,000 for men, but increased from 31.6 to 34.6 per 100,000 for women, in the nineties (NCHS 2002). By all indications, lung cancer mortality will decline only after the prevalence of smoking declines. (Unfortunately, increases among women counterbalance the declines among men.)

The second leading cause of cancer death among women is breast cancer (lung cancer is first). Many people believe that improved early detection and treatment have reduced mortality from breast cancer, but the evidence shows otherwise. Age-adjusted mortality due to breast cancer has remained fairly stable since the 1950s, increasing some in the decade of the eighties, and decreasing some in the nineties (American Cancer Society 1997; Bailar and Smith 1986; NCHS 2002). As in lung cancer, early detection creates an illusion of improved survival. Breast examinations and mammograms detect cancers at an early stage, before spreading. The earlier cancers are detected, the longer the average time between detection and death. Early detection finds smaller tumors, creating the illusion of longer survival, first, because the tumors are found earlier so people would live longer even without any treatment (Feuer and Wun 1992; King and Schottenfeld 1996; Lantz, Remington, and Newcomb 1991; Miller, Feuer, and Hankey 1991; Newcomb and Lantz 1993). Any apparent increase in the incidence of breast cancer or in the apparent increase in survival may be due to the increased use of mammography screening. Take two women both aged fifty and with the same size small tumors; one has her first mammogram when she is fifty, but the other does not have one until she is sixty. Thus, the first woman's tumor is seen ten years earlier than the second's. Both live to age seventy. The woman who got her mammogram at age fifty has survived twenty years since diagnosis, but the woman who got her first mammogram at age sixty has only survived ten years since diagnosis. Even without any treatment at all, the woman with the earlier detection has survived ten years longer. Thus, a lot of what appears to be a benefit of early detection and treatment is not real. Second, many of the small cancers would not spread and become fatal, even if undetected and untreated (Bailar and Smith 1986). The immune system successfully fights off many cancers, just as it does infectious diseases like flus and colds. Unfortunately, cancer treatments like chemotherapy depress the immune system and interfere with our own body's ability to fight off cancers.

Does marriage improve women's survival by increasing the early detection and treatment of breast cancer? Using data from a cancer center on 910 married and 351 widowed women with breast cancer, Neale et al. (1986) found that married women are less likely than widows to delay seeking treatment after noticing symptoms like a lump or change in the breast. However, adjusting for age, socioeconomic status, and stage of the disease, they found that earlier detection and treatment do *not* increase ten-year survival. Married women with breast cancer do live longer than widowed women with breast cancer, but their increased survival is not due to earlier detection, because the latter does not lengthen survival. This study is important because it statistically adjusts for the stage of disease (how much the cancer has spread). Married women are diagnosed and treated earlier in the disease, but the salutary effect of marriage on subsequent length of survival is not explained by finding the cancer at an earlier stage.

Summing Up

Marriage has positive effects on health that are *not* due to early detection of disease or treatment of disease. At the same level of health, married people do visit the doctor more than the nonmarried, but this is not what accounts for their low levels of disease, distress, and death. Instead, their good health is probably due to fewer economic hardships, more social support, and more regulation of risky behaviors. Married people experience less economic hardship than the nonmarried, which reduces stress and improves health. Married people also have higher levels of social support, especially emotional support, than the nonmarried. Most of the effect of social support on health appears to be mediated by improved psychological well-being, not by health behaviors (since the married score worse on some behaviors, and because social support itself does not improve health lifestyle). Married people lead a more orderly and regulated life.

Well-educated people have more stable and supportive relationships with others. In particular, they are more likely to be married, which protects health. Marriage, more than other types of supportive relationships, may be the protective factor. General social support improves psychological well-being, which in turn is associated with physical health, but support is not associated with a healthy lifestyle. Looking at the two aspects of health, subjective health is improved by social support, but physical functioning is not. This may be because subjective health has a larger psychological component. Feelings of poor health include feeling run-down, tired, lacking energy, and general feelings of malaise, which are also associated with depression. Marriage influences feelings of good health in part by decreasing economic hardship and in part by increasing social support. Marriage's positive impact on physical functioning remains even after adjustment for economic well-being and support, indicating that something else about marriage influences good physical functioning, probably the regulation married life provides.

| 6 |

Age and Cumulative Advantage

Education's varied and enduring consequences produce health advantages for the better-educated that accumulate and grow over the life course (Ross and Wu 1996). Many things in life produce effects that fade over time as individuals adjust to their circumstances, as tastes and times change, or as enthusiasms wane. Education's effects work the opposite way, growing with time. That is because education transforms the person, putting the individual's life on a different track. Education acts as a structural element of the individual's life, like a structural beam in a building. Many other elements of life depend on education and take shape with respect to it. To fully understand education's positive impact on health one must envision that benefit unfolding across the lifetime. Education's health-related effects are present at every age. Even if they were small in any one year, they accumulate and compound over a lifetime, producing ever larger health differences between persons with different levels of education.

By definition, a cumulative advantage is a benefit acquired by successive addition (O'Rand 1996). Education's cumulative health advantage rests on three underlying phenomena: permeation, accumulation, and amplification. The first of these, permeation, means that education affects many aspects of life. In the other chapters of this book we discuss a range of things influenced by education that in turn affect health, including habits, interpersonal relationships, family responsibilities, occupational exposures and opportunities, economic sufficiency and security, neighborhood qualities, autonomous and creative activities, and a sense of controlling one's own life. In this chapter we define and describe the other two forces behind education's cumulative advantages: accumulation and amplification.

After defining and describing the processes of accumulation and amplification, we summarize and discusses three current and interrelated scientific questions pertaining to cumulative advantage: Do the positive effects of education on health continue to grow throughout life, or do they diminish in old age? Does education slow the physical decline at every age or simply delay the inevitable until a sudden precipitous decline in old age?

Does education reduce the amount of the lifetime spent with serious chronic disease and impairment, or does it increase that period of burden by keeping alive those who would otherwise die of their diseases and infirmities? We argue that the differences in health across levels of education grow throughout life. The cumulative benefits do not suddenly disappear at the end. As a result, the well-educated enjoy a longer healthy life with less time spent sick or impaired near the end.

ACCUMULATING EFFECTS

Accumulation refers to gathering many smaller effects into a larger one. Some accumulations benefit health and others harm it. Education tends to speed or advance the beneficial accumulations and slow or delay the detrimental ones. Accumulation occurs when consequences, once present, tend to stay present. The health-related consequences of education accumulate on many levels, from the socioeconomic down to the cellular.

Socioeconomic Accumulation

On the socioeconomic level, for example, individuals generally stay in the same line of work, accumulating experience and seniority and gaining access to the more desirable and lucrative positions. Generally the norms and rules in an organization, occupation, or profession lay out a sequence of stages and discourage both skipping ahead or going backward in line (Rosenbaum 1984). As a consequence, the extrinsic and intrinsic work rewards that influence health tend to accumulate. Some rewards almost take on a life of their own, becoming accumulations of accumulations. For example, pay generally increases the longer someone works, with each raise a multiple of the previous amount. That means the raises generally get larger as pay increases. As income goes up larger amounts get used to acquire wealth in the form of durable goods, real estate, savings, and investments, which accumulate over time (Crystal and Shea 1990). Some of that wealth generates income or capital gains, increasing the rate of accumulation.

The rising levels of pay, income, and wealth all insulate against economic hardship and enhance the sense of control over one's own life, thereby improving health. The relatively small education-based differences in prosperity at the beginning of adulthood grow over the life course. Meanwhile the base level of health risk grows with age, so the impact of economic hardship on health also tends to grow. A year of economic troubles might multiply the risk of serious impairment or chronic disease by roughly the same percentage for older persons as for younger ones, but a higher base level of serious health problems makes the amount of the increase much greater for older persons. By these and other mechanisms, the accumulating socioeconomic differences across levels of education become accumulating health differences.

Behavioral Accumulation

Accumulation happens on the behavioral level too. Humans naturally form habits, which are recurrent and often unconscious patterns of behavior acquired through frequent repetition, established dispositions of the mind or character, and customary manners or practices. Habits relevant to health include physical and social activities, diet, smoking, and drinking. Education influences many habits and activities by increasing the sense of control over one's own life, which is itself a learned and stable worldview summing a lifetime of experience, as discussed in Chapter 3. The sense of control influences a person's habitual approach to risks and problems. The more control someone feels they have, the more effort they make to detect and avoid risks and the more actively and practically they respond to problems that arise. That tends to make individuals more effective. In addition, a higher sense of control generally reduces the psychophysiological distress associated with crises by reducing the sense of helplessness and hopelessness. The stability of activities, health-related behaviors, and sense of control create persistent effects present throughout long portions of life.

Humans also form sustaining personal relationships, which can be viewed as habits of association and interaction. Relationships tend to be stable over time. Education generally improves the quality of relationships, making them seem to the participants more fair, equal, respectful, and sustaining. Partly because of that, education makes marital relationships more enduring, increasing the prevalence of marriage and reducing the risk of exposure to the stress of divorce. Marriage, marital quality, and social support all contribute to health, as discussed in Chapter 5. To the extent that education's health-promoting interpersonal consequences persist, they contribute to its accumulating health benefits (Berkman, Glass, Brissette, and Seeman 2000).

Biological Accumulation

The socioeconomic and behavioral accumulations necessarily influence health through biological mechanisms, many of which accumulate too. Health science knows of many biological accumulators that affect health, and probably will discover many more. The accumulation of body fat may be the most obvious one, and the best known because of its place in popular culture. It serves as a good example of biological accumulators in general.

Body Fat: A Typical Bioaccumulator

The buildup of body fat happens slowly over a period of years. An individual who eats ten calories a day more than he or she burns will accumulate a pound of fat a year. Start doing that at age twenty and it adds up to ten pounds of excess fat by age thirty, and thirty pounds of excess fat by age fifty(ten calories is the number in one Life Saver candy or one-fifth of an Oreo cookie). It is roughly the amount of energy burned in eight minutes of sitting or sleeping. Make that two Life Savers a day or two-fifths of an Oreo and it adds up to sixty extra pounds by age fifty. Make it an entire Oreo a day and it adds up to 150 extra pounds by age fifty, which is more than enough body weight for an entire second person.

The ugly fact is that, once gained, body fat persists. There is no quick way to get rid of it. It takes about eight hours of jogging to burn one pound of fat. It takes over a year of jogging an hour a day to burn fifty pounds of fat. On the other hand, not accumulating the fat takes much less intensive effort. Two extra minutes a day of gardening, light bicycling, or brisk walking will burn the ten calories of excess food a day that adds up to fifty pounds of fat by age fifty. So will an extra minute and a half of jogging, racquet ball, tennis, moderate bicycling, swimming, or stair climbing. So will an annual one-week vacation with a couple of hours of hiking each day rather than lounging. Seemingly small differences in habits add up greatly over time. Two candy bars a week rather than two apples adds up to six pounds of extra fat in a year. It takes about 4,700 minutes of brisk walking to burn those extra calories. That is seventy-eight hours, or almost ten 8-hour days, but it is only about thirteen minutes a day over the 365 days of the year. A person who habitually parks an extra five minutes away, and takes stairs instead of elevators and escalators, easily burns an extra six pounds of fat a year instead of accumulating it. Lifestyle differences may look small on any given day, but they add up greatly over the years.

Desirable and Undesirable Accumulators

The human body has many less obvious biological accumulators that influence health (Marieb 1994; Memmler et al. 1996; Thibodeau and Patton 1997). Many of the desirable ones contribute to aerobic capacity, which is the ability to burn oxygen. The desirable biological accumulators include vital capacity of the lungs, the number and sensitivity of insulin receptors on cell membranes, the ratio of slow to fast muscle fibers, the number of mitochondria and nuclei in muscle cells, and the number of small arteries supplying the heart and skeletal muscles. Some undesirable biological accumulations get defined as diseases or medical conditions when they progress beyond a clearly dangerous point. They include high resting blood pressure, buildup of fatty plaque in arteries, a low ratio of high-density to low-density lipoprotein in the blood, cellular resistance to insulin and the resulting increase in blood glucose, declining bone density, deposits of uric acid crystals in the soft tissues of joints, softening and fraying of cartilage, and the calcification of ligaments.

Accumulations and Critical Events: The Heart Attack Example

Some undesirable accumulations eventually provoke damaging and deadly crises such as embolism, fibrillation, heart failure, infarction, hemorrhage, stroke, shock, or respiratory arrest. A heart attack provides a good example (Libby 2002; Marmot and Mustard 1994; Memmler et al. 1996; Rozanski, Blumenthal, and Kaplan 1999). The slow accumulation of fatty plaque in an artery feeding blood to the heart diminishes the amount of blood that can flow through it to feed the heart tissue. The narrower the artery the more likely that a situational demand for the heart to pump more blood will cause a crisis. As the heart pumps harder and faster to supply blood to the rest of the body it needs more blood itself. The occluded coronary artery cannot supply it fast enough. The heart tissue gets starved for oxygen, resulting in the death of some heart tissue. Sometimes the fatty plaque ruptures, releasing substances that clot the blood (Libby 2002; Marmot and Mustard 1994). The resulting thrombus breaks away and clogs a downstream artery supplying part of the heart, starving that portion of oxygen and resulting in its death. Either way, the damaged heart has less muscle to meet future demands, and a tendency to become uncoordinated and unable to pump at all. Dangerous and damaging medical events, like a heart attack, often result from the decline of desirable accumulations such as aerobic capacity and the development of undesirable ones such as the buildup of fatty plaques in arteries.

Stress, Allostatic Load, and Neuroendocrine Accumulators

Most of the better understood biological accumulators influenced by education reflect elements of health lifestyle such as smoking, diet, and exercise. However differences in the levels of stress over the lifetime probably also influence biological accumulators directly, apart from health lifestyle. As used here, the word "stress" refers to a specific neuroendocrine reaction, called the stress response, to external events or conditions, called stressors. The stress response is a two-phase activation of the sympathetic nervous system and the hypothalamus, pituitary, and adrenal glands. The short-term alarm phase releases epinephrine (adrenaline) and norepinephrine, which increases heart rate, respiration rate, blood pressure, and blood glucose, and also dilates the small passageways of the lungs. The longer resistance phase releases aldosterone, which increases blood volume and blood pressure, and also cortisol, which increases blood glucose and depresses inflammation and immune function (Marieb 1994; see also Chapter 4).

Much current biobehavioral research examines "allostatic load," which is the impact of intense, recurring, or chronic stress on neuroendocrine accumulators that influence health (McEwen 1998,2000; Taylor, Repetti, and Seeman 1997). Allostasis refers to the fluctuation in physiological systems to meet demands from external events or exposures. The nervous and endocrine systems regulate those responses. Allostatic load refers to persistent and potentially harmful changes in the regulatory system itself in response to its own history of activity. On a biological level the hypothetical accumulators involve changes in the size or layout of structures in the nervous and endocrine systems, and changes in the receptivity or sensitivity of various tissues to neurotransmitters or hormones. These alterations change the individual's characteristic physiological response to stressors. The harmful changes include hair-trigger activation, failure to relax in a normal amount of time, failure to adapt to a stressor with experience, or abnormal suppression of response (Evans et al. 1994; McEwen 1998,2000; Rozanski et al. 1999; Sapolsky 1998). Some of the changes represent learned, habitual responses of parts of the brain that activate the sympathetic nervous system and control the hypothalamic-pituitary-adrenal axis, and some represent deterioration of neurons in one of the control centers. Both changes increase the entire body's exposure to hormones such as epinephrine, aldosterone, and cortisol. That exposure over time affects the state of other accumulators such as resting blood pressure, body fat, and insulin resistance. We think that education reduces allostatic load by giving individuals the skills, resources, standing, and confidence to master their own lives and cope with its challenges effectively and efficiently.

Because biological research on the cumulative effects of stress over the lifetime is fairly new, most of it addresses well-known accumulators such as blood pressure, body fat, and insulin resistance. Current and future research probably will find other significant biological accumulators. Some of the most interesting current research looks at the effects of chronic stress on functioning of the immune system, as reviewed in Chapter 4 (Cohen et al. 1991; F. Cohen et al. 1999; Cohen and Herbert 1996; Glaser and Kiecolt-Glaser 1998; Glaser et al. 1999; Herbert and Cohen 1993; Irwin et al. 1997). That research suggests two candidate accumulators: a decreased ability to produce the natural killer lymphocytes that detect and destroy cells showing abnormalities of the sort produced by genetic transcription errors or viral invasions, and decreased ability to produce antibodies and T-lymphocytes keyed to the detection and destruction of specific invaders.

Prevention and Correction

Education's health benefits flow primarily from the "ounce of prevention" taken regularly, which forestalls damaging and deadly crises, and also improves recovery from the injuries and crises that do happen. However, education also increases the likelihood of sensible and effective responses among those who experience a health crisis. For example, among middle-aged cigarette smokers who have a heart attack, the probability of quitting goes up dramatically with the level of education (Wray, Herzog, Willis, and Wallace 1998). Only about a third of smokers with less than a high school degree quit after a heart attack, compared to over 80 percent of those with four years of college or more. Higher education improves the odds of a healthy response at every step. Education reduces the likelihood of ever smoking. Among those who smoke, education increases the likelihood of quitting before a health crisis occurs. Among smokers who have a health crisis such as a heart attack, higher education increases the odds of quitting in response to the crisis.

Undesirable accumulations typically can be reversed, even after a crisis, but generally only over a period of time as a result of concerted and multifaceted effort. Education helps individuals to avoid undesirable accumulations that need correction, to correct undesirable accumulations before they precipitate a crisis, and—failing that—to heed the implications of the crisis and take the difficult but necessary corrective action.

AMPLIFYING EFFECTS

Education's amplifying effects form the third element of cumulative advantage. We have seen that education has pervasive and accumulating effects. Many of those consequences either influence each other or regulate each other's effects on health. Scientific research invariably uses analytic methods that conceptually isolate specific consequences or pathways of effect. That allows scientists to understand and describe the parts and how they work. It is important to remember, though, that all of these analytic elements exist together, each within a context of the others. The relationships among the parts produce phenomena of their own. In particular, mutual effects progressively concentrate various desirable outcomes together in more-educated individuals and progressively concentrate various undesirable outcomes together in less-educated individuals. Feedback and structural amplification are the two generic forms of mutual effect that concentrate advantage in some and disadvantage in others over time. Together with education's pervasive and accumulating effects they produce a cumulative advantage in health for the better-educated.

Feedback Amplification

Feedback occurs when the current state of a system produces effects that lead to a change in its state. All feedback takes one of two forms: deviation suppressing or deviation amplifying. In deviation-suppressing feedback a change in one direction has consequences that lead to corrective changes in the opposite direction. The body's homeostatic mechanisms provide the classic examples of deviation-suppressing feedback. For example, the hypothalamus monitors body temperature, keeping it in an acceptable range. When the body starts to get too cold (below 36.1°C, 97°F) the hypothalamus constricts the blood vessels near the skin, reducing the loss of heat to the environment, which brings body temperature back up, which signals the hypothalamus to relax the constriction of the blood vessels, which keeps the body from getting too hot (above 37.8°C, 100°F). Unlike deviation-suppressing feedback, which keeps things balanced, static, proportional, or similar, deviation-amplifying feedback makes things change, develop, differentiate, or diverge.

Deviation-Amplifying Feedback

In deviation-amplifying feedback, a change in one direction has consequences that lead to more changes in the same direction. Rather than bringing things back toward the starting or target state, deviation-amplifying feedback propels them away from the original state in the direction of the deviation. Body fat again provides a good example. The more body fat individuals have, the less they feel like exercising, and the less they exercise the more fat they add. On the other hand, the less body fat individuals have, the more they feel like exercising, and the more they exercise the less fat they add. Over time that deviation-amplifying feedback has two effects. First, the differences among individuals in body weight grow over time, and so do the differences in amount of exercise. Second, two beneficial accumulations (low body fat and high aerobic capacity) get increasingly paired in some individuals, whereas their detrimental opposites (high body fat and low aerobic capacity) get increasingly paired in others. Amplification works both ways, accumulating the advantages in some individuals and the disadvantages in others.

The Sense of Control and Physical Functioning

The feedback between physical functioning and the sense of control over one's own life amplifies one of the most important links between education and health. In doing so it magnifies over the life course the advantage in both of those accumulators enjoyed by the better-educated. The feedback helps enlarge the education-based differences that develop in levels of both physical impairment and the sense of control. It also helps increasingly concentrate good physical functioning and a firm sense of personal control together in the better-educated, while concentrating physical impairment and a weak sense of control together in the less well-educated.

Psychologists studying adaptation in old age emphasize the self-reinforcing dynamics of function and morale. Rodin's (1986a, 1986b) ideas exemplify the point of view. According to Rodin, old age increases environmental challenges to the sense of control and physiological vulnerability to the effects of helplessness. The combination multiplies dysfunction and disease, which further degrades the sense of control and physiological competence. The mutual reinforcement of physical functioning and the sense of control intensify the long-run impact of conditions such as low income, widowhood, and chronic disease, and of events such as forced retirement, death of a spouse, diagnosis with a serious disease, or occurrence of a health crisis such as a stroke. According to Rodin, interventions that bolster the personal sense of control among older persons reduce the rate and amounts of biological decline by counteracting the downward spiral.

Rodin's research and ideas primarily look at short-run effects among persons in nursing homes over periods ranging from several months to several years. They necessarily treat educational attainment and its influence across the life course as immutable history at that point. Nevertheless, the research and ideas have clear implications for long-run development of effects. Those implications generally find support in the results of research such as ours looking at adults of all ages living in the general community, and comparing across age groups or following cohorts as they age. Figure 6.1 illustrates one such analysis. It uses advanced structural equation modeling to estimate the strength of the deviation-amplifying feedback between impairment and the sense of control, and to measure the fit between the patterns predicted by the model and those actually observed in the data (Bentler 1995).

The results corroborate the hypothesized amplifying feedback. They imply that a higher sense of control decreases the probable level of impairment and a lower sense of control increases it. Likewise, they imply that higher impairment decreases the sense of control and lower impairment increases it. Together these create a "double-negative" feedback. Anything that boosts the sense of control thereby decreases the level of impairment, which further improves the sense of control. Likewise, anything that decreases the sense of control thereby increases the level of impairment, which further degrades the sense of control. If this model is correct, then it and the data imply that the feedback amplifies the effects of other things on impairment and on the sense of control by around 50 percent. High

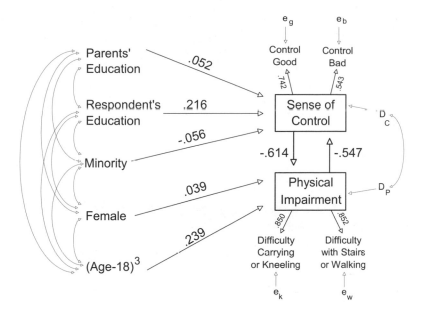

Figure 6.1. Structural equation model estimating the strength of the deviation-amplifying feedback between impairment and the sense of control. The results imply that feedback amplifies effects of social differences and of random shocks by 50 percent. Fit indexes above 99.4 percent indicate that the model reproduces observed variances and covariances well.

model fit statistics indicate that the implications of the model correspond to the patterns observed in the data quite well.

The feedback between physical impairment and the sense of control has three important implications. First, it amplifies the long-term effects of structural variables on each of the two accumulators (sense of control and physical impairment). Structural variables include sociodemographic attributes such as sex, race, and age and socioeconomic ones such as education. The persistent, lifelong effects of such attributes get enlarged by the feedback. Second, it amplifies the effects of short-term random shocks to each of the two accumulators. The effects of psychosocial crises such as layoffs, bouts of unemployment, or episodes of economic hardship get enlarged when a weaker sense of control slackens the brakes on the accumulation of physical impairment, further degrading the sense of control. Likewise, the effects of health crises such as injuries, infections, flare-ups of chronic diseases, and critical events such as heart attacks and strokes get

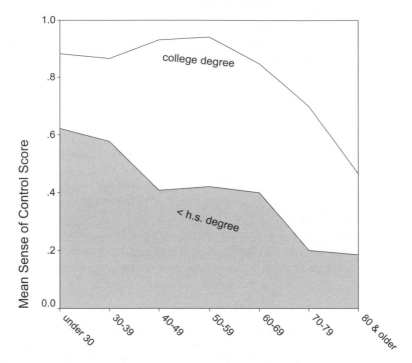

Figure 6.2. Comparison of mean sense of control scores by age group for those with a college degree and those with no high school degree.

enlarged when the increased physical impairment undermines the sense of control, thereby undermining efforts to lessen or reverse the resulting physical impairment. Third, structural effects and random shocks on either side can set the feedback in motion. Psychosocial conditions and events produce amplifying health effects, and vice versa. Disadvantage or loss on one side produces reverberating effects on both sides.

The amplifying feedback between the sense of control and physical impairment helps create growing differences across levels of education in both accumulators with increasing age. Figures 6.2 and 6.3 illustrate the mirror patterns. Figure 6.2 shows the relationship between age and the average sense of control for persons with less than a high school degree compared to those with four years of college or more. For the low-education group the sense of control starts out relatively low among the young adults and drops progressively in successively older age groups. For the high-education group, in contrast, it starts out relatively high among the young adults, stays high or perhaps even increases until the

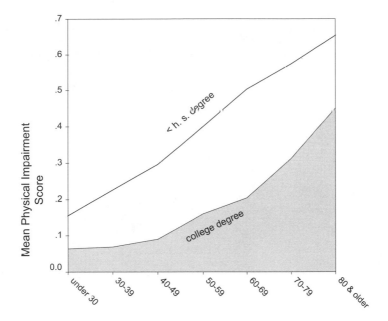

Figure 6.3. Comparison of mean physical impairment scores by age group for those with a college degree and those with no high school degree.

fifties age group, and then begins to drop in successively older age groups. The pattern suggests that differences in the sense of control between persons with high versus low education get larger up until late middle age, because those with high education delay the decline in sense of control until then. Figure 6.3 shows the mirror pattern for physical impairment. Among persons with low education the level of impairment starts relatively high in early adulthood and rises progressively in successively older age groups. Among those with high education it starts relatively low and stays low through the forties. It rises somewhat in the next two age groups, but mostly rises in oldest age groups of persons in their seventies and eighties and above. The difference between education groups in levels of impairment increases progressively until the sixties age group.

The static comparisons across age groups look consistent with the idea of a cumulative advantage for the better-educated in both the sense of control and physical impairment, due in part to the amplifying feedback between the two accumulators. The changes over a three-year period reinforce that view. Figure 6.4 shows the average change in sense of control between 1995 and 1998 by age and level of education at the beginning,

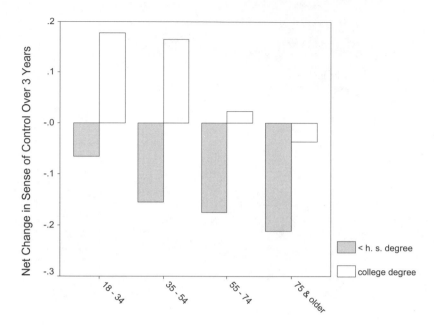

Figure 6.4. Comparison of mean three-year change in sense of control by age group for persons with a college degree and those with no high school degree, adjusting for initial sense of control and sex.

adjusting for sex and initial sense of control. The adjustment means that the figure compares the different changes in sense of control over the period observed among persons in different age or education categories but otherwise similar in terms of sex and initial sense of control. Figure 6.4 shows a net decrease in sense of control among persons with less than a high school degree in every age group. The size of the decrease gets larger in older age groups. In contrast, the young and middle-aged adults with four years of college or more have substantial net increases in sense of control over the period. Among the college-educated only the oldest persons ages seventy-five and up have a net decrease in sense of control.

Net changes in physical impairment show a pattern that mirrors the one for sense of control. Figure 6.5 shows the changes adjusting for sex and initial level of impairment. The persons with less than a high school degree show net increases in physical impairment in all four age groups, with moderate net increases among the young and middle-aged adults, somewhat larger net increases among older persons within ten years of age sixty-five, and substantially larger ones among the oldest adults age seventy-five and up. In contrast, the college-educated show net decreases in

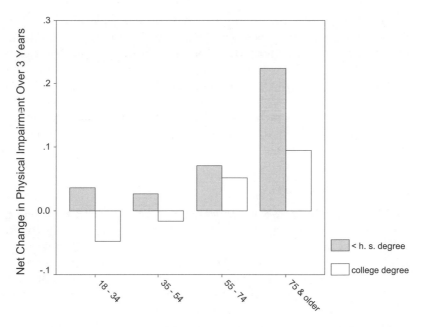

Figure 6.5. Comparison of mean three-year change in physical impairment by age group for persons with a college degree and those with no high school degree, adjusting for initial physical impairment and sex.

physical impairment among the young and middle-aged adults. Net increases in physical impairment appear only among the older and oldest age groups of college-educated. In age groups where the college-educated have net increases in impairment, the adults with less than a high school degree have larger net increases, particularly among the oldest adults.

Taken together, the models and results support the idea that one's sense of control and level of physical impairment affect each other, producing feedback amplification of differences among individuals in both as they accumulate over the life course. American adults with low education begin adulthood with a relatively low sense of control and relatively high impairment for young persons. Each disadvantage leads to subsequent undesirable changes in the other, producing parallel degradation in sense of control and physical functioning throughout adulthood. In contrast, adults with high education begin with a relatively high sense of control and low impairment, and manage to delay the deterioration in control and functioning until old age. The advantageous sense of control among the well-educated helps them delay the rise of physical impairment, and the good physical functioning in turn reinforces the sense of control.

Feedback amplification among education's consequences magnifies its effects on health. In the process it concentrates advantageous outcomes together in those with high education and disadvantageous outcomes together in those with low education. As a consequence, education-based differences in health grow in adulthood, particularly in young adulthood and middle age. The next section describes the distinct process of structural amplification, in which low education worsens the consequences of difficult situations that it also makes more likely, giving extra impetus to the downside disadvantages.

Structural Amplification

Problems faced by the poorly educated more often than by the well-educated frequently also degrade health more severely for the poorly educated. Low income, for example, reduces the health of the college-educated much less than it does the health of persons without high school degrees, as shown in Chapter 4. In large part that is because low income creates more difficulty paying bills and buying necessities for the poorly educated than for the well-educated, who have more of other personal and interpersonal resources to help them manage on a low income. Poverty would not harm the poor as much as it does if they had more education and the other kinds of resources higher education provides. In reality, though, the effect of education on income means that persons with low income disproportionately lack the higher levels of education that would help them avoid the harmful effects of low income on their health. Similarly, low education worsens the impact on subjective health of psychosocial strains and of risky health behaviors such as smoking and lack of exercise (Cohen, Kaplan, and Salonen 1999) that are more common among the poorly educated. These are instances of what we call structural amplification (Ross, Mirowsky, and Pribesh 2001). Often the same thing that would make a situation less destructive also helps individuals to avoid or escape it (Harnish, Aseltine, and Gore 2000), and so it is not common among those in the situation. Conversely, the same thing that makes a situation more destructive often leads individuals to be in it, multiplying the damage.

Higher education helps individuals to avoid risky situations and, failing that, to get out of them sooner while limiting the harm done when in them. Education makes individuals more resourceful in two senses of the word. For one thing, it gives them more of the society's standard resources of various kinds, including contacts, sources, knowledge, autonomy, prestige, pay, income, and skill at finding, evaluating, using, and communicating information. More importantly, though, education makes individuals better at turning whatever they find available into resources for meeting needs and solving problems. People often think of resources as things of inherent value and use that may or may not be available. Actually, though, resources are created and not just found. Collectively and individually, people make resources out of things that they find available. All things have intrinsic properties, but nothing has intrinsic value or usefulness. Humans create the worth and utility of things by understanding their properties and inventing ways to use them. Being resourceful means acting deliberately, energetically, and imaginatively, especially in difficult situations.

Resource Substitution

Education makes individuals more adept at resource substitution, which means using one thing in place of another, and finding ways to achieve ends with whatever materials, relationships, and circumstances present themselves. Resource substitution and the structural amplification of disadvantage are, in many ways, opposite faces of the same phenomenon. Higher education makes individuals better at acquiring whatever they need, and better at turning to use whatever they find available. As a result, higher education tends to increase an individual's store of the society's standard resources while improving the individual's ability to improvise resources. A greater capacity for resource substitution makes the absence of any one standard resource less harmful for the better-educated. Conversely, lower education leaves individuals less adept at acquiring and inventing resources, increasing the individual's dependence on each standard resource.

Figure 6.6 illustrates a typical instance of resource substitution. It shows the difference in average physical impairment scores between individuals who have someone who helps them when they are sick and those who do not. The greater mean impairment associated with not having someone who helps depends on the level of education. Persons with college degrees tend to have little physical impairment even if they have no one who nurses them when sick. Persons with less than a high school degree tend to have relatively high levels of impairment, *especially* if they have no one who helps them when sick. Compared to those with college degrees, individuals without high school degrees apparently depend much more heavily on having someone to help them when sick in order to maintain physical functioning. However, those with less than high school degrees are twice as likely to lack that kind of help. They need it more, but they have it less.

Cascading Sequences

Structural amplifiers often stack up in cascading sequences. The capacity for resource substitution helps the better-educated to avert problems or ameliorate outcomes at each step. In contrast, the relative lack of resources

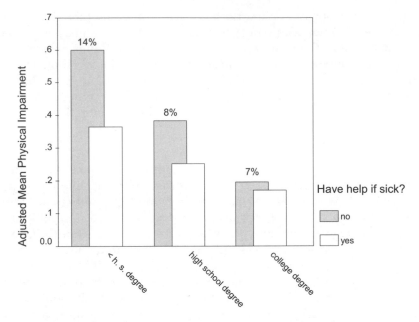

Figure 6.6. Example of structural amplification, comparing the mean physical impairment of persons with or without someone who will take care of them if sick, by level of education, adjusting for age, age-squared, and sex. The numbers above the bars show the percentage at each level of education without someone to help.

and resourcefulness among the poorly educated exacerbates the outcomes at each step. Figure 6.7 illustrates, showing the cascading sequence of chronic disease, physical impairment, and poor subjective health. About 65 percent of the adults in our sample with less than a high school degree report having a potentially serious diagnosis compared to about 36 percent of the college-educated. Individuals with less than high school degrees have the greatest increment in physical impairment associated with having a serous diagnosis, as well as having the greatest prevalence of diagnoses, as shown in the top panel. That combination of exposure to chronic disease and vulnerability to it helps concentrate serious impairment among the poorly educated. About 27 percent of the adults with less than a high school degree report having a great deal of difficulty with at least one of the physical functions on our list, compared to about 10 percent of the college-educated. In the next step, shown in the bottom panel of Figure 6.7, individuals with less than a high school degree also have the greatest increment in the likelihood of feeling unhealthy associated with impairment. The higher prevalence of impairment combines with greater

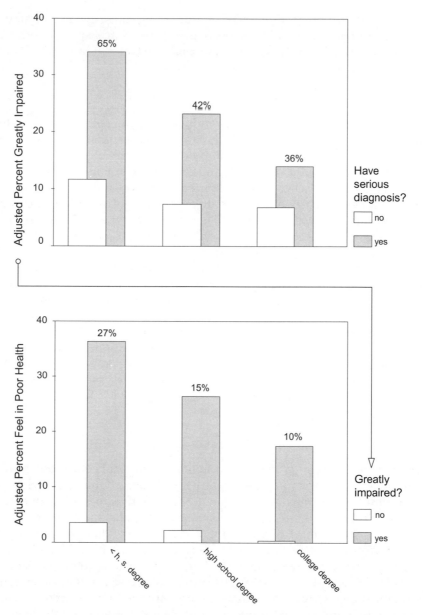

Figure 6.7. Example of cascading structural amplification, comparing the percentage greatly impaired among persons with and without a serious diagnosis, and the percentage feeling in poor health among persons with and without a great impairment, by level of education, adjusting for age, age-squared, and sex. The numbers above the bars show the percentage at each level of education with at least one of the serious diagnoses (top) and at least one great impairment (bottom).

difficulty managing it to help concentrate poor subjective health among persons with less than a high school degree. Cascading sequences of structural amplification help concentrate problems of all kinds, including health problems, among the poorly educated.

Amplification of Misfortune

The same resources and resourcefulness that can soften the impact of difficult but avoidable circumstances can soften the impact of unavoidable or random ones too. For example, widowhood is an undesirable and stressful state generated by events and conditions largely beyond the individual's control. Low education sharpens the association of widowhood with physical impairment, just as it sharpens the association of chronic disease with physical impairment. Technically the magnification of widowhood's effect does not fit the definition of structural amplification because the resources that make widowhood more manageable probably are not less common among the widowed. Nevertheless, the magnified effects of unavoidable or even random events and situations such as widowhood add to the concentration of poor health outcomes among the poorly educated. For that reason we include it here in our discussion of structural amplification. Even though a particular risk to health may be unavoidable, its effects still will be worst among the poorly educated. That adds to the concentration of problems among the poorly educated, often setting in motion deviation-amplifying feedback and cascading structural amplification that further concentrate problems.

DECLINE SLOWED OR ONLY DELAYED?

The pervasive, accumulating, and amplifying effects of education produce cumulative health advantages for the better-educated that grow with age. That raises a question. Do the differences in health across levels of education grow without limit, or do they reach a peak at some point in the life cycle and then diminish? One thing is certain. Everyone dies, no matter how well educated. Death abolishes any advantages in health an individual might have had. Even so, the differences in health among those who remain alive may continue to grow, as may differences in the risk of dying anytime soon. Many current topics in population-based research on health pertain to whether accumulated advantages dwindle in the general retrenchment of old age. In this section we summarize a number of the related issues and give our views on them. In brief, we think the health advantages associated with higher education continue to grow throughout life, including the retirement years (Ross and Wu 1996). The evidence remains equivocal, however, and might go against our view. No matter how this debate turns out, the researchers on both sides generally agree on three important things. The differences in health across socioeconomic strata grow until at least late middle age and probably well into old age, remain considerable in old age, and favor the well-educated and the well-to-do of all age groups.

On the surface of it, there seem to be several reasons to expect that education's effects on health might diminish in old age after having grown until sometime in late middle age or early old age (Beckett 2000; House et al. 1994). The various arguments all refer to one or both of two underlying forces. One set of arguments refers to the socioeconomic life-cycle in modern democratic welfare states. Those arguments assume that the socioeconomic advantages associated with a higher level of education diminish in old age, suggesting that the health advantages do too. Another set refers to biologically programmed senescence. They assume that the physical decline inevitable in old age diminishes the health advantages accumulated over a lifetime. The following subsections argue against those views, questioning whether socioeconomic differences diminish in old age, and pointing out that current theories of biological aging imply larger cumulative advantages or disadvantages in old age, not smaller ones.

The Socioeconomic Life Cycle

Education's effects on health might wax and wane if its effects on income, wealth, and access to medical care do. Modern democratic states use the competition for position and wealth as an engine driving continuous economic, technical, political, and cultural development, but do not want those who fare poorly in the competition to suffer unduly, particularly after the game is over. Individuals coming of age together start out with relatively few differences in personal income, wealth, and influence. Those differences grow enormous by late middle age. Some individuals accumulate little or nothing, working for minimum wages when they can find a job, possessing no savings, property, or pension, known by perhaps a dozen other human beings but significant at most to one or two who are equally destitute and powerless. Others direct the labor and actions of thousands, earn millions of dollars a year, have personal wealth rivaling that of entire nations, or shape enduring aspects of science, technology, politics, or culture. What happens in old age to this enormous variance in prosperity?

Clearly, the *average* levels of income and wealth in the United States decline in old age, following peaks sometime around ages fifty and sixty, respectively. This leads some individuals to assume that the enormous inequality of income and wealth in middle age shrinks in old age too.

However, decline in average income and wealth does not necessarily produce greater equality. In the United States the inequality of income (measured by the Gini coefficient) grows steadily after age fifty-nine (Crystal and Waehrer 1996). This implies an even larger growth in wealth inequality, because wealth provides an increasing fraction of household income in successively older age groups, and because inequality of wealth exceeds inequality of income at all ages (Davern and Fisher 2001). At any given level of income, the oldest Americans have the greatest amount of wealth and the greatest inequality of wealth. These patterns are especially marked for wealth in the form of stocks, bonds, mutual funds, and the like. Social Security income exerts some equalizing effect, but not enough to overcome the differences based on savings, investments, private pensions (often keyed to peak lifetime earnings), and government-sponsored programs such as IRA and 401k plans that allow tax-deferred saving (Crystal, Shea, and Krishnaswami 1992; Dannefer 1987). It should be no surprise that the U.S. social security system does not reduce economic inequality in old age. It was not designed to do that. Social Security mostly redistributes income from adults who are employed to those who are retired, not from retirees who are wealthy to those who are poor.

Some individuals also assume that Medicare and similar programs reduce health inequalities by assuring access to needed medical care for all retirees. Supposedly that somehow counteracts the cumulative differences in health resulting from a lifetime of differences in exposures, behaviors, incidents, and stress. That expects a lot, and there is little reason to think Medicare does or ever could meet those expectations. Sole reliance on government-sponsored medical insurance, including Medicare, appears to accelerate declines in health, as detailed in Chapter 4. Universal medical care systems in the United Kingdom, Canada, and other countries did not reduce socioeconomic disparities in health for their populations, even though those countries provide care over the whole lifetime. Partly that is because no country provides its poorest and neediest citizens the level of medical services available to its richest ones (although some small, wealthy countries such as Kuwait might come close). Mostly, though, it is because medicine generally does not make people healthy (Evans 1994; Evans and Stoddart 1994). Most often medicine simply manages the course of a disease, attempting to slow the deterioration and forestall damaging and perhaps deadly events. Too often medicine's dangerous interventions create additional pathology from side effects, errors, and accidents. Systems such as Medicare and Medicaid in the United States and the National Health in the United Kingdom do what they can. The practical limits of welfare politics and medical science combine to assure that such systems do not undo the health advantages or disadvantages of a lifetime.

We generally see little reason to expect socioeconomic convergence in old age. However we do see one important exception to that rule. Older Americans apparently need less income to avoid economic hardship (Mirowsky and Ross 1999). Older Americans use income more efficiently, know the economic pitfalls and avoid them, typically already own a home and the standard household durables, have already raised their children, and have Social Security and Medicare helping to protect them from destitution. As a result, the low income associated with low education generates less economic hardship among seniors than it does among younger adults, particularly those raising children. The differences in economic hardship across levels of education diminish in old age. Since economic hardship contributes to health problems in all age groups, that probably slows somewhat the old-age growth of differences in health across levels of education. Even so, other forces drive a continuing expansion of the cumulative differences, including the forces of biological senescence on neuroendocrine and cellular levels described in the next section.

Biological Senescence, Life Span, and Healthy Life Expectancy

As humans get old they become increasingly frail and susceptible. No matter how healthy individuals have been throughout life, eventually they age physically and die. This fact of human existence can mislead observers into assuming that old age eliminates the health advantages associated with higher education. Most young persons enjoy good health, and most old ones eventually bear disease and disability, seemingly regardless of their socioeconomic status. While true in a sense, this does not mean that health differences diminish. It is true that, at every level of education, most older adults were healthier when they were younger. Nevertheless, among seniors of the same age, the ones with lower levels of education have declined in health longer and farther, if they survive at all. That gets more and more true at successively older ages. High death rates among the unhealthiest individuals, who are disproportionately poorly educated, may compress the health differences among the survivors somewhat. The healthiest of the poorly educated survive, making the poorly educated group a little healthier on average than it would have been. Even so, we think the differences in health continue to grow in old age, as individuals with lower levels of education acquire more numerous and varied diseases and disabilities that have progressed to more serious levels.

Current biological theories and studies of senescence imply that the differences among individuals in biological decline increase with the age of the survivors. Several biological accumulators increase the variability of organic decline as individuals born about the same time age. The ultimate biological aging clock ticks at a variable speed determined by the rate at which cells must divide to repair or replenish tissues, and it ticks only a limited number of times. It seems likely that biological aging clocks tick faster for the poorly educated, making them biologically older than the well-educated who were born about the same time. We briefly describe the biological aging clocks below. However, it is more important for social scientists to understand the implications than the mechanisms. If the biological theory described below is correct, then the process has three properties: it acts as an accumulator on the level of molecules, cells, and tissues; it is advanced by stress and disease and in turn eventually increases susceptibility to disease, thereby creating deviation-amplifying feedback; and it makes individuals with a history of exposures and problems more susceptible to the acquisition, progression, and debilitation of disease, thereby structurally amplifying health disadvantages.

Biologists say that every species has an upper limit on the longest duration of life that members of the species can achieve (Perez-Campo et al. 1998). Many biologists think that limits on the repair and replacement of cells enforce the life span limit. Some tissues have cells that do not get replaced when they die. In humans the muscle cells, fat cells, and most neurons do not get replaced. A mature human can lose those cells more or less quickly, but cannot replace them once lost. More commonly, tissues have cells that can divide only a limited number of times (Hayflick 1998). Chromosomes have ends called telomeres that get shorter each time the cell divides. Once a telomere gets too short its cell no longer can divide and replenish its tissue. The more cell lines that reach their limit, the more the tissue degenerates and loses its ability to function.

Damage to the nuclear DNA in cell lines adds to the degeneration of tissues. Nuclear DNA contains the code inherited from both parents that cells use as instructions for manufacturing proteins and other needed chemicals. Damage to nuclear DNA most often gets repaired well enough for the cell line to continue, although with accumulating errors progressively increasing disorder in the molecular processes of the cell line. Sometimes the errors disrupt a cell enough to invite its destruction by the immune system. Sometimes the errors make the cell susceptible to viral invasion or other disease processes, leading to its destruction. Sometimes, though, genetic damage frees a cell line from the telomere's limits on division, but the result is not good: tumors and cancers.

Damage to mitochondrial DNA in cells and cell lines also adds to the degeneration of tissues (Hayflick 1998; Wallace 1997). Mitochondria contain specialized DNA inherited only from one's mother. Every cell contains hundreds of mitochondria with several loops of DNA. The mitochondrial DNA contains the code needed to make special proteins that form parts in a structure that manufactures a molecule called adenosine triphosphate

(ATP). That molecule, ATP, provides the energy needed for cellular processes. The food a person eats gets made into glucose that circulates throughout the body and enters cells when insulin unlocks the ports. Once inside a cell, the glucose gets broken into parts that the mitochondria use to make ATP, creating heat and carbon dioxide as byproducts. Apparently the process that makes the ATP also creates toxic byproducts called oxygen free radicals, which are highly reactive molecules that can damage components of the cells, including the proteins making ATP and the DNA templates for making those proteins. The more damage there is to the proteins making ATP, the more free radicals get produced, doing even more damage. The resulting molecular disorder spreads throughout the cell and accumulates within it. The division of a cell over many generations concentrates the damaged mitochondria in subsets of the offspring, creating concentrations of impaired cells within the organs they compose. In cells that do not divide, like those of the muscles, shortages of ATP in a region served by a damaged mitochondrion stimulate the replication of that mitochondrion, adding to the accumulation of damaged energy-producing units. Both types of accumulation progressively impair cells and thus the tissues and organs they compose.

The third biological aging accumulator operates on the level of the brain and endocrine system, and may work as an amplifier of the other two. Research on animals shows that exposure to severe or chronic stress creates persistent anomalies in the structure and function of the endocrine system, and also in parts of the brain that regulate endocrine response (Sapolsky 1998; Selye 1976). Research on humans suggests similar effects of severe or chronic stress. The structures involved activate and regulate the body's response to threats, called the fight or flight syndrome. Apparently the system also reshapes itself in response to chronic stress, somewhat like muscles getting larger and more efficient from exercise. Unlike greater strength and stamina, though, a beefed-up stress response produces undesirable effects, particularly in the context of modern society, where neither fighting nor fleeing are useful or even feasible.

A part of the brain called the pituitary initiates the stress response in the endocrine system, which releases cortisol and other hormones. According to current theory, that initiation is regulated by two other parts of the brain (LeDoux 1996; McEwen 1998, 2000; Sapolsky 1998). The amygdala signals the pituitary to activate the hormonal stress response and the hippocampus signals it to deactivate the response. Together the balance of "go" and "stop" signals regulates the phasing (rise and fall) and intensity of the stress response.

The hippocampus happens to have many receptors for cortisol, and thus serves a thermostat-like control function. When blood cortisol levels are high or rising rapidly, the hippocampus signals the pituitary to cut back the release of cortisol by the adrenal glands. Unfortunately, the high sensitivity to cortisol means that high levels of it can damage the hippocampal neurons. Cortisol increases each neuron's need for fuel and oxygen. Under peak load a neuron can suffer a deficit of fuel or oxygen and die. To protect themselves from frequent exposure to high cortisol, the neurons cut the filaments of their dendrites that receive signals from other neurons. Over time the trimming of dendrites lowers the responsiveness of the hippocampus to high or rising cortisol. (It also impairs some memory functions.) While that protects the neurons in the short run, it reduces the ability of the hippocampus to counteract the "go" signals from the amygdala during exposure to stress. As a result the levels of epinephrine, norepinephrine, and cortisol rise faster with less provocation, peak higher, and stay high longer. That in turn puts the hippocampal neurons at even greater risk. Eventually the hippocampus fails to shut off the production of cortisol even in the absence of stress.

The loss of hippocampal dendrites and neurons reflects the cumulative lifetime exposure to the fight-or-flight hormones. It also increases current exposure to those hormones, particularly cortisol. Too much circulating cortisol produces fatigue, thinning muscles, adult-onset diabetes, hypertension, osteoporosis, reproductive decline, and immune suppression (Sapolsky 1998). The diabetes and hypertension degrade the circulatory system and kidneys, which in turn degrades or puts at risk other organ systems. The stress hormones mobilize the body's energy resources for intense physical activity. In doing so they delay the allocation of the body's resources to the repair of tissues. In addition, the mobilization of energy for action that never occurs may accelerate the accumulation of mitochondrial free-radical damage mentioned previously. Current theory focuses on how the free-radical damage accumulating from the production of ATP makes the life span of a species inversely proportional to its metabolic rate, ultimately limiting how long any member of the species can live. Among modern humans, though, differences in the rate at which free-radical damage accumulates may reflect lifetime differences in the frequency and intensity of the stress response. A sedentary lifestyle might magnify the rate of accumulation, by causing a failure to use mobilized energy.

Each organ system has a limited capacity for regeneration, sometimes called organ reserve. Infections, toxins, injuries, and exposures to physical extremes tend to use up that capacity. So does chronic damage from high blood glucose, high blood pressure, poor circulation, psychophysiological stress, and so on. As an organ system nears the end of its reserve, its susceptibility to problems increases. The biological aging clocks measure the declining ability to shut off cortisol release, the accumulation of molecular disorder in cells, and the depletion of limited cell divisions, rather than time itself. The accumulating atrophy, errors, and divisions inevitably increase with time, but more rapidly for some individuals than others.

Education helps individuals to live longer because it helps make them healthier and biologically younger for their chronological age. Many persons mistakenly believe that humans are living longer because medical advances keep the diseased and impaired alive longer (Evans and Stoddart 1994; Lomas and Contandriopoulos 1994). On the contrary, people are living to older ages being physically younger, and having had fewer health problems throughout life (Crimmins and Saito 2001; Freedman and Martin 1988). The active, healthy, and disability-free life expectancy generally increases along with overall life expectancy itself. (The chief exception occurs when measuring the average length of life free of diagnosed chronic disease. Chronic diseases can appear to start earlier and last longer on average because of deliberate efforts to find cases at earlier stages and because of the broadening of diagnostic criteria and the proliferation of diagnostic categories.) Education increases the expected number of healthy years and decreases the expected number of unhealthy years, as well as increasing the total years of life expectancy (Crimmins and Saito 2001).

The Trend Toward Bigger Effects of Education

The differences in health and healthy life expectancy among persons of the same age but different levels of education continue to expand. We think that is because the better-educated persistently lead in incorporating advances in knowledge into their own choices and ways of life. Advances in science and technology favor society as a whole, but disproportionately favor those who know how to find, evaluate, and use information to best advantage. The more thorough and accurate society's store of knowledge becomes, the more effective education becomes.

Figures 6.8 and 6.9 graph the correlation between education and the odds of surviving another decade, by age and year of birth. The figures illustrate two things. First, the correlation between education and the odds of continuing to live another decade get stronger as persons age. Second, the correlation is getting stronger at each age in younger generations. The figures illustrate statistics published by Lauderdale, an epidemiologist at the University of Chicago, based on U.S. census data from 1960, 1970, 1980, and 1990 (Lauderdale 2001). She calculated the odds of surviving from one census to the next for native-born U.S. whites who went beyond high school compared to those who never finished high school. Our figures show her results for the women, but the patterns are similar for white men. (Statistics for blacks were not included because of uncertainty about year of birth in the older generations. Foreign-born were excluded because the

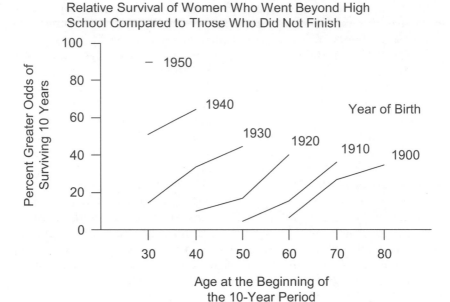

Figure 6.8. Increasing correlation between education and the odds of surviving
another ten years, within birth cohorts as they aged, for native-born U.S. white
women alive in the 1960, 1970, or 1980 census. Each point represents the
improvement in odds of continued survival for women who went beyond
high school compared to those who never finished. [Based on analyses by
Lauderdale (2001).]

process of immigration favors unusually healthy individuals, and also
because excluding them simplifies calculations.)

Following up the women who were born about the same time shows
that the correlation between education and the odds of continuing to survive increases as they age. Figure 6.8 shows that, as a cohort of women
ages, the survival advantage associated with higher education gets larger.
For example, the women born around 1910 were about age fifty in the 1960
census. The ones who went beyond high school had a 4.6 percent higher
odds of surviving to age sixty than the ones who never finished high
school. At age sixty the better-educated survivors had a 15.6 percent
higher odds of surviving to age seventy. At age seventy the better-educated among the remaining survivors had 36.0 percent better odds of living to age eighty. The correlation between education and the odds of
surviving another ten years increases among the survivors as they age. A
similar increase in the correlation with age appears in every one of the

Relative Survival of Women Who Went Beyond High
School Compared to Those Who Did Not Finish

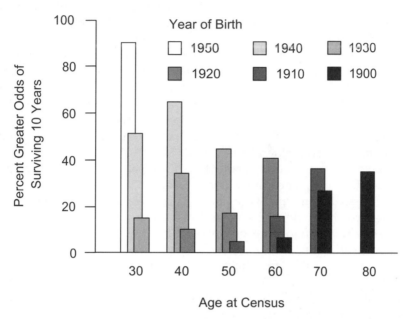

Figure 6.9. Increases across birth cohorts in the age-specific correlation between
education and the odds of surviving another ten years, for native-born U.S.
white women alive in the 1960, 1970, or 1980 census. Each point represents the
improvement in odds of continued survival for women who went beyond
high school compared to those who never finished. [Based on analyses by
Lauderdale (2001).]

cohorts born from around 1900 to around 1940. (Because data from the
2000 census was not available at the time of the analysis, the cohort born
around 1950 shows only the greater odds of surviving over a single interval from age thirty to forty.) Clearly, the correlation between education and
subsequent survival increases over the life course for white women. The
same is true for white men. The longer these Americans born about the
same time survive, the more important education becomes to subsequent
survival. Mortality eliminates the poorly educated more severely at every
step, and yet the correlation of education with the odds of making it to the
next step grows.

At each age, the members of newer cohorts show a stronger correlation
between education and the odds of surviving another ten years. Figure 6.9

shows the same information as in Figure 6.8, but in a manner that emphasizes the growth in age-specific correlations across generations. For example, when the women born around 1910 were about fifty years old the ones
who went beyond high school had a 4.6 percent better odds of surviving
another ten years than did the ones who never finished high school. By the
time women born around 1920 were about age fifty the ones who went
beyond high school had 17 percent better odds of continued survival.
Within a decade after that, when the women born around 1930 were about
fifty years old, the survival advantage associated with the higher education shot up to 44.5 percent. Although the age-specific odds of continued
survival improved at all levels of education over the last half of the century, they improved most rapidly for the better-educated. That trend got
stronger in successive generations.

Researchers sometimes mistake the historical trend toward bigger
effects of education on health for a decline in education's effect in old age.
The rising breadth and quality of knowledge make education more useful
and effective. The oldest among us lived their lives when humankind
knew less about staying prosperous and healthy. Under those circumstances education had less of a positive effect on health throughout life.
That is one reason why the effect of education on health can appear to
diminish in old age when it actually increases in persons born about the
same time as they get older. (Look at the back row of bars in Figure 6.9.
They show the correlations by age group in the 1980 census, which are
lowest in the oldest age groups.)

No one knows for certain whether the patterns and trends of the twentieth century will continue through the twenty-first. Certain things follow
logically if they do. If it remains true that education's correlation with subsequent survival gets larger as a cohort ages, then those correlations will
explode at older ages. Look in Figure 6.8 or 6.9 at the correlation for
women born around 1950 and about age thirty in the 1980 census. If that
correlation gets larger as those women age, it will be enormous when they
are in their sixties, seventies, and eighties. Even if that correlation remains
constant as the cohort ages, the cumulative effect over the life course will
be quite large. The odds of surviving from age thirty to age fifty will be 3.6
times greater for the women who went beyond high school than for the
ones who never finished. The odds of surviving from age thirty to age 60,
70, 80, or 90, respectively will be 6.8, 13.0, 24.6, and 46.6 times greater. As
it stands now, those cumulative values look like conservative estimates.

EDUCATION'S CUMULATIVE ADVANTAGE

The advantages or disadvantages in health associated with level of education accumulate during all of adulthood, over many areas of life, and at all

levels of organization from the socioeconomic down to the molecular. Over short periods the increments or decrements in any one accumulator may be quite small and seemingly insubstantial. Individuals might not notice the changes, and even scientists might have difficulty measuring them against the background of random fluctuations and measurement errors. Even so, the accumulated differences grow substantial over long periods of time—the three to four decades between school and retirement and two or three decades after retirement. Some of the positive or negative accumulations affect each other, creating feedback that amplifies the effects of persistent attributes such as education and also the effects of events such as job losses, disease episodes, economic crises, and personal losses. Benefit begets benefit and deficit begets deficit, accelerating the growth of differences among individuals who began adulthood about the same time, concentrating various good outcomes together in some of them and various bad outcomes together in others. Cascading sequences of structural amplification multiply the accumulation and feedback. The same traits that make the well-educated less likely to be in risky situations make them less susceptible to the risks if in those situations. In particular, a greater capacity for resource substitution makes the well-educated less dependent on any one heath resource such as income or marriage. The obverse is also true. The same traits that make the poorly educated more likely to be in risky situations make them more susceptible to those risks. A smaller capacity for resource substitution magnifies the harm from lacking or losing a standard resource. Education's pervasive, accumulating, and amplifying effects create the cumulative advantages and disadvantages in health that emerge and grow over the lifetime.

| 7 |

Specious Views of Education

We think that formal schooling develops real skills and abilities that make individuals resourceful and capable of achieving many things, including health. Readers from the biological and physical sciences may be surprised to learn that many scholars in the social sciences take exception to the idea that formal education teaches anything inherently and broadly useful. In this chapter we contrast our view of education as learned effectiveness with four alternatives: education as credential, as reproducer of inequality, as false satisfier, and as spurious correlate. The four critical and disparaging views of education share one element in common that distinguishes them from the human-capital view. They deny that education's apparent benefits result from the productive skills and habits of general value that people learn in school. In support of their views, the critics cite empirical observations that seem to refute education's cultivation of human capital, or they give alternative interpretations of education's apparent benefits that the observations seem not to rule out. Each critical view draws on observations or arguments that can create an appearance of validity, which is why we call them specious rather than simply wrong.

In the sections that follow we summarize and critique the evidence and arguments given in support of each disparaging view of education. Some critics portray education as a credential operating merely as a symbolic token that opens social gates. Others portray it as a reproducer of inequality, merely training individuals for the attitudes and behaviors appropriate to their inherited social status. Some portray education as a false satisfier that functions to make both winners and losers in the competition for status see the outcome as fair and satisfactory. Finally, some critics portray education as a spurious correlate of desirable outcomes that falsely appears to produce them because it results from the same advantageous social or genetic inheritance that creates those subsequent outcomes.

After rebutting the critical views we try to explain why so many social scientists might want to argue that education imparts nothing of intrinsic effectiveness. We trace the critical views of education to discoveries made in the 1960s and 1970s. Research in that period found that educational attainment predicted subsequent occupational status, personal earnings, and household income among U.S. males, apparently acting both as a main avenue of upward mobility and as the nearly exclusive link between the social status of one generation and the next (Blau and Duncan 1967; Davies 1995; Sewell and Hauser 1975). Critics of social inequality often saw these findings as implicit justification for the social and economic inequalities that exist. If education develops abilities that enable individuals to achieve better outcomes, then the resulting inequality might seem inevitable, functional, and fair. The wish to delegitimize social and economic inequality stimulated what we call the ideological project, which attempts to discredit education's real value, portraying it instead as a system of channels and barriers that at most teach acceptance of and conformity to one's rank. More recently the ideological project seems to have elicited an odd counterproject: an attempt to portray inequality of attainments as inevitable and good because it reflects preordained differences in natural ability. We have no sympathy for ideological projects and counterprojects, and encourage readers to evaluate arguments about education's role on scientific rather than ideological grounds.

EDUCATION AS CREDENTIAL

The credentialist view maintains that education produces an artificial effect. In this view, education has real consequences but only as a mark of status. Education's effect is purely symbolic, acting as a token that opens social gates, and not by imparting anything of inherent and general usefulness related to worker performance (Berg 1970; Collins 1979). Early credentialists often speak as if academic degrees themselves open social gates (Berg 1970, Collins 1979). More recent credentialists emphasize that persons in power open social gates, choose which credentials to accept, and favor credentials that distinguish persons similar to themselves from others. For example, Lieberson (1985) argues that whites use the credential of a degree as a stumbling block put in the way of minorities to keep them from getting good jobs. He claims whites attach academic requirements to better jobs in order to reserve them for whites. He suggests that schooling does not help individuals get good jobs by training them in skills employers value. Lieberson asserts that if African-Americans attained the same level of education as whites, then whites would simply put another obstacle to success in place. He predicts that if blacks' educational attainment becomes equal to that of whites, educational attainment will no longer determine who gets a good job that pays well. Instead, whites will erect another barrier to success (ibid.:166). (Ironically, credentialist policies could make the prediction appear to come true. If social promotions make

levels of education equal but not the amount of ability, employers probably would use standardized tests to screen applicants.) Credentialists support their view by arguing that the skills used on most jobs are learned on
the job and not taught in school. They point to workplace studies showing
little or no correlation between job performance and academic ability or
educational attainment.

Much of the credentialist argument relies on blurring the distinction
between the general skills and abilities of broad usefulness in many jobs
and the distinctive skills needed for a particular job. When Collins (1979)
argues that most skills are learned on the job, not in school, he equates
"skills" with those specific to a job such as operating a particular kind of
machine. Collins might be right that most job-specific skills are learned on
the job. However, general cognitive skills learned in school help a worker
read the instructions for machine operation, figure out the cause of a
machine malfunction and fix it, or explain to a coworker how the machine
works, all of which increase effectiveness on the job. Indeed, human-
capital theory views formal education as specifically charged with the
responsibility of developing skills and abilities of general value. The evidence shows that schooling does increase general cognitive skills that do
improve job performance (Pascarella and Terenzini 1991; Spaeth 1976;
Hyman et al. 1975; Kohn and Slomczynski 1993). Still, the argument that
smart employees perform no better than those who lack general mental
ability led to a 1971 court decision making it illegal to use intelligence tests
as a basis for civilian hiring (Herrnstein and Murray 1994), and many
social scientists endorse the claim that education does not improve work
skills (Burris 1983).

The credentialists frequently support their arguments by reference to
studies using small samples of individuals in the same occupation, often
at the same workplace. The small size and preselected homogeneity of
each sample weights heavily against finding statistically significant correlations between education and job performance. Collins (1979) points to
several studies measuring the correlation between school grades and job
performance among individuals with roughly the same years of education
doing similar kinds of jobs. The studies find little or no correlation of
school grades with job performance. Those studies have several problems.
First, grades alone provide only a weak indication of cognitive skill
because schools have different grading standards. That is one reason why
college and postgraduate admission tests were developed. Second, comparing only individuals with a similar level of education minimizes the
possibility of observing the effects of additional years of education on job
performance. Finally, individuals in the same occupation generally have
been screened and selected for a similar level of general cognitive ability.
Limiting each sample to one occupation implicitly limits it to a narrow

range of cognitive abilities, in effect holding constant the very thing that links education to performance. Berg (1970) cites similar kinds of evidence against an association between education and productivity, based on samples limited to secretaries, bankers, insurance agents, technicians, or manufacturing employees.

Using narrowly selected samples introduces biases that are clear mathematically, although difficult to express in words (Winship and Mare 1992). The trick of using preselected samples also appears in attacks on standardized educational admissions tests, where the biases may be a little easier to see. SAT scores, for example, have relatively little correlation with the academic performance of students in any one college or university, for three reasons. First, the explicit admissions criteria and tacit selection processes restrict the variance in scores at any one school. The relatively small differences in scores within a school narrow the range of observable consequences. Second, students admitted with relatively low scores for the school often have compensating traits likely to contribute to success, such as special abilities in the arts or sports or unusual determination in overcoming a physical or social disadvantage. On the other hand, students who come with unusually high scores for the school often are seeking an easier program that leaves time for other pursuits. As a result, within any one college or university lower admissions test scores partly indicate greater determination or special skills that help compensate for the lower general ability prior to admission. Finally, students gravitate to programs within a college or university with requirements and grading standards appropriate to their level of ability. Studies that use students from one college or university and ignore these selection phenomena produce biased results. Studies limited to one occupation produce similar biases. They narrow the observed variance in education, assure that unusually low or high levels of education imply countervailing traits, and typically ignore the fact that organizations often move the less able or less motivated individuals to less demanding posts.

Oddly, credentialist research typically omits any attempted demonstration that academic credentials might have the token effects the view claims. Degrees presumably act as the main credentials. If education acts solely as a credential then the degrees, rather than the years of schooling, should have the major effects. The association of desirable outcomes with education should happen in steps, with clear risers at twelve and sixteen years associated with having the high school and college degrees. Viewed purely in terms of credentials, another year of schooling should produce no benefit unless it completes a degree sequence. In contrast, if the time spent in training develops effective abilities, then additional years should produce benefits even when they do not complete a degree sequence. In our research we find that the years of schooling, more than the level of the highest

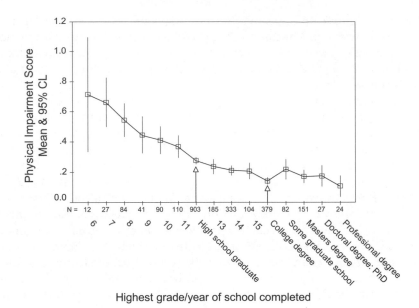

Figure 7.1.   Mean physical impairment scores by highest grade or degree.

degree, predict subsequent health and well-being (Reynolds and Ross 1998; Ross and Mirowsky 1999). Our analyses do show steps at twelve and six-teen years, but as small deviations from a general association of health with years of education. Figure 7.1 illustrates the pattern for physical impair-ment, but other health measures show similar patterns. Our analyses find that the small deviation associated with the high school degree is statisti-cally significant (larger than the margin of error) but the one associated with the college degree is not. More importantly, our analyses consistently show that the number of years of education predicts statistically significant differences in health adjusting for the level of the highest degree.

EDUCATION AS REPRODUCER OF INEQUALITY

Another set of critics portrays education as a reproducer of inequality that merely copies social status from one generation to the next. They argue that the educational system encourages and promotes children based on signs of family social status, and trains them to accept their status and behave in ways appropriate to it. Reproductionists differ from credential-ists in emphasizing that the educational and occupational systems select and reinforce observable attitudes and behaviors that are qualities of the individuals, and not merely certificates or tokens bestowed on the individuals. Like the credentialists, the reproductionists deny that education progressively develops productive abilities that subsequently create a gradient of status attainments. Some reproductionists, however, say that education does reinforce in students the attitudes, skills, or manners suitable to their stations. Others say that the education system merely grades and promotes students based on signs of status learned in the home. Either way, reproductionists portray the rewarded traits as otherwise useless manifestations of status culture that provide the signs occupational gatekeepers match to positions.

The scholars who portray education as a reproducer of inequality emphasize one or more of the steps in a three-part process: (a) detection of the family's status through signs such as clothing, manners, interests, or neighborhood, (b) positive reinforcement of attitudes and behaviors appropriate to the child's social status and negative reinforcement of ones that are inappropriate, and (3) the grading and channeling of students into academic and occupational strata based on the detected and reinforced signs of family status. We divide reproduction arguments into two categories, depending on whether they emphasize explicit or implicit tracking, as described below.

Explicit Tracking

Marxist and neo-Marxist scholars often emphasize education's relatively explicit tracking according to social class. In this context "Marxist" refers to a scholarly tradition with its origins in the academic work of Karl Marx, and not a political affiliation. Marx saw an inherent conflict of interest between the social classes in capitalist economies that should lead workers to rebel against the system. Workers produce more goods and services than they need to survive. Owners of the means of production (land, tools, machines, raw materials, etc.) expropriate the surplus product. Each class serves its own interests best by taking as much of that surplus for itself as possible. A capitalist social system, by nature and definition, favors taking it away from the workers and giving it to the owners. Workers acting rationally on their own behalf would rebel against such a system. Even Marx had to admit that workers rarely do rebel. Working-class quiescence poses a challenge to Marx's idea about class conflict that needs to be explained (Davies 1995). Marx saw religion as the main institution promoting the status quo in eighteenth- and nineteenth-Century England and Europe. Many researchers see education as the main institution serving that function in the twentieth-century United States.

Education, according to the reproductionist view, advantages those from high social class origins but disadvantages those from working-class and lower-class backgrounds, thus reinforcing the status quo. Each year of education means something different for upper-, middle-, working-, and lower-class students (Bowles and Gintis 1976). Differential treatment across class origins lies at the heart of Bowles and Gintis's well-known radical interpretation of schooling in the United States (1976). According to them, school policies and personnel reproduce the inequality by sorting, segregating, labeling, tracking, and differentially socializing students according to social origins (ibid.). In particular, schools train upper- and middle-class students to be independent, creative, and ambitious, while training the lower- and working-class ones to be obedient, punctual, quiet, and submissive (Bowles and Gintis 1976; Oakes 1982). Scholars who see status reproduction through explicit tracking say education legitimates and reproduces inequality mostly in two steps: students attend different types of schools according to family economic means, and schools then sort students into vocational, general, and college tracks. This placement into types of schools and tracks then defines the type of education one receives. For example, schools teach college track students intellectual skills and encourage them to show initiative and innovation. They teach vocational and general track students manual skills and command them to be punctual, orderly, and obedient to authority. The first track trains future supervisors, managers, and owners, the latter tracks train industrial laborers and, more recently, clerical workers and low-level service workers such as fast-food employees.

The arguments claiming explicit reproduction of inequality have one fatal shortcoming. They ignore the sequential development of skills and abilities. Children from higher-status backgrounds generally start school at a more advanced point in the sequence and move ahead more quickly. The result can appear like tracking based on family social status when it actually results from attempts to provide challenging but not overwhelming courses for each level of ability. Likewise, the emphasis on discipline for children from lower-status neighborhoods and families can falsely seem like differential training for submission, deference, and subservience. Actually, all children must learn to get to school on time, be quiet and attentive in class, obey the teacher, and not disrupt the classroom by fighting, yelling, running around, and so on. Otherwise they and others cannot learn anything else. Children from higher-status families generally learn these desirable and useful behaviors earlier, and so can go on to other things earlier. Children from higher-status families are *more obedient* in school: they fight less often, do homework more regularly, get in trouble less, and so on (Ainsworth-Darnell and Downey 1995). Marxist and other radical critics of schooling created experimental alternative schools that did not require silence and obedience, but instead allowed all children the freedom to be themselves in an unrestrictive environment (Aronowitz and Giroux 1993). Those schools typically failed to teach children adequate basic skills like reading and math (Davies 1995). Rather than revising their ideas, some experimenters blame the larger capitalist order for the failure (e.g., Aronowitz and Giroux 1993).

Studies of American high schools consistently find that they do not base tracking on family socioeconomic status (Heyns 1974; Alexander, Cook, and McDill 1978). American schools track students based on past achievements and measured abilities, not on parental status (Heyns 1974; Alexander et al. 1978). American children from higher-status families have higher average achievement and ability, which makes them more likely to get into advanced classes and programs. Among students with the same level of achievement and ability, family status has no influence on the likelihood of getting in. Things may be a little different in other countries. One study in Great Britain finds that, given the same level of achievement and ability, boys from higher-status families are more likely to get into advanced classes and programs (Kerckhoff 1993). Also, both higher family status and advanced-track membership improve subsequent academic performance and teachers' evaluations. Even in the British study, though, grades and test scores are the big link between family status and advanced placement. In the United States they are the only link. They also account for the kinds of advice, counseling, encouragement, and learning resources a student gets (Heyns 1974).

Performance-based placement does indirectly reinforce and amplify the differences in academic performance and achievement across levels of family status. Other things being equal, students placed in more advanced courses wind up with more advanced skills. They often learn more quickly too. As a result, performance-based placement preserves and often enlarges the existing differences in academic ability across levels of family status. Differences between schools also contribute to the effect. Schools set goals and design programs for the level and range of abilities most common in the populations they serve. That also preserves and perhaps enlarges the existing differences in academic ability among the populations. Adapting curricula to different needs and abilities has the unintended consequence of reinforcing those differences. The Marxist critique portrays efforts to advance the abilities of all students as subjugating those from lower- and working-class families while favoring students from middle- and upper-class families. That portrait is false at its core, and malicious in appearance and effect if not intent.

Implicit Tracking

Post-Marxist European social criticism also portrays formal education as a system for reproducing inequality that imparts nothing truly productive. However it emphasizes the affinity that individuals of similar status have for each other because of shared culture, rather than the domination of one class by another as a result of conflicting economic interests. Implicit tracking occurs when high-status individuals and their cultural agents in the academic world select and promote students based on interests and activities cultivated in the family and consistent with those of high-status adults in general. Bourdieu's (1977) thoughts on what he calls cultural capital exemplify the view. His emphasis on status culture owes more to the German sociologist Max Weber's (1968) writings at the end of the nineteenth-century than to Marx's somewhat earlier political economics. Nevertheless, Bourdieu joins with Marxist scholars in the effort to delegitimize social inequality by disparaging formal education's contribution to ability and productivity.

Bourdieu claims formal education simply transmits social status from one generation to the next without adding skills of any real value. He argues that the educational system merely selects and promotes prestigious cultural interests. Cultural capital embodies the culture of the dominant class: its behavior, habits, tastes, lifestyles, and attitudes. It consists of going to museums, concerts, the theater, and lectures, of reading literature, and of developing an appreciation for the arts and some skill in one or more of them. Cultural self-development requires time and money, so the resulting knowledge and ability act as forms of conspicuous consumption. Much of cultural capital's social value results from its apparent lavish impracticality. Because the possession of this cultural capital is a sign of being from a higher social status, children from high-status families get rewarded by teachers and encouraged at school. As a result they do well in school, complete high school, and go on to college. According to Bourdieu, schools do not teach the dominant culture, they simply reward students who learn it at home.

Bourdieu's concept of cultural capital seems to have spread like a virus, generating much talk and interpretive gloss but little science. We found three quantitative analyses of survey data attempting to evaluate the empirical validity of Bourdieu's ideas. The studies support some of his assertions and contradict others, but do not question his core aspersions: (1) that developing and having cultural interests, activities, and abilities has no practical value, and (2) that formal schooling does not develop habits and skills that make students more able and resourceful. Taken together, the studies generally confirm that students with cultural interests, activities, knowledge, and skill do well in school (Aschaffenburg and Maas 1997; DiMaggio 1982). One study distinguishes in-school from out-of-school training in the arts (Aschaffenburg and Maas 1997). It finds that training from both sources correlates with a higher probability of progressing to the next stage of education, but the correlation is stronger for training outside school. The studies confirm that student interest and participation in high culture increases with parental social status, but perhaps much less so in the United States than in Europe (DiMaggio 1982; Katsillis and Rubinson 1990). The U.S. studies suggest that schools here do favor students who show signs of cultural development, but those signs only moderately reflect high family status (Aschaffenburg and Maas 1997; DiMaggio 1982). The researchers argue that, in the United States, cultural capital operates more as an avenue for status attainment than as a means of passing status from one generation to the next. This partial contradiction of Bourdieu's ideas leaves unquestioned his aspersion that formal education merely promotes prestigious but otherwise impractical interests, activities, and abilities.

Apart from its shaky empirical foundation, the theory of cultural capital rests on the bizarre assumption that going to museums, concerts, and theaters, reading literature, and practicing the fine arts and humanities provides no knowledge or ability of practical use. In the theory of cultural capital, mastering cultural knowledge and artistic skill has no value other than forging a symbolic key that opens desirable social positions. To us that view seems obviously false, but it is worth mentioning some things that contradict it. First, cultural and artistic skills are communication skills. When individuals develop themselves culturally and artistically they develop the ability to apprehend and express perceptions, ideas, and sentiments. One of the U.S. studies found such a high correlation between vocabulary and cultural knowledge that their effects on grades could not be distinguished (DiMaggio 1982:194). Second, high culture attempts to transcend the limits of time and place, by connecting the individual to the cultures of other societies and to the enduring traditions of the past. Individuals who know a lot about high culture also tend to know a lot about popular culture, history, politics, current events, science, technology, business, and economics. Such broad interest makes available a range of ideas and possibilities. Third, many traits developed in the pursuit of culture and the arts have broad practical value. Habits of exploration, reflection, judgment, practice, and design make individuals more effective in all aspects of life. Such habits constitute the resourcefulness behind the phenomena of resource substitution described in Chapter 6. In our research, we find that the creativity of daily activities increases with the level of education and predicts better health outcomes net of earnings, household income, workplace autonomy, and traits such as sex and age (in Chapter 4, see section, "Education and the Autonomy and Creativity of Work," and Figures 4.16 and 4.17). By all indications, formal education cultivates and promotes awareness, openness, creativity, and self-discipline, and those traits have broad practical value.

The Core Fallacy of Status Reproduction

The theories that portray education as merely transcribing status from one generation to the next share a core fallacy. Whether Marxist or neo-

Marxist ideas about explicit tracking, or post-Marxist ideas about implicit tracking, they assume that education provides fewer benefits to individuals from lower-status families. Indeed, some of the Marxist and neo-Marxist ideas imply that longer education simply lengthens exposure to a stifling and dispiriting discipline for low-status students. Empirical research in the United States provides a deluge of observations that reveal the core fallacy of status reproduction. Surveys of the general population consistently find that, at each level of parental education and occupational status, greater personal education correlates with better adulthood outcomes by a variety of measures that include the sense of control, economic well-being, emotional well-being, and physical health (e.g., Reynolds and Ross 1998; Ross and Mirowsky 1999).

Scientific surveys do not find that individuals from low-status families get fewer benefits from staying in school longer. If anything, empirical research shows just the opposite. Individuals from low-status families gain the most from additional education. Figure 7.2 shows three instances from our 1995 U.S. data. The panel on the bottom shows a stronger positive correlation between personal education and feeling in control of one's own life for individuals whose parents had less than a high school degree than for those whose parents had a high school or higher degree. That pattern contradicts the idea that formal education oppresses individuals from low-status backgrounds, stifling their self-determination. The panels in the middle and on top show a similar pattern for subjective health and physical functioning. The improvements associated with higher educational attainment are greater for individuals from low-status backgrounds. Almost all the differences in health associated with status of origin occur among individuals who do not finish high school themselves. For individuals who have high school or college degrees, their parents' education makes little or no difference to health. This illustrates a general principle: *a person's own educational attainment overcomes the undesirable effects of disadvantaged origins.*

The interaction between personal and parental education creates an intergenerational instance of resource substitution. (See Chapter 6 for a general discussion of resource substitution and its effects.) Individuals from higher-status families develop beneficial personal resources in the home as well as in school, and thus depend less on schooling for those resources. Formal education helps individuals from low-status backgrounds develop effective personal resources. It gives them training they otherwise would not get. Individuals from lower-status backgrounds depend more on their own educational attainments for health and a sense of control over their own lives. The knowledge, skill, and resourcefulness developed through formal schooling give them independence, health, and well-being they otherwise would find extremely difficult to achieve.

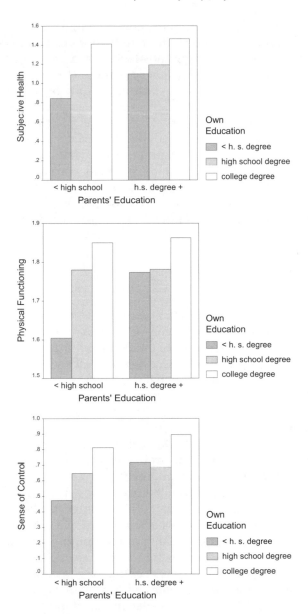

Figure 7.2. Subjective health, physical functioning, and sense of control by education and parents' education, adjusting for age, sex, and race.

As usual, the structural amplification of disadvantage shadows the phenomenon of resource substitution. In the intergenerational case, individuals from low-status backgrounds tend to acquire less education, and also fare less well with little personal education. That tends to concentrate low education and poor outcomes within a family over multiple generations. Individuals from low-status backgrounds depend more on formal education to gain control of their own lives and create good outcomes for themselves, but they tend to get less formal education than individuals from middle- or high-status backgrounds. Disparaging formal education will not help Americans to correct this problem. Formal education tries to give every child the knowledge, skill, and ability that otherwise only those from advantaged backgrounds would enjoy. Any solution to the problem of disadvantaged origins lies in the direction of raising the levels of education in successive generations, particularly for low-status families.

EDUCATION AS FALSE SATISFIER

A third view of education sees it as a system for getting members of all social strata to accept their relatively advantaged or disadvantages positions. All complex societies have hierarchies of power, prestige, and reward. To operate peacefully and efficiently, all societies need to justify their inequality in terms of values that their institutions promote. U.S. society took shape in opposition to a system that justified social inequality by reference to gradations of nobility and standing ascribed at birth and transmitted through family lines. American society justifies inequality by reference to individual ability and effort. The system of formal education persuades members of all social strata to accept the inequality in autonomy, authority, income, wealth, and quality of life as proper and fitting. Schools do not have to exhort students to accept their advantages or disadvantages. The process itself carries the message, to the extent that the desirability of the jobs individuals get is proportional to the length and difficulty of their studies and the quality of their grades. Members of prestigious, highly paid professions such as law or medicine feel comfortable with their advantages in part because of the long, arduous academic competition. Individuals in less desirable jobs can see that others in better positions studied longer and harder to get them. While they may wish for better, they understand that better positions require training they have not had. Viewed as a *false* satisfier, the educational system produces acceptance of inequality even if the academic competition is unfair or irrelevant to the skills needed in the desirable jobs, and even if those jobs get rewarded out of proportion to the value they produce.

On a theoretical level, the view of education as false satisfier seems close to reproductionist views, particularly in the Marxist tradition. We address it separately for two reasons. First, the educational system could create broad satisfaction with unequal outcomes regardless of the relationship between parental status and educational attainment. Even if students from all backgrounds had equal chances of making it to any given level of education, an apparently competitive system would persuade individuals to see their advantages or disadvantages later in life as proportional to their personal effort and ability. Success in school would operate as a major sign of effort and ability. That could happen even if outcomes in the competition were in fact random, as in a game of chance, so long as most persons believed the competition tested effort and ability. Second, the research that seems to support the view of education as false satisfier comes out of the empirical and pragmatic study of job satisfaction. It generally does not come out of efforts to confirm theories designed to delegitimize social inequality. Nevertheless, the facts uncovered by those studies suggest that differences in education do, in a sense, justify unequal job rewards in the minds of workers.

Empirical surveys repeatedly find that workers with different levels of education report about the same degree of satisfaction with their jobs (Gordon and Arvey 1975; Quinn and de Mandilovitch 1977; Quinn, Staines, and McCullough 1974; Weaver 1978; Andrisani 1978; Hodson 1989). This unexpected observation has two faces. Some critics of education focus on the fact that higher education apparently does not provide more satisfying jobs (e.g., Berg 1970; Quinn and de Mandilovitch 1977). Students work longer and harder in school in order to have more satisfying work later (Glenn and Weaver 1982:46). The critics say that, if education does not provide more satisfying jobs, then perhaps it has little real value in life. Those criticisms miss a larger implication of the results. Individuals with relatively low levels of education, in jobs with relatively low pay and poor conditions, generally report being satisfied with their jobs. They are no more likely to report feeling dissatisfied than better-educated workers with higher pay and better working conditions.

Satisfaction judgments represent perceptions of personal outcomes relative to the norm for individuals like oneself. The absence of an overall correlation between education and job satisfaction exists because education has two contradictory effects. On one hand, higher education leads to more rewarding jobs in terms of pay, autonomy, prestige, and recognition. Among workers with similar levels of education, those getting the highest rewards are the most satisfied with their jobs. On the other hand, higher education leads individuals to expect better outcomes as their due. Among workers getting similar levels of rewards, the ones with higher levels of education feel less satisfied with their jobs and the ones with lower levels of education feel more satisfied. The null correlation exists because education on average increases the expectations and the rewards in proportion. Individuals judge their outcomes in reference to those enjoyed by others of similar education. (Age, seniority, organizational rank, and occupational status also define reference points.) Workers with low education feel satisfied with their jobs because they judge their own jobs by reference to those that others like themselves have. Satisfaction with low wages and poor conditions implies a degree of resignation and submission to the inequalities correlated with education.

Studies of job satisfaction mislead to the extent that they treat satisfaction as measuring the quality of life. Satisfaction judgments balance personal outcomes against reasonable expectations. Acceptance of disadvantage may be more mature, effective, and comfortable than hostility and resentment, but it does not signify a high quality of life. Measures that represent the desirability of outcomes apart from expectations consistently show that higher education yields a higher quality of life. It lowers the average levels of depression, anxiety, and malaise, and increases the average levels of happiness, joy, and enthusiasm (Mirowsky and Ross 1989; Ross and Van Willigen 1997). The well-educated enjoy fuller employment, higher pay and household income, lower economic hardship, more rewarding and self-expressive work, higher levels of social support, and a stronger sense of control over their own lives, as documented in this book and elsewhere (Bird and Ross 1993; Kohn 1976; Kohn et al. 1990; Kohn and Schooler 1982; Ross and Reskin 1992; Ross and Wu 1995; Ross and Mirowsky 1989; Ross and Van Willigen 1997). As a practical matter, employers need to mind the satisfaction of their workers. Otherwise the workers perform indifferently or go elsewhere. Society, though, needs to mind the well-being of its members. Clearly, higher education produces greater well-being.

Formal education's role in shaping expectations and justifying unequal outcomes raises questions about the legitimacy of those effects. The view of education as false satisfier portrays it as a phony or irrelevant competition that merely instills acceptance of inequality. We think that education's benefits are valid and true in three important senses. First, education produces benefits in proportion to effort and ability, in keeping with the values of American culture. Longer schooling and more advanced studies require greater effort, and yield greater ability. All individuals can freely affirm or reject these standards, but education clearly meets them. Second, education produces real benefits, not just acceptance of inequality. It measurably improves the likely subjective quality of relationships and activities, and the likely degree of emotional well-being and physical health. Education benefits everyone in proportion to the length of their training.

There is no evidence that it makes life worse for any social strata. Formal education makes persons from all social origins better than they would have been otherwise. Indeed, additional education improves most the outcomes of persons from low-status origins. Third, education produces its benefits mostly apart from access to lucrative and desirable jobs. Statistical analyses consistently show positive effects of education on health and other desirable outcomes apart from the ones mediated by earnings, income, and occupational status. In most cases those other paths outweigh the job-related ones. In addition, our research finds that education acts as a substitute for income, diminishing the negative impact of low income on health. These observations contradict the idea that education operates largely as a false satisfier creating acquiescence to unjust inequality but little else of value.

EDUCATION AS SPURIOUS CORRELATE

Some critics argue that the length of schooling reflects an unmeasured factor that produces education's seemingly beneficial effects. Portrayed as a spurious correlate, educational attainment merely stands in for the unseen factor that actually produces the benefits. Critics of education speculate on a variety of possible hidden factors. Some argue that the real determinants of success are family *social* origins. In such views, wealthier and more powerful families send their children to school longer, embed them in more influential and privileged networks, get them more enjoyable and lucrative positions, and transfer wealth to them. Surveys rarely measure completely the wealth and power of an adult's family of origin. Education might simply stand in for those unmeasured aspects of advantaged social origins and falsely appear to produce their desirable consequences. Health scientists sometimes espouse variants of this view, arguing that poor nutrition, infection, and exposure to lead or other chemicals during gestation and childhood can slow or limit intellectual development. That in turn undermines both performance in school and later prosperity, well-being, and health in adulthood. Surveys of adults generally cannot measure prenatal and childhood exposures, so educational attainment might stand in for them. Some critics argue that family *genetic* origins determine both educational attainment and adulthood outcomes. No one can yet specify the genes and alleles that shape intellectual predisposition, or the biological structures and processes for which they code, so no one can measure them either. As a result, critics can argue that educational attainment merely stands in for those unspecified genetic and biological factors that actually produce adulthood prosperity, well-being, and health. In fact, no survey can measure all the things, known or unknown, imagined or unimagined, that might create a spurious correlation between educational attainment and the desirable outcomes in life that include health.

The logical possibility of spurious correlation is the black hole of empirical science. An enormous variety of procedural and statistical methods attempt to minimize the risk of confounding—of thinking that one thing causes another when in fact it merely stands in for something else that has the effect. Only one method can unequivocally rule out the possibility of spurious correlation: the randomized, controlled experiment. Randomly assigning cases to a treatment group or a control (no-treatment) group assures that any differences between the groups are either random or caused by the treatment. With large enough groups the random differences average out. That happens for every possible confounder, measurable or not, suspected or not. Any remaining difference in outcome must result from the treatment.

Randomized, controlled experiments on humans have ethical and practical limitations. With regard to education, we can imagine a lottery that allows some students to continue in school and forces others to quit and join the workforce. If we keep that control group from returning to school, and follow both groups for decades, we can see if the randomized access to continued education produces better health. With large enough groups the randomization would rule out a spurious association between better health and longer education. The human cost of the experiment would be great if longer education actually does produce better outcomes, because the experiment denies longer education to members of the control group. However, we want to do the experiment because we suspect that education produces those benefits. That is the moral dilemma. Practically speaking, families and authorities would not cooperate with the experiment because they believe education works, and they have the right and responsibility to act on those beliefs.

The standards of scientific practice require that researchers try to imagine possible confounders, measure them, and use procedures of observation or analysis that adjust for them. Researchers who suspect that a seemingly causal association is actually spurious must demonstrate the validity of their suspicions. Sometimes advocates misuse the concept of spurious association to defend against unwelcome evidence. For example, defenders of the tobacco industry often argued that genetic predispositions or other unknown traits might lead to smoking and be the real but hidden cause of lung cancer and other health problems associated with it. No one has ever randomly assigned individuals to become smokers or not, so the possibility of a spurious association has never been decisively ruled out. On the other hand, no one has ever shown that the association of smoking with lung cancer, heart disease, and many other health problems vanishes once a specific hypothetical confounder gets taken into account.

Over the years researchers examined many possibilities, and the results always failed to disconfirm smoking's destructive effect. The same may be said of education's benefits. Over the years researchers examined many possible confounders, and consistently failed to disconfirm education's beneficial effects on adulthood outcomes.

Family and Neighborhood Resources and Standards

One challenge comes from research comparing the effects of school quality to those of family and neighborhood intellectual resources and standards. In the 1960s, policymakers wanting to reduce social inequality in America thought that spending more on schools in disadvantaged neighborhoods might help. Students at schools that spend more per student have higher test scores on average. Based on the correlation alone, it appears that the differences among schools in their average scores might be reduced considerably by eliminating the differences in expenditures. The problem is that wealthier schools are in wealthier neighborhoods where parents often have strong educational backgrounds and intellectually stimulating jobs, where households often have books, magazines, globes, encyclopedias, dictionaries, and other educational materials, where families sometimes go to museums and galleries or play intellectual games like Scrabble, and where family and neighborhood standards promote studying and high educational aspirations. That raises a question. Does the spending per student produce the higher test scores, or does it merely stand in for family and neighborhood wealth and standards?

In a classic study of elementary and secondary schools, Coleman and his colleagues found that differences among schools in resources, amount spent per pupil, curriculum, and quality of teachers contribute relatively little to the differences among students in test scores (Coleman et al. 1966). Family differences in the parents' education and interest in the child's schooling, household income, number of children, and books in the home contribute the most to the children's differences in test scores. The family characteristics of other students in the school contribute the next most. School quality accounts for little once those other things are taken into account. Coleman's results gave little reason to think that equalizing school resources can overcome the differences in test scores associated with family and neighborhood status. Coleman based his conclusions on methods of data analysis that few quantitative social scientists now would consider adequate. Subsequent research finds some important and valuable school effects. In particular, teachers with higher measured ability improve their students' corresponding measured ability more rapidly, particularly in mathematics and science. Nevertheless, subsequent research largely confirms the basic implications of the earlier findings. The students at wealthier schools perform better academically mostly because of family and neighborhood intellectual culture rather than the amount spent per student classroom hour. However, those findings do not rule out the possibility of improving the outcomes of students from disadvantaged backgrounds by spending more on longer training.

Coleman and his colleagues might have been more optimistic about the benefits of schooling if they had considered quantity rather than quality. Even as critics of education were claiming that the quality of schooling could not overcome family background effects on achievement (Coleman et al. 1966; Jencks 1972), others had clear evidence that the quantity of schooling improved achievement, even among children of the same age (Wiley 1976). The number of hours per day school meets, the number of days in the school year, and the average daily attendance have large effects on average verbal, reading, and math scores (ibid.). The more time children spend in school, the higher their abilities. Spaeth (1976) argues that the quantity of schooling improves success in many realms of life because it indicates the duration of exposure to intellectually complex and challenging environments, which improves cognitive abilities.

A remarkable confirmation comes from another study of the period. Heyns (1978) compared the amount of cognitive development over the summer quarter to the average amount over the school year quarters among sixth- and seventh-graders in the Atlanta public schools. She found that cognitive abilities improved most during the school year. The test scores of white students improved during the summer, but not as much as during the school year. The test scores of black students declined over the summer:

> What Heyns's analysis reveals is that schools do, in fact, play an important constructive role in fostering cognitive development, especially for disadvantaged minorities. Schooling, in effect, compensates partially for cognitive deficits in the home and community environments of disadvantaged youngsters; by implication, were it not for the school's intervention, the gap between the test scores of advantaged and disadvantaged youngsters would be even greater. (Alexander, Natriello, and Pallas 1985:411)

Heyns's findings provide another example of the principles of resource substitution and structural amplification discussed earlier. Later studies comparing dropouts to continuing students find similar effects of duration (Alexander et al. 1985; Shavit and Featherman 1988). Cognitive ability improves faster for the young persons who stay in school than for those from similar backgrounds who drop out. While cognitive ability improves faster for more advantaged students, the gap between students and dropouts grows faster for individuals from less advantaged backgrounds.

The same students most inclined to drop out of school lose the most ground by doing it.

Intelligence as Predestination

Another challenge comes from social scientists who argue that educational attainment merely stands in for genetically inherited intelligence. Their theories emphasize the functional benefits of hierarchies that stratify occupations according to intellectual demands and select individuals with the native capacities to meet those demands (Gottfredson 1985; Herrnstein and Murray 1994). In this view, education merely selects and promotes intelligent individuals. The duration and increasing rigor of academic competition ejects individuals who attempt schooling beyond their level of intelligence. As a result, educational attainment indirectly measures native intelligence, which employers value and reward.

Intelligence is the capacity to acquire and apply knowledge and to think and reason. The view that education merely selects for preordained intelligence rests on questionable assumptions. In their controversial book, Herrnstein and Murray (1994) correlate a wide range of positive social outcomes with a test of intelligence at the beginning of adulthood. Few social scientists doubt the positive correlations, but many take exception to Herrnstein and Murray's interpretation of them. Most of the book simply ignores the likely contribution of education to intelligence. A technical appendix defends the omission by arguing that education's apparent benefits are mostly spurious, due to its correlation with intelligence. The appendix presents statistical models showing that, among individuals with similar cognitive test scores, differences in education have relatively small correlations with positive outcomes such as employment, job performance, earnings, per capita family income, and quality of child-parent relationships. In contrast, among individuals with similar levels of education, differences in test scores have relatively large correlations with those positive outcomes. Herrnstein and Murray interpret this as showing that most of education's effects are spurious. Their interpretation necessarily *assumes* that differences in length of education do not produce the differences in test scores. The top panel of Figure 7.3 represents Herrnstein and Murray's interpretation of the results they present. The middle panel shows an alternative interpretation that fits their results equally well. It says that education creates desirable adulthood outcomes by increasing intelligence. The statistics that Herrnstein and Murray report cannot distinguish between those two interpretations.

In all likelihood, intelligence and length of education influence each other and each directly improves adulthood outcomes. The bottom panel

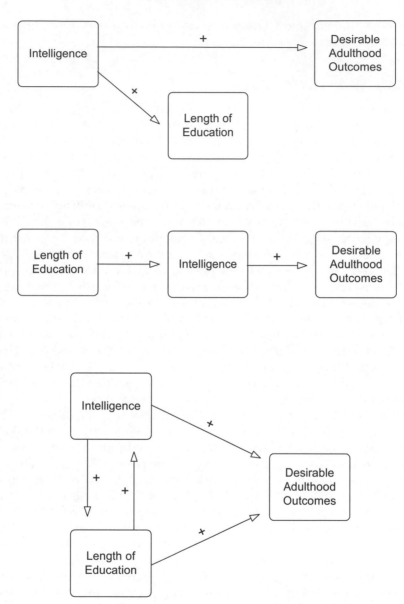

Figure 7.3.   Three views of the causal relationships among intelligence, length of education, and desirable adulthood outcomes.

of Figure 7.3 illustrates the causal interpretation implied by the results of studies other than Herrnstein and Murray's (Alexander et al. 1985; Farkas, England, Vicknair, and Kilbourne 1997; Shavit and Featherman 1988). It has two main features. First, intelligence and education have deviation-amplifying feedback effects. Students with higher test scores are more likely to remain in school and advance to the next level, and students who remain in school increase their scores more rapidly than others who were at a similar level originally but dropped out (Alexander et al. 1985; Shavit and Featherman 1988). Second, among persons with similar levels of education, higher test scores correlate with better outcomes but, among persons with similar test scores, longer schooling *also* correlates with better outcomes (Farkas et al. 1997). In other words, education produces desirable outcomes partly by developing intellectual skills, but also by developing other effective traits such as a sense of control over one's own life.

The core fallacy of Herrnstein and Murray's view lies in seeing intelligence as a fixed and preeminent trait. Based on that assumption, they argue that giving more or better education to children from disadvantaged families will do little good. In their view, education most benefits intelligent children, who have intelligent and therefore successful parents. A partial truth in that view hides a larger error. Children from more advantaged families do show greater intellectual ability and do advance their ability more. The U.S. Department of Education's statistics show that the children of college-educated parents have reading, mathematics, and science scores by age thirteen that the children of parents without high school degrees only achieve four years later, at age seventeen (Campbell, Hombo, and Mazzeo 2000). The children of parents with low education start behind and stay behind. That does not make their education futile. As noted above, staying in school most benefits children from disadvantaged backgrounds.

The longer that the children of poorly educated parents stay in school the higher the level of intellectual performance they achieve. That in turn sets the level at which their own children enter the system. In the United States, each generation attains a higher level of education than the previous one, as illustrated in Figure 7.4. The intergenerational ladder of educational attainment produces a corresponding ladder of intellectual ability. Researchers who see intelligence as a trait fixed at birth deplore the fact that smarter individuals generally have fewer children (e.g., Herrnstein and Murray 1994). If intelligence is a fixed genetic trait, then modern humans are getting less intelligent with each generation, and have been for some time. That is a logical inference given the premise and long-standing demographic patterns, but empirical observations fail to confirm its alarming implications. On the contrary, average IQ scores increased greatly over the twentieth century (Dickens and Flynn 2001.) Economists often say that human capital has been increasing faster than other forms of

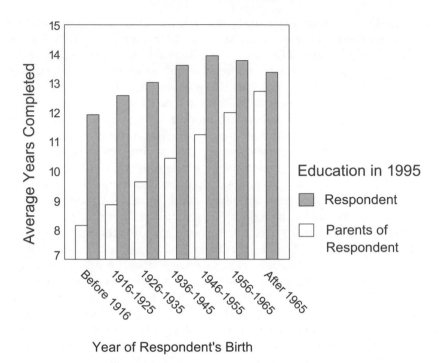

Figure 7.4. The intergenerational ladder of educational attainment.

capital (e.g., Schultz 1962). In fact, in the 1950s and 1960s economists revived and named the concept of human capital when they realized that wealth and productivity were increasing faster than could be explained by the growth of physical capital. Without the intergenerational ladder of educational attainment, average adulthood intelligence probably would trend down, and the inequalities based on family of origin would increase. The educational system upgrades the intellectual abilities of individuals, families, and society.

Passing Tests of Spurious Association.

Good scientific practice requires that scientists address the possibility of spurious association. There is no good evidence that education's positive correlation with health is spurious, but no one has ever eliminated or ever will eliminate all possible confounders from contention. Still, each failed attempt to demonstrate spuriousness strengthens the inference that education improves health. Modern statistical techniques called structural-equation modeling allow researchers to test "What if" scenarios. For example, what if an unmeasured factor produces the positive correlation between a person's own education and that of their parents? Can that factor also account for all of the correlation between education and health? The methods cannot say whether such a factor really exists or what it might be (family social standing, genetic inheritance, or something else). The methods *can* calculate the likelihood that such a factor, if it exists, might account for education's correlation with health. They show it is unlikely. Other scenarios produce similar results. Suppose that an unmeasured factor creates a spurious association between education and earnings. Can it account for the correlation between education and health? Unlikely. So far, education's apparently beneficial effect on health cannot be explained away by reference to specific confounders, whether measured directly or inferred speculatively.

EDUCATION, INEQUALITY, AND HEALTH

The Ideological Project and Counterproject

The views of education as mere credential, reproducer of inequality, false satisfier, and spurious correlate often seem preposterous. To us, as mainstream health researchers, they appear plainly unrealistic and oddly disparaging. The four critical views of education are not disgruntled cries for stronger training. They portray education as meaningless certification irrelevant to job performance but handy to bigoted employers, as browbeating subjugation of lower- and working-class children alongside sycophantic coddling of middle- and upper-class children, as the lauding and elevation of children displaying the elaborately useless cognitive ornamentation of the upper classes, as a phony or irrelevant contest for position that beguiles both winners and losers into accepting the outcomes as due, or as a spurious manifestation merely standing in for the advantages preordained by social or genetic inheritance. Like us, many readers will be surprised that these critical views of education have any currency. We wonder why social theorists would use their intellects to strenuously malign an institution as constructive as the educational system. We wonder why professors, lifelong students, and teachers themselves, would buy and sell such ideas.

As human beings and scientists, we have tried to make sense of what seems a senseless attack. What is it about education that provokes such belittling criticism? What justifies the attempted destruction of education's reputation as a constructive force? Only one answer makes sense to us: the desire to delegitimize social inequality. Social science has a core mandate to describe and explain the nature, causes, and consequences of social inequality. Social science has other goals too, but that is one of the most central. That scientific concern readily becomes a human and social one—a sincere and worthy desire to improve society by reducing any harm done by inequality. That leads many social scientists to define social inequality as a social problem and to speak against it. The discovery of education's role in the attainment and transmission of socioeconomic status made it for many the target of that critical speech. We call the efforts to delegitimize social inequality, by disparaging education, the ideological project. We call the efforts to defend inequality, by portraying education as a contest of native intelligence, the ideological counterproject. However well-intentioned these efforts might be, they distort reality and demean an institution that gives individuals the ability to make their own lives prosperous, meaningful, enjoyable, healthy, and long.

We see two main problems with the ideological project. First, it substitutes sociopolitical goals for scientific ones. An effort to delegitimize inequality is not, at core, an effort to understand it. The strenuous search for reasons to view inequality as illegitimate exaggerates some of education's features and disregards others. The resulting caricatures probably cannot guide actions effectively. Second, the ideological project presumes that education's value lies in providing access to lucrative social positions. It erroneously equates money with well-being and disadvantage with dispossession. The money fallacy and the zero-sum fallacy exaggerate some things and disregard others, distorting interpretations of education's impact on health.

The Money Fallacy

Generally speaking, prosperity is healthier than poverty. Most people believe that, and the scientific evidence supports it. The problem lies in the interpretation. Mistaken assumptions about economic inequality lead to erroneous conclusions. The money fallacy is that earnings, income, and wealth are the sole or central aspects of prosperity. In our research we repeatedly find that money is only one means of achieving well-being and health, and generally not the most powerful one. Increases in personal earnings and household income have their biggest effects near the bottom of the socioeconomic ladder. There are two reasons why. One is that economic sufficiency is more important to well-being and health than economic abundance. Once the basic needs are met, there is not much more that money can buy to improve health (and quite a bit it can buy that will make health worse). The other reason is that low education increases the need for money. By developing effective skills and habits, education develops the capacity for resource substitution. Resourceful individuals with little income or wealth find other means toward fulfillment and health. It is generally the combination of low education with low income that makes low income into poverty. If everyone with little income or wealth were a college-educated philosopher, artist, monk, or volunteer pursuing an unpretentious and virtuous life, then income and wealth might have little or no correlation with health. Over two millennia ago the Greek philosophers codified a minimalist lifestyle that is quite inexpensive. The Greeks believed that the prescribed vegetarian diet, moderation in drink, and daily walks would sustain a long and healthy life. Modern health science supports that belief.

The Zero-Sum Fallacy

The second major fallacy is that the benefits enjoyed disproportionately by some individuals ultimately must come from others who have been deprived of those benefits. By necessity, a science must limit its purview to specific phenomena. Social scientists who study inequality tend to see a low position in the hierarchy as the source of the problems correlated with it. That creates a zero-sum view of outcomes. To balance the equation, the advantages of some individuals imply the disadvantages of others. In that view, the prosperity, well-being, and health enjoyed by better-educated individuals must somehow create the distress, impairment, disease, and early death disproportionately suffered by the poorly educated. That view has no basis except in the operating restrictions that bracket the study of inequality. Social scientists who study aggregate trends rather than concurrent differences find that all strata can rise together, and typically do. This certainly has been true of the historical declines in age-specific mortality rates, and the corresponding increases in life expectancy. The well-educated do live considerably longer than the poorly educated, but the poorly educated live longer today than in the past. In fact, the poorly educated live longer now than the well-educated did in the past. Partly that is because the lowest strata now have much more education than historically (typically eight to eleven years rather than zero to six). Partly it is because greater education in one part of society benefits the society as a whole. Raising the average level of education, particularly in disadvantaged families, improves aggregate prosperity and health, to the benefit of all.

EDUCATION: THE SOLUTION, NOT THE PROBLEM

In the long run, formal education provides the most likely solution to the health problems later in life associated with being from a disadvantaged family. A person's own educational attainment overcomes the undesirable effects of disadvantaged origins. Education improves health because it makes individuals more effective, increasing personal control over their own lives. Formal schooling develops real skills and abilities that make individuals resourceful and capable of achieving many things, including health. It produces desirable outcomes partly by developing intellectual skills, but also by developing other effective traits. Formal education culti-vates and promotes awareness, openness, creativity, and self-discipline. It instills habits of exploration, reflection, judgment, practice, and design. Such traits and habits constitute much of the resourcefulness behind the phenomenon of resource substitution.

Education makes persons from all social origins better than they would have been otherwise, but improves most the outcomes of persons from disadvantaged families. The improvements in health associated with higher educational attainment are greatest for individuals from low-status backgrounds. Unfortunately, this means that the same students most inclined to drop out of school will suffer the most harm from living with little education. The interaction between personal and parental education creates intergenerational structural amplification. Individuals from lower-status backgrounds depend more on their own educational attainments for health and a sense of control over their own lives. The knowledge, skill, and resourcefulness developed through formal schooling give them inde-pendence, well-being, and health they otherwise would find extremely difficult to achieve. Formal education tries to give every child the knowl-edge, skill, and ability that otherwise only those from advantaged back-grounds would enjoy. Any solution to the problem of disadvantaged origins lies in the direction of raising the levels of education in successive generations, particularly for low-status families.

Education helps individuals to become active agents in their own lives. The choices individuals make for themselves increasingly determine health and survival. That drives education's increasing importance to health and survival. Social policies that treat unequal or inadequate income and wealth as the core problem miss the point. Redistributing money from the wealthy to the poor probably would improve average levels of health, to the extent that losses at the upper end have less effect than gains at the lower end. Redistribution policies have problems, though, apart from resistance among the well-to-do. One is that they are partially zero-sum, so that the negative health effects on those taxed even-tually limits the average gains that can be made. More importantly, they do not make persons independent agents. Among individuals with little education, money is an inefficient means toward personal control, well-being, and health. It takes a great deal of money to compensate for low education. On the other hand, somewhat more education increases access to money while decreasing dependence on it. And there is no zero-sum. Greater education in one part of society benefits society as a whole. That is particularly true of greater education among those from disadvantaged backgrounds. Education puts the power where it needs to be. Not in the hands of those who redistribute. In the hands of those who, through edu-cation, gain control of their own lives.

| 8 |

Conclusion: Self-Direction Toward Health

Education improves health because it develops productive abilities. An individual's level of education indicates learned effectiveness because getting an education is learning effectiveness. Individuals learn effectiveness through other channels too, but formal education institutionalizes its development. Schooling builds in individuals a greater capacity to control their own lives. That helps individuals achieve whatever they want, including health.

Education has a powerful influence on health for several reasons. Its array of consequences is present in many aspects of life throughout the entire lifetime. Those consequences are uniformly positive with regard to health. Many of those positive consequences accumulate across the lifetime, producing ever larger health advantages. The accumulators operate on all levels, from the economic down to the intracellular. Education's consequences often amplify each other. Some of them bolster each other, producing feedback amplification. Some of them substitute for one another, so that others compensate for a shortfall on any one of them. Education's greatest benefit is that it develops the capacity for resource substitution. It helps individuals to acquire an array of standard resources, making the individual less dependent on any one of them. Perhaps more importantly, it develops the capacity to improvise resources—to find or invent new ways to solve problems or achieve goals.

The capacity for resource substitution is a major element of health-promoting learned effectiveness. Education develops the capacity to find out what needs to be done and how to do it, and develops habits and skills of self-direction. Together those prove effective when seeking health. They make individuals better at identifying and avoiding risky situations or habits, quicker to exit the risky situations or correct the risky ways, and better able to manage health problems that occur, minimize the damage, and return to health as fully and quickly as possible.

In writing this book we came to realize a number of things about education and health. Many interesting and surprising discoveries resulted from empirical tests of specific hypotheses. Observations like that are the usual product of research reported in scientific journals. Many others, though, came from asking how the various specific observations and ideas might together explain the association of health with social status. Those reflections crystallized a coherent and distinct view of the association that repeatedly underscores education's place as the fundamental aspect of social status connected to health. To us these realizations come as discoveries. Some readers may consider it odd to be surprised by them, while others may remain skeptical of their validity. In science, each cycle of discovery ends at the beginning of the next. These are the realizations to which we have come and with which we end.

LEARNED EFFECTIVENESS TOPS ACCESS TO LUCRATIVE POSITIONS

Education is more important than standing and rank and more important than income and wealth in connecting better health with higher social status. Partly that is because education lies upstream, at the headwaters of achieved social status. That makes any direct health benefit of standing and rank or of income and wealth also an indirect benefit of education. The opposite is not true. The health benefits of education include but also exceed those mediated by standing and rank or by income and wealth. Education's connection with health cannot be reduced to its impact on access to advantageous and lucrative positions. Indeed, education's health benefits in America today mostly come from its other consequences. Like many sociologists, we were inclined to expect that education's benefits throughout life would be largely if not entirely explained by occupational and economic status. Instead, we found that education produces health in addition to prosperity, because both are desirable ends made achievable through learned effectiveness.

LEARNED EFFECTIVENESS PROVIDES CONTROL OVER LIFESTYLE AND CIRCUMSTANCES

In today's America, education improves health largely because it increases control over one's own life, thereby encouraging and enabling a healthy lifestyle. Education gives individuals the intellectual tools they need to gain control of their own lives. That in turn gives individuals the knowledge, motivation, and discipline to adopt healthy practices such as exercising, eating a balanced diet, restricting caloric intake, not smoking, drinking in moderation, not driving or operating machinery while intoxicated, wearing seatbelts, washing hands frequently, and brushing and flossing. The elements of a healthy lifestyle have nothing in common with each other except that they improve health. In seeking health, individuals weave these disparate habits and practices into a coherent lifestyle designed to preserve and promote health. That lifestyle defends successfully against a broad range of diseases and impairments while improving the sense of physical well-being.

Modern nations have instituted increasingly successful programs for public, occupational, and environmental heath that protect all members of their populations, but particularly the persons of lowest status who otherwise would be most at risk. Ironically, the success of those programs creates a residual and growing association between status and health mediated by behaviors with a strong and irreducible element of personal choice and self-determination. This does not imply wayward self-destructiveness on the part of the poorly educated. Rather, it implies that they lack the tools needed to gain effective control of their own lives. Given those tools they would seek health as willingly and effectively as others do.

Control of one's own life, and the healthy lifestyle it promotes, form the main bridge between education and health, but not the only one. Two aspects of poverty also connect low education to poor health. Having difficulty paying bills or buying necessities and living in a neighborhood rife with signs of social disorder and physical decay undermine health too. Apparently they erode health by posing direct threats that activate the neuroendocrine stress response. In the short run that response creates symptoms of psychophysiological distress such as faintness, shortness of breath, stomach aches, heart palpitations, cold sweats, weakness, tiredness, and sleep disturbances. In the long run, if frequent or intense, it reduces immune function, accelerates the accumulation of body fat and atherosclerotic plaque, and perhaps also raises blood pressure and insulin resistance. Those accumulations in turn increase the risk of disease and death.

Individuals who feel in control of their own lives feel less threatened when faced with economic hardship or neighborhood disorder, which helps protect them from the detrimental physiological effects. Unfortunately, repeated or prolonged exposure to threatening circumstances often undermines the sense of control needed to cope with them, because chronically exposed individuals infer that they are helplessness to avoid or escape those threats.

Education has two additional benefits that improve health in ways that cannot be explained entirely by a greater sense of control or a healthier lifestyle. Better-educated individuals are better at creating and maintaining supportive personal relationships. They also are better at finding work that allows productive creativity. The supportiveness of relationships and the creativity of work provide many practical benefits, but they also seem to meet inherent human needs. Precisely how they do so is not entirely clear. They may protect against the neuroendocrine stress response, by making situations seem less threatening. Apart from that, though, supportive relationships and creative work may promote other physiological responses that improve vitality in the short run and the balance of healthy and unhealthy accumulations in the long run. Whatever the physiological mechanisms, human health benefits from caring relationships and self-expressive work.

EDUCATION HAS PERVASIVE, CUMULATIVE, SELF-AMPLIFYING BENEFITS

Education's beneficial effects are pervasive, cumulative, and self-amplifying. An individual's learned abilities remain available at all times and in all situations. A person may lose a powerful, prestigious, and lucrative position. A person's wealth may vanish in a market reversal. The knowledge, skill, habits, and orientations used to acquire that position and wealth remain. The quality of universal constructive presence, combined with cumulative effect, creates much of education's powerful impact. Education's overall, long-term impact can be enormous even if any one part of it is small in itself and even if the entire gain in benefit is small over the short run. Education does have specific consequences with substantial measurable effects on health, even in the short run. Lower rates of smoking and higher levels of physical activity stand out. Nevertheless, the broad range of education's beneficial effects, combined with the accumulation of beneficial effects over time, gives education an overall impact that far exceeds any specific one.

Self-amplification leavens those varied and cumulative health effects. Some of education's beneficial outcomes have each other as consequences, as when perceived control over one's own life encourages a healthier lifestyle that improves physical function that bolsters the sense of control. Many of education's beneficial consequences act as backup systems for each other, as when education increases the probable level of household income but also reduces the correlation of low income with trouble paying bills and buying necessities. The growing store of economic, social, psychological, and physical resources helps individuals delay the onset of disease and disability, slow or reverse their progression once present, and manage a fuller and better life in their presence.

LACK OF EDUCATION TURNS LOW INCOME INTO PRIVATION

Education reduces the negative effect of low income on health. Differences in income have larger effects on health among persons with low education and smaller effects among those with high education. Oddly, that helps create what economists would call a diminishing marginal effect of greater income on health. The higher the level of income, the smaller the effect on health of any specific dollar amount added to it or subtracted from it. That happens partly because higher education reduces the effect of differences in income on health while it also increases the average level of household income. Individuals with low income often do not have the higher levels of education that would help them preserve health despite the lack of economic resources. That makes them depend more on income to achieve any given level of health, and that makes their health more sensitive to differences in income. On the other end, individuals with high incomes typically also have the higher educations that help them to be healthy anyway. That makes their health considerable less sensitive to differences in income.

The interaction between low education and low income suggests a third option for reducing the effects of economic inequality on health. The two standard options focus on the fact that additional income improves health most at the low end of the income scale. Both options try to move the population up out of the income range associated with substantial decrements in health. One strategy tries to increase income across the board. The other tries to redistribute income from the wealthiest portion of the population to the poorest. Both of those strategies treat the relationship of low income with poor health as fixed and try to move the bulk of the population up out of the range of privation. A third option focuses on reducing the unhealthy impact of low income, thereby lowering the boundary and intensity of destitution. The moderating effect of education suggests that the privation associated with low income can be reduced by raising the lowest levels of education in a society. Policies aimed at raising the average level of education in the 20 or 30 percent of households with the lowest income might have two beneficial effects on average levels of health: Higher minimum levels of education should help raise many of the lowest household incomes, reducing the fraction of incomes in the zone of privation. In addition, though, higher levels of education among those with low incomes might reduce the degree of economic hardship and poor health associated with having low income. In effect, raising the lowest levels of education might reduce the amount of income needed for a comfortable and healthy life at the same time that it raises the lowest incomes.

STRUCTURAL AMPLIFICATION CONCENTRATES PROBLEMS

Structural amplification concentrates poor health in a minority of persons with multiple related disadvantages. Structural amplification exists when the factors that make a situation less damaging also are less common among those in the situation. Effective traits and corrosive situations create structural amplification. In the first case, a stable personal characteristic that makes a situation less damaging also helps individuals to avoid or escape the situation. As a result, the effective trait is relatively uncommon among persons in the situation, amplifying the situation's harmful effect. By not developing effective traits, such as perceived control over one's own life, the poorly educated disproportionately fall into stressful situations such as unemployment, single parenthood, economic hardship, or neighborhood disorder, and also suffer worse consequences in those situations. In the second case, a difficult situation corrodes the traits or resources that protect individuals against its harmful effects. Resources as varied as accumulated wealth, perceived control, marital commitment, emotional support, and cardiorespiratory fitness that protect individuals in difficult situations also get diminished or strained in those situations.

Ineffective individuals often move through a cascading sequence of corrosive situations made worse at each step by the predisposing traits and conditions that led into those situations. Imagine a teenage girl from a low-income household who might not have started having sex except that her family only could afford to live in a neighborhood with a lot of unemployed young men hanging out on the streets. Sexual activity probably would not have led her to become an unwed mother if her family had been college educated, but none of them had finished high school. Being an unwed mother probably would not have caused her to drop out of school if she had been from a middle-class family, but she was not. She might have stayed in school had she been doing well, but no one ever taught her good study habits, and home was often too crowded or noisy to think. She might have stayed in school had there been a program for pregnant girls, but the district had no money for it and the principal did not like the idea of having pregnant girls around. Being a dropout might not have made her chronically unemployed had she not been an unwed mother, but jobs were hard to find near home and when she had one she missed work a lot. The chronic unemployment might have given her time for exercise, but she was home with her child a lot, mostly watching television for entertainment. She might have exercised more when her child was older, but by that time she had put on a lot of weight, and had aches and pains in her joints too. Besides, she did not know of any gyms or pools in her neighborhood, and the streets and parks did not look safe. She did not have any friends who exercised. Most of the women she knew got heavy, so she figured it was normal. The inactivity might not have caused her to have high blood pressure and too much cholesterol and glucose in her blood had she eaten more fruits, vegetables, and grains, less fat (particularly the saturated kind) and sugar, and fewer calories overall. The serum cholesterol might not have made her coronary artery occlude had she exercised more.

Without that occlusion she would not have shed a thromboembolism when she was served an eviction notice for nonpayment of rent, creating an infarct and fibrillation that she might have survived had she not been obese, diabetic, and out of condition.

Cascading structural amplification creates a grim reality, but one with cause for hope. In theory, the chain can be broken at any step. If the absence of a particular resource magnifies the harm at a specific step, then averting that step or providing that resource may break the chain. Realistically, the most effective strategies probably avoid the risky situations and supply the protective resources at many points. This underscores the importance of educational attainment as a critical point in the chain, and the importance of formal education as a system for developing abilities with pervasive, cumulative, and self-amplifying benefits.

RESOURCE ACCUMULATION AND SUBSTITUTION IMPLY STRUCTURAL AMPLIFICATION

Over time the continuous acquisition, application, and evaluation of knowledge helps the individual to avoid corrosive situations while accumulating many protective resources. Education develops the ability to find, evaluate, and use information. In the process it orients individuals toward thoughtful management of their own lives, encouraging the recognition and development of personal values and goals, the awareness that choices and actions have consequences, and the habit of considering likely consequences when making choices. Education teaches individuals first to edit their own behaviors and then to compose their own futures. Imagine an individual living within the means provided by interesting and productive work, living with a supportive and committed partner, eating right, exercising regularly, refraining from damaging habits, taking reasonable precautions, planning and saving for the future, and keeping a lively interest in all things that might nudge that future in a better direction. That individual avoids crises when possible, but handles them studiously when necessary, drawing on ample resources and creative habits.

Resource substitution provides alternative means toward desired ends, making their achievement depend less on any one resource. To a large extent, resource substitution and structural amplification are positive and negative faces of the same phenomenon. Individuals with many resources at their disposal suffer less from a loss or deficit than those with few resources would suffer from the same loss or deficit. Education helps individuals acquire more resources quantitatively as in higher wages and incomes, qualitatively as in more stable and fulfilling jobs and marriages, and numerically as in the variety of economic, social, and physiological advantages. The health of well-educated individuals depends less on the quantity, quality, or presence of any one resource, because the store of others compensates. Conversely, the health of poorly educated individuals depends more on the quantity, quality, or presence of any one resource, because little else compensates.

NO ONE LOSES WHEN SOMEONE GAINS CONTROL

Education helps individuals advance their own health and well-being without harming anyone else's. Each person who adopts healthy ways makes it easier for others to do the same. Individuals who gain control of their own lives relieve themselves and others of the undesirable consequences produced by an ill-managed life. The intellectual capacities developed through education do give individuals a greater ability to exploit others who lack the same capacities, but they also lead most individuals to realize that liberation is more rewarding than domination.

Some health scientists argue that low social status in and of itself degrades health and increases the risk of death. If true, then individuals higher in the hierarchy enjoy better health at the expense of others lower down, which could explain the correlation between status and health. In support of this view, the scientists point to two sets of facts. First, the subordinate animals in ape, monkey, and rodent social hierarchies usually show many signs of chronic neuroendocrine stress while the dominant ones show few signs of it. If other social animals with neuroendocrine systems similar to ours suffer physiologically from subordination then it is a reasonable guess that humans might too. Second, the mortality rates of men in the British civil service increase substantially with each step down the hierarchy, even though none of them on any level are deprived or destitute. That is true even within categories of men who have similar profiles on some major risk factors such as smoking, cholesterol levels, and blood pressure. Perhaps the stress of subordination damages the health of those lower down to the benefit of those higher up among humans as among other social animals. Perhaps, but apes, monkeys, and rodents achieve dominance through violence and threats of violence—something guaranteed to generate a neuroendocrine response but as rare among British civil servants as poverty and material privation. Perhaps, instead, hierarchical status in the British civil service comes from preparation and performance in school and on the job, which develop the ability to achieve health as well as status.

Formal education is not a contest establishing who gets to bite whom, who gets to eat first, and who gets to have sex. It is a system for developing each individual's capacity for self-determination and productive creativity. That we have such a system both reflects and enlarges the great difference between us and other species. We can and regularly do produce better outcomes for everyone by helping individuals gain control of their own lives. Every individual, over the course of a lifetime, either produces more of value than they consume or consumes more than they produce. By increasing individual productivity, education makes net producers of those who otherwise would become net consumers, not by working them hard while starving them out, but by helping them to do things that others reward. Everyone gains.

Money for programs to increase levels of education, particularly at the low end, must come from somewhere. It would be nice to think that we Americans might reallocate some of the money from our spending on medical care. Each year we spend about 13.5 percent of our gross domestic product (GDP) on health, most of which goes to medical care. About 95 percent of that goes to medical services, supplies, insurance, facilities, and administration, leaving about 2 percent for research and 3 percent for non-medical public health programs. It totals about $1,150 billion a year, or $4,170 per man, woman, and child living in the country. For that kind of money we could buy around 7.7 million new $150,000 homes each year, or 38.5 million new $30,000 cars. More to the point, we could build 38,500 new schools costing $30 million each, or hire 23 million additional teachers on $50,000 salaries, or give every one of our 68.6 million students in kindergarten through graduate school an extra $16,760 per year to spend on tuition, books, computers, and so on. Of course, that would leave nothing for medical care. If we spent the same fraction of our GDP on medical care as the Canadians do, that would save us roughly a fourth of the total: enough for 9,625 new schools each year or 5.75 million additional teachers or $4,400 per current student. If we spent the same fraction as the Japanese it would save us double that amount. A reduction of medical expenditures in that range probably would not hurt the health of Americans and might actually improve it. The U.S. life expectancy at birth is about two years less than in Canada and three or four years less than in Japan.

It would be nice to think that we Americans might reallocate those expenditures, but it does not seem likely any time soon. The medical industries and professions resist, and so do voters and workers. So far the efforts to control medical expenditures fail to stop their growth, let alone reverse them. Legislation opposes rational, outcomes-based allocation of medical dollars rather than promoting it. On the whole, we Americans demand as much medical care as we can get, regardless of the costs and benefits. So, where can the money come from to increase the lowest levels of education in America? Who will pay?

Consider this. Persons with earnings, those who work or invest, produce the wealth that supports everyone. If we workers and investors can help someone become more effective and productive then we may reasonably expect to benefit in the future. When someone becomes more productive everyone can benefit because there is more to go around. Workers can expect higher wages and lower taxes. Investors can expect higher returns. The money we spend on helping individuals become more effective will profit us in the future and, just as true, the money we do not spend will cost us. Increasing future levels of education acts as a form of saving for retirement, because the prosperity of retirees depends on the productivity of workers. Unlike medical expenditures, greater educational expenditures can improve average levels of health, and decrease disparities in health, while paying for themselves over time.

EDUCATION: THE ANSWER

So, we end with our answer to one of the most important scientific questions of our day. Why does health increase with social status? Not because of the money, much less the authority, but because learned effectiveness creates the ability to achieve something everyone wants: health. Education develops the skills, habits, and attitudes that help individuals take control of their own lives. Whenever someone does, everyone gains.

| 9 |

Data and Measures

ASOC: U.S. NATIONWIDE SURVEY

Baseline Sample

Our analyses use the 1995 survey of Aging, Status, and the Sense of Control (ASOC). It is a national telephone probability sample of U.S. households. The National Institute on Aging supported the data collection. Sampling, pretesting, and interviewing were conducted by the Survey Research Laboratory of the University of Illinois. Respondents were selected using a prescreened random-digit dialing method that decreases the probability of contacting a business or nonworking number and decreases standard errors compared to the standard Mitofsky-Waksberg method, while producing a sample with the same demographic profile (Lund and Wright 1994; Waksberg 1978). The ASOC survey has two subsamples, designed to produce an 80 percent oversample of persons aged sixty or older. The survey was limited to English-speaking adults. The main sample draws from all households; the oversample draws only from households with one or more seniors. In the main sample the adult (eighteen or older) with the most recent birthday was selected as respondent. In the oversample the senior (sixty or older) with the most recent birthday was selected. Up to ten call-backs were made to select and contact a respondent, and up to ten to complete the interview once contact was made. Interviews were completed with 71.6 percent of contacted and eligible persons: 73.0 percent for the main sample and 67.3 percent for the oversample. The final sample has 2,592 respondents ranging in age from 18 to 95.

The following statistics compare the demographic characteristics of the ASOC sample to those for the U.S. population as a whole (U.S. Bureau of the Census 1995). These statistics are weighted to compensate for the oversample of seniors. For ASOC and the U.S., respectively, the percentage female is 56.2 and 51.2, the percentage white is 85.1 and 82.9, the percentage married (excluding cohabitors and the separated) is 55.7 and 55, and the mean household size is 2.67 and 2.59. For persons age 25 or older the percentage with a high school degree is 85.1 and 80.9, and the percentage with a college degree is 25.6 and 22.2. The mean household income is $43,949 and $41,285. The mean household income in thousands by age group in ASOC and the U.S., respectively, is $40.5 and $37.5 for 25- to 34-year-olds, $47.1 and $49.5 for 35- to 44-year-olds, $53.8 and $57.8 for 45- to 54-year-olds, $51.8 and $44.8 for 55- to 64-year-olds, and $32.4 and $26.0 for those 65 or older.

Follow-Up Sample

Some of our analyses look at the changes in health over time. The ASOC survey reinterviewed 1,344 members of the initial sample (or 53.6 percent) in 1998, approximately three years after the baseline 1995 interviews. Follow-up surveys inevitably lose cases for a variety of reasons. The *random* component of attrition does not bias estimates of regression coefficients. It does reduce the power of significance tests somewhat because of the smaller sample size. Attrition also can affect sample representativeness. The *nonrandom* component of attrition can bias regression estimates. That raises the issue of whether self-selection makes the sample differ from the population in ways that may produce biased answers to the study's questions. Regressions that adjust for the determinants of attrition produce unbiased estimates (Winship and Radbill 1994). However, concern arises when unobserved residual changes in the outcome under study, like health, may covary with the tendency to remain in the sample. Our longitudinal models adjust for the hazard of attrition, so that readers may be reassured that outcome-dependant attrition does not bias estimated effects of education on health.

Health Measures

Self-reported health is the respondent's subjective assessment of his or her general health in response to the question, "Would you say your health is very poor, poor, satisfactory, good, or very good?" It combines the subjective experience of acute and chronic, fatal and nonfatal diseases, and general feelings of well-being, such as feeling rundown and tired or having backaches and headaches. Thus, it measures health as defined by the World Health Organization—as a state of well-being and not simply as the absence of disease. Self-reported health correlates highly with more "objective" measures such as physician's assessments and with measures of morbidity, like having heart disease or diabetes, and it predicts mortality net of chronic and acute disease, of physician assessment made by clinical exam, of physical disability, and of health behaviors (Davies and Ware

1981; Idler and Benyamini 1997; Liang 1986). In fact, self-assessed health is a *stronger* predictor of mortality than is physician-assessed health (Mossey and Shapiro 1982).

Physical functioning is assessed by musculoskeletal and sensory impairment. The first describes difficulty with physical mobility and functioning in daily activities. Respondents were asked "How much difficulty do you have (1) climbing stairs; (2) kneeling or stooping; (3) lifting or carrying objects less than 10 pounds, like a bag of groceries; (4) preparing meals, cleaning house or doing other household work; (5) shopping or getting around town?" The second form of physical impairment is sensory impairment, which assesses difficulty seeing and hearing. Respondents were asked "How much difficulty do you have (1) seeing, even with glasses; (2) hearing?" (For those with a hearing aid, "Hearing, even with your hearing aid?"). Responses were "a great deal of difficulty," "some difficulty," and "no difficulty." Indexes of physical functioning average the responses to the seven questions.

Serious chronic conditions are coded in response to the questions: "Have you ever been diagnosed or told by a doctor that you have (1) heart disease, (2) high blood pressure, (3) lung disease like emphysema or lung cancer, (4) breast cancer, (5) any other type of cancer, (6) diabetes, (7) arthritis or rheumatism, (8) osteoporosis (brittle bones)?"

Subjective life expectancy is measured in response to the question, "To what age do you expect to live?"

Vigor is assessed by asked respondents, "On how many days in the past week (from 0 to 7) did you (1) feel physically fit, and (2) have lots of energy?"

Enthusiasm is measured by asking respondents, "On how many days in the past week, did you (1) enjoy life, (2) feel happy, (3) feel hopeful about the future?" These questions are from the Center for Epidemiological Studies' Depression scale.

Discomfort is measured by three physical symptoms also recorded in days per week: "On how many days did you have (1) backaches, (2) headaches, (3) any other sorts of aches and pains?"

Malaise is assessed by asking respondents, "On how many days in the past week (from 0 to 7) have you (1) had trouble getting to sleep or staying asleep; (2) felt that everything was an effort; (3) felt you just couldn't get going; (4) had trouble keeping your mind on what you were doing." These questions are from the Center for Epidemiological Studies' Depression scale.

Depression is measured as the frequency of unpleasant symptoms of depressed mood, using three items from the Center for Epidemiological Studies' Depression Scale. Respondents were asked to indicate, "On how many of the past seven days have you (5) felt sad; (6) felt lonely; and (7) felt you couldn't shake the blues?" Responses are coded in days per week from 0 to 7.

Anxiety is measured as the number of days in the past week the respondent (1) felt anxious, (2) felt tense, or (3) felt restless.

Sense of Personal Control Index

The sense of control is the belief that you can and do master, control, and shape your own life. It is measured by a 2 × 2 index that balances statements claiming or denying control over good or bad outcomes (Mirowsky and Ross 1991). Claiming control over good outcomes: (1) "I am responsible for my own successes, (2) I can do just about anything I really set my mind to." Claiming control over bad outcomes: (3) "My misfortunes are the result of mistakes I have made, (4) I am responsible for my failures." Denying control over good outcomes: (5) "The really good things that happen to me are mostly luck, (6) There's no sense planning a lot—if something good is going to happen it will." Denying control over bad outcomes: (7) "Most of my problems are due to bad breaks, (8) I have little control over the bad things that happen to me." Responses to control questions (1 through 4) are coded –2, strongly disagree; –1, disagree; 0, neutral; 1, agree; 2, strongly agree. Responses to lack of control questions (5 through 8) are coded 2, strongly disagree; 1, disagree; 0, neutral; –1, agree; –2, strongly agree. A mean score sense-of-control index was created from these questions, coded from low sense of control (–2) to high sense of control (2) (alpha reliability = .68). This measure is conceptually similar to the personal control component of Rotter's (1966) locus-of-control scale (modified for community surveys by using Likert scale responses rather than forced-choice responses) and to Pearlin et al.'s (1981) mastery scale. The major difference is that the scale balances statements claiming control against those denying control, and statements about good outcomes against those about bad outcomes.

Healthy Lifestyle Indicators

Walking is measured as the number of days walked per week. Respondents were asked, "How often do you take a walk?" Open-ended responses are coded into number of days walked per week.

Strenuous exercise is measured by asking respondents, "How often do you do strenuous exercise such as running, basketball, aerobics, tennis, swimming, biking, and so on?" Open-ended responses are coded into number of days of exercise per week.

Smoking compares persons who report that they never smoked (never smoked), with those who report that they have smoked but who do not currently smoke (quit smoking), and those who report that they currently smoke seven or more cigarettes a week (current smoker).

Alcohol consumption is measured first by asking respondents about frequency of drinking: "On average, how often do you drink any alcoholic beverages such as beer, wine, or liquor?" Frequency is coded in number of days per week based on open-ended responses. Quantity is measured with response to the question, "On the days that you drink, on average, how many alcoholic drinks do you have?" Quantity is coded as the number of drinks per day (from a low of 0 for nondrinkers to a high of 25 drinks per day). Quantity × frequency scores are computed by multiplying the number of days per week a person drinks times the number of drinks reported for the average day. Scores are categorized because the effect of drinking on health is likely nonlinear, with both abstainers and heavy drinkers reporting worse health than moderate drinkers. Abstainers report that they never drink or drink less than one drink a year, moderate drinkers drink up to 4 drinks a day, and heavy drinkers drink more than 4 drinks a day.

Degree of overweight is measured by relative body weight (weight/height^2). Of the various weight-relative-to-height measures, weight/height^2 is the most adequate because it is least correlated with height and highly correlated with skinfold measures indicating body fat (Roche, Siervogel, Chumlea, and Webb 1981). Relative weight is based on self-reported weight and height. Self-reported weights and scale weights are highly correlated; the small error that does exist is the tendency for people who weigh a lot to somewhat underestimate their weights. Almost all excess weight among Americans is due to fat, not muscle. We examine relative weight as a continuous variable, coded from low to high levels of relative weight; and we examine obesity define as a relative body weight score of 27 or greater.

Supportive Relationships

Marriage contrasts people who are currently married or living together as married with those who are not married (single, separated, divorced, or widowed).

Social support is measured by responses to four questions. The first two assess emotional support, and the second two, instrumental support. Respondents were asked "How much do you agree with the statements: 'I have someone I can turn to for support and understanding when things get rough,' 'I have someone I can really talk to,' 'I have someone who would help me out with things, like give me a ride, watch the kids or house, or fix something,' and 'I have someone who would take care of me if I were sick'" (coded 1, strongly disagree; 2, disagree; 3, agree; 4, strongly agree). The social support index is the mean response.

Measures of Economic Well-Being

Household income is assessed using a set of questions that maximize response while conserving precision (Ross and Reynolds 1996). The interviewer first asks for the exact income for all members of the household from all sources. If the respondent does not report an exact household income then the interviewer probes for approximate income ("Can you tell me, is it more than X or less than X?") Annual household income equals the exact dollar amount if reported, and the categorical approximation otherwise. Reported household incomes range from $600 to $800,000. We usually show income in thousands of dollars.

Economic hardship is assessed by asking respondents three questions: "During the past 12 months, how often did it happen that (1) you had trouble paying the bills; (2) you did not have enough money to buy food, clothes, or other things your household needed; (3) you did not have enough money to pay for medical care?" Responses are "never," "not very often," "fairly often," and "very often." The responses can be averaged to produce an index of economic hardship, or they can be examined separately. This is a modification of Pearlin's economic strain index (Pearlin et al. 1981).

Aspects of Employment and Work

Employment status compares people who are employed full-time and those employed part-time, with those who are not employed for pay.

Occupations are scored according to the *Dictionary of Occupational Titles*, which assess conditions such as the degree to which the occupation involves work that is outdoors, wet, cold, noisy, and so on. These are linked to census codes of the person's occupation, like secretary, but do not reflect the person's actual work on their own job.

Work includes any productive activity, either paid or unpaid. We asked employed and nonemployed persons to describe the work, tasks, or activities they mostly do during the day. Respondents were then asked about the subjective rewards of their primary daily work. Paid work is considered the primary daily work of people working for pay twenty hours per week or more. Unpaid work includes reported activities such as housework, childcare, care for an ill or elderly family member, volunteer work, and gardening and home repair.

Creative work is an index of four standardized items indicating the degree of routinization of daily tasks, problem-solving, enjoyment, and opportunities for learning on the job, as reported by respondents. *Task variety* assesses whether the work or daily tasks involve (1) "doing the same thing in the same way repeatedly," (2) "the same thing in a number of different ways," or (3) "a number of different kinds of things." Work that involves *solving problems* is measured by the amount of agreement with the statement, "In my work, I have to figure out how to solve problems." Responses were coded 1, strongly disagree; 2, disagree; 3, agree; and 4, strongly agree. Work that provides opportunities for *learning* is measured by the amount of agreement with the statement, "My work gives me a chance to develop and to learn new things." Responses were coded 1, strongly disagree; 2, disagree; 3, agree; and 4, strongly agree. Task variety, problem-solving, and learning load .623, .815, and .769, respectively on a single factor, distinct from work autonomy, described next.

Autonomous work is an index of two standardized items indicating decision-making autonomy and freedom from supervision on the job. *Decision-making autonomy* is measured with responses to two questions. "Some people have supervisors or someone else who tells them what to do, while others make their own decisions. Who usually decides *how* you will do your work? Who usually decides *what* you will do in your work?" Responses to the two questions were coded 1, someone else decides; 2, you and someone else decide about equally; or 3, you decide; and summed. *Freedom from supervision* is measured with response to the question, "How free do you feel to disagree with the person who supervises your work?" Responses are coded 1, not at all free; 2, somewhat free; 3, largely but not completely free; 4, completely free; 5, no one supervises my work. Decision-making autonomy and freedom from supervision load .745 and .849, respectively on a single factor, distinct from creative work.

Status of Origin

Parents' education is measured as the number of years of formal schooling completed by one's mother and father. It is the average of one's mother's and father's years of schooling if both are reported. When one parent's education is unknown, we use the other's. Knowledge of parents' education is adjusted whenever parents' education is included. Unknown parental education is a variable coded 1, if the respondent did not know either his/her mother's or father's education; 0.5, if the respondent knew one but not the other; and 0, if the respondent knew both.

CCH: ILLINOIS STATEWIDE SURVEY

The Sample

Our analysis of neighborhood effects on health uses another data set called Community, Crime, and Health (CCH), which is a probability sample of Illinois households with linked census tract information, based on addresses. Census tracts are the best approximation of neighborhoods. Where tract information was missing, we used zip codes. Respondents were interviewed by telephone and were selected into the sample by random-digit dialing. There are 2,470 respondents, age 18 and older in wave 1, collected in 1995.

Distinctive Measures

Neighborhood disadvantage is an index of the percentage of tract households with children headed by women and the percentage of tract households below the federal poverty line.

Perceived neighborhood disorder refers to conditions and activities, both major and minor, criminal and noncriminal, that residents perceive to be signs of the breakdown of social order. The index [the Ross-Mirowsky Perceived Neighborhood Disorder Scale (1999)] measures physical signs of disorder such as graffiti, vandalism, noise, and abandoned buildings, and social signs such as crime, people hanging out on the street, people drinking, or using drugs.

Physical Disorder and Order
  (1) There is a lot of graffiti in my neighborhood.
  (2) My neighborhood is noisy.
  (3) Vandalism is common in my neighborhood.
  (4) There are lot of abandoned buildings in my neighborhood.
  (5) My neighborhood is clean.
  (6) People in my neighborhood take good care of their houses and apartments.

Social Disorder and Order
  (7) There are too many people hanging around on the streets near my home.
  (8) There is a lot of crime in my neighborhood.
  (9) There is too much drug use in my neighborhood.
  (10) There is too much alcohol use in my neighborhood.
  (11) I'm always having trouble with my neighbors.
  (12) My neighborhood is safe.
  (13) In my neighborhood, people watch out for each other.

To create a mean score disorder scale, disorder items scored 1, strongly disagree; 2, disagree; 3, agree; 4, strongly agree, and order items scored 1, strongly agree; 2, agree; 3, disagree; 4, strongly disagree (alpha reliability = .92, mean = 1.81).

References

Abbott, Robert D., Yin Yin, Dwayne M. Reed, and Katsuhilo Yano. 1986. "Risk of Stroke in Male Cigarette Smokers." *New England Journal of Medicine* 315: 717–20.

Aday, L. A., R. Andersen, and G. V. Fleming. 1980. *Health Care in the U.S. Equitable for Whom?* Beverly Hills, CA: Sage.

Ainsworth-Darnell, James W. and Douglas B. Downey. 1998. "Assessing the Oppositional Culture Explanation for Racial/Ethnic Differences in School Performance." *American Sociological Review* 63:536–53.

Alexander, Karl L., Martha Cook, and Edward L. McDill. 1978. "Curriculum Tracking and Educational Stratification: Some Further Evidence." *American Sociological Review* 43:47–66.

Alexander, Karl L., Gary Natriello, and Aaron M. Palas. 1985. "For Whom the School Bell Tolls: The Impact of Dropping Out on Cognitive Performance." *American Sociological Review* 50:409–20.

American Cancer Society. 1997. "Breast Cancer Facts and Figures." Retrieved November 1, 2000 (http://www.cancer.org.).

American Heritage Dictionary of the English Language. 1992. 3d ed. Boston, MA: Houghton-Mifflin. Retrieved November 1, 2000 (http://www.ohiolink.edu. db/ahd.html).

Andrisani, Paul J. 1978. "Internal-External Attitudes, Personal Initiative, and Labor Market Experience." Pp. 101–33 in *Work Attitudes and Labor Market Experience: Evidence from the National Longitudinal Surveys,* edited by Paul J. Andrisani. New York: Praeger.

Aneshensel, Carol S., Ralph R. Frerichs, and George J. Huba. 1984. "Depression and Physical Illness: A Multiwave, Nonrecursive Causal Model." *Journal of Health and Social Behavior* 25:350–71.

Angell, M. 1993. "Privilege and Health: What Is The Connection?" *New England Journal of Medicine* 329:126–27.

Anson, Ofra. 1989. "Marital Status and Women's Health Revisited: The Importance of a Proximate Adult." *Journal of Marriage and the Family* 51:185–94.

Aronowitz, Stanley and Henry Giroux. 1993. *Education Still under Siege,* 2d ed. Westport, CT: Bergine and Garvey.

Aschaffenburg, Karen and Ineke Maas. 1997. "Cultural and Educational Careers: The Dynamics of Social Reproduction." *American Sociological Review* 62:573–87.

Atkinson, Thomas, Ramsay Liem, and Joan H. Liem. 1986. "The Social Costs of Unemployment: Implications for Social Support." *Journal of Health and Social Behavior* 27:317–31.

Auster, R., I. Leveson, and D. Sarachek. 1969. "The Production of Health: An Exploratory Study." *Journal of Human Resources* 4:411–36.

Bailar, John C. 1976. "Mammography: A Contrary View." *Annals of Internal Medicine* 84:77-84.

Bailar, John C. and Elaine M. Smith. 1986. "Progress Against Cancer?" *New England Journal of Medicine* (May 8):1226–32.

Bandura, Albert. 1986. *Social Foundations of Thought and Action.* Englewood Cliffs, NJ: Prentice-Hall.

Basavaraj, Sudha. 1993. "Smoking and Loss of Longevity in Canada." *Canadian Journal of Public Health—Revue Canadienne de Sante* 84:341–45.

Becker, Gary S. 1962. "Investment in Human Capital: A Theoretical Analysis." *Journal of Political Economy* 70:9–49.

Becker, Gary S. 1964. *Human Capital.* New York: Columbia University Press.

Beckett, Megan. 2000. "Converging Health Inequalities in Later Life—An Artifact of Mortality Selection?" *Journal of Health and Social Behavior* 41:106–19.

Bentler, P. M. 1995. *EQS Structural Equations Program Manual.* Encino, CA: Multivariate Software, Inc.

Berg, Ivar E. 1970. *Education and Jobs: The Great Training Robbery.* New York: Praeger.

Berk, Marc L. and Amy K. Taylor. 1984. "Women and Divorce: Health Insurance Coverage, Utilization, and Health Care Expenditures." *American Journal of Public Health* 74:1276–78.

Berkman, Lisa F. and Lester Breslow. 1983. *Health and Way of Living: The Alameda County Study.* New York: Oxford University Press.

Berkman, Lisa F., Thomas Glass, Ian Brisette, and Teresa E. Seeman. 2000. "From Social Integration to Health: Durkheim in the New Millennium." *Social Science and Medicine* 51:843–57.

Berkman, Lisa F. and S. Leonard Syme. 1979. "Social Networks, Host Resistance, and Mortality: A Nine-year Follow-up Study of Alameda County Residents." *American Journal of Epidemiology* 109:186–204.

Berlin, Jesse A. and Graham A. Colditz. 1990. "A Meta-Analysis of Physical Activity in the Prevention of Coronary Heart Disease." *American Journal of Epidemiology* 132:612–28.

Billings, J. and N. Teicholz. 1990. "Uninsured Patients in District of Columbia Hospitals." *Health Affairs* 9:158–65.

Bird, Chloe E. and Catherine E. Ross. 1993. "Houseworkers and Paid Workers: Qualities of the Work and Effects on Personal Control." *Journal of Marriage and the Family* 55:913–25.

Blau, Peter M. and Otis Dudley Duncan. 1967. *The American Occupational Structure.* New York: Wiley.

Blaxter, Mildred. 1987. "Evidence on Inequality in Health from a National Survey." *Lancet* 2:30–33.

Bloom, David E. and James Trussel. 1984. "What Are the Determinants of Delayed Childbearing and Permanent Childlessness in the United States?" *Demography* 21:591–611.

Bourdieu, Pierre. 1977. "Cultural Reproduction and Social Reproduction." Pp. 487–511 in *Power and Ideology in Education,* edited by J. Karabel and A. H. Halsey. New York: Oxford University Press.

Bowles, Samuel and Herbert Gintis. 1976. *Schooling in Capitalist America*. New York: Basic Books.

Bowling, Ann. 1987. "Mortality after Bereavement: A Review of the Literature on Survival Periods and Factors Affecting Survival." *Social Science and Medicine* 24:117–24.

Brown, C. 1980. "Equalizing Differences in the Labor Market." *Quarterly Journal of Economics* 94:113–31.

Brown, Julia S. and Barbara Giesy. 1986. "Marital Status of Persons with Spinal Cord Injury." *Social Science and Medicine* 23:313–22.

Bruce, Martha Livingston and Philip J. Leaf. 1989. "Psychiatric Disorders and 15-Month Mortality in a Community Sample of Older Adults." *American Journal of Public Health* 79:727–30.

Brunner, Eric. 1997. "Stress and the Biology of Inequality." *British Medical Journal* 314:1472–75.

Burris, Val. 1983. "The Social and Political Consequences of Overeducation." *American Sociological Review* 48:454–67.

Burstin, H. R., S. R. Lipsitz, and T. A. Brennan. 1992. "Socioeconomic Status and Risk for Substandard Medical Care." *JAMA* 268:2383–87.

Cairns, John. 1985. "The Treatment of Diseases and the War against Cancer." *Scientific American* 253:51–59.

Campbell, J. R., C. M. Hombo, and J. Mazzeo. 2000. *NAEP 1999 Trends in Academic Progress: Three Decades of Student Performance*, NCES 2000-469. Washington, DC: US Department of Education.

Canadian Task Force on the Periodic Health Examination. 1979. "The Periodic Health Examination." *Canadian Medical Association Journal* 138:617–26.

Canadian Task Force on the Periodic Health Examination. 1988. "The Periodic Health Examination." *Canadian Medical Association Journal* 121:1194–1254.

Carstairs, Vera and Russell Morris. 1989. "Deprivation and Mortality: An Alternative to Social Class?" *Community Medicine* 11:210–19.

Caspersen, Carl J., Bennie P. Bloemberg, Wim H. Saris, Robert K. Merritt, and Daan Kromhout. 1992. "The Prevalence of Selected Physical Activities and their Relation with Coronary Heart Disease Risk Factors in Elderly Men: The Zutphen Study, 1985." *American Journal of Epidemiology* 133:1078–92.

Cherlin, Andrew J. 1981. *Marriage, Divorce, Remarriage*. Cambridge, MA: Harvard University Press.

Cohen, Francis, Margaret E. Kemeny, Kathleen A. Kearney, Leonard S. Zegans, John M. Neuhaus, and Marcus A. Conant. 1999. "Persistent Stress as a Predictor of Genital Herpes Recurrence." *Archives of Internal Medicine* 159: 2430–36.

Cohen, S. and T. B. Herbert. 1996. "Health Psychology: Psychological Factors and Physical Disease from the Perspective of Human Psychoneuroimmunology." *Annual Review of Psychology* 47:113–42.

Cohen, S., G. A. Kaplan, and J. T. Salonen. 1999. "The Role of Psychological Characteristics in the Relation between Socioeconomic Status and Perceived Health." *Journal of Applied Social Psychology* 29:445–68.

Cohen, S., D. A. Tyrrell, and A. P. Smith. 1991. "Psychological Stress and Susceptibility to the Common Cold." *New England Journal of Medicine* 325:606–12.

Cohen, Sheldon and S. Leonard Syme. 1985. *Social Support and Health.* Orlando, FL: Academic.

Coleman, James S., Ernest Q. Campbell, Carol J. Hobson, James McPartland, Alexander M. Mood, Frederic D. Weinfeld, and Robert L. York. 1966. *U.S. Department of Health, Education and Welfare Office of Education. Equality of Educational Opportunity.* Washington, DC: U.S. Government Printing Office.

Collins, Randal. 1979. *The Credential Society: An Historical Sociology of Education and Stratification.* New York: Academic.

Crawford, Robert. 1986. "Individual Responsibility and Health Politics." Pp. 369–77 in *The Sociology of Health and Illness,* 2d ed., edited by P. Conrad and R. Kern. New York: St. Martin's.

Crimmins, Eileen M. and Yasuhiko Saito. 2001. "Trends in Healthy Life Expectancy in the United States, 1970–1990: Gender, Racial, and Educational Differences." *Social Science and Medicine* 52:1629–41.

Crystal, Stephen and Denis Shea. 1990. "Cumulative Advantage, Cumulative Disadvantage, and Inequality among Elderly People." *Gerontologist* 10:437–43.

Crystal, Stephen, Denis Shea, and S. Krishnaswami. 1992. "Educational Attainment, Occupational History, and Stratification as Determinants of Later-Life Economic Outcomes." *Journals of Gerontology Social Sciences* 47:S213–21.

Crystal, Stephen and K. Waehrer. 1996. "Later-Life Economic Inequality in Longitudinal Perspective." *Journals of Gerontology Social Sciences* 51:S307–18.

Dannefer, Dale. 1987. "Aging as Intracohort Differentiation: Accentuation, the Matthew Effect, and the Life Course." *Sociological Forum* 2:211–37.

Darrow, Sherri L., Marcia Russell, M. Lynne Copper, Pamela Mudar, and Michael R. Frone. 1992. "Sociodemographic Correlates of Alcohol Consumption Among African-American and White Women." *Women and Health* 18:35–51.

Davern, Michael E. and Patricia J. Fisher. 2001. "Household Net Worth and Asset Ownership: 1995." *U.S. Census Bureau Current Population Reports,* Household Economic Studies, Series P70–71. Washington, DC: U.S. Government Printing Office.

Davies, Allyson Ross, and John E. Ware. 1981. *Measuring Health Perceptions in the Health Insurance Experiment.* R-2711-HHS. Santa Monica, CA: Rand Corporation.

Davies, Scott. 1995. "Leaps of Faith: Shifting Currents in Critical Sociology of Education." *American Journal of Sociology* 100:1448–78.

Davis, Karen and Diane Rowland. 1983. "Uninsured and Underserved: Inequities in Health Care in the United States." *Milbank Memorial Fund Quarterly/Health and Society* 61:149–76.

Deyo, R. A. 1998. "Using Outcomes to Improve Quality of Research and Quality of Care." *Journal of the American Board of Family Practice* 11:465–73.

Deyo, R. A., D. Cherkin, D. Conrad, and E. Volinn. 1991. "Cost, Controversy, Crisis: Low Back Pain and the Health of the Public." *Annual Review of Public Health* 12:141–56.

Dickens, William T., and James R. Flynn. 2001. "Heritability Estimates Versus Large Environmental Effects: The IQ Paradox Resolved." *Psychological Review* 108:346–69.

Diderichsen, F. 1990. "Health and Social Inequalities in Sweden." *Social Science and Medicine* 31:359–67.

DiMaggio, Paul. 1982. "Cultural Capital and School Success: The Impact of Status Culture Participation on the Grades of United States High School Students." *American Sociological Review* 47:189–201.

Doornbos, G. and D. Kronhout. 1990. "Educational Level and Mortality in a 32-year Follow-Up Study of 18-Year-Old Men in the Netherlands." *International Journal of Epidemiology* 19:374-79.

Downey, Geraldine and Phyllis Moen. 1987. "Personal Efficacy, Income and Family Transitions: A Longitudinal Study of Women Heading Households." *Journal of Health and Social Behavior* 28:320–33.

Duncan, John J., Neil F. Gordon, and Chris B. Scott. 1991. "Women Walking for Health and Fitness." *Journal of the American Medical Association* 266:3295–99.

Elder, Glen H. and Jeffrey K. Liker. 1982. "Hard Times in Women's Lives: Historical Influences Across Forty Years." *American Journal of Sociology* 88:241–69.

Elo, Irma T. and Samuel H. Preston. 1996. "Educational Differentials in Mortality: United States, 1979–85." *Social Science and Medicine* 42:47–57.

Epstein, A. M. 1996. "Use of Diagnostic Tests and Therapeutic Procedures in a Changing Health Care Environment." *Journal of the American Medical Association* 275:1197–98.

Evans, Robert G. 1994. "Introduction." Pp. 3–16 in *Why Are Some People Healthy and Others Not?* edited by Robert G. Evans, Morris L. Barer, and Theodore R. Marmor. Hawthorne, NY: Aldine de Gruyter.

Evans, Robert G., Matthew Hodge, and I. Barry Pless. 1994. "If Not Genetics, Then What? Biological Pathways and Population Health." Pp. 161–88 in *Why Are Some People Healthy and Others Not?* edited by Robert G. Evans, Morris L. Barer, and Theodore R. Marmor. Hawthorne, NY: Aldine de Gruyter.

Evans, Robert G. and Gregory L. Stoddart. 1994. "Producing Health, Consuming Health Care." Pp. 27–64 in *Why Are Some People Healthy and Others Not?* edited by Robert G. Evans, Morris L. Barer, and Theodore R. Marmor. Hawthorne, NY: Aldine de Gruyter.

Farkas, George. 1996. *Human Capital or Cultural Capital? Ethnicity and Poverty Groups in an Urban School District.* Hawthorne, NY: Aldine de Gruyter.

Farkas, George, Paula England, Kevin Vicknair, and Barbara S. Kilbourne. 1997. "Cognitive Skill, Skill Demands of Jobs, and Earnings among Young European American, African American, and Mexican American Workers." *Social Forces* 75:913–38.

Feinleib, Manning. 1985. "Epidemiology of Obesity in Relation to Health Hazards." *Annals Of Internal Medicine* 103:1019–24.

Feldman, Jacob J., Diane M. Makuc, Joel C. Kleinman, and Joan Cornoni-Huntley. 1989. "National Trends in Educational Differentials in Mortality." *American Journal of Epidemiology* 129:919–33.

Feuer, E. J. and L. M. Wun. 1992. "How Much of the Recent Risk in Breast Cancer Incidence Can Be Explained by Increases in Mammography Utilization?" *American Journal of Epidemiology* 136:1423–36.

Fischer, Claude S., Michael Hout, Martin Sanchz Jankowski, Samuel R. Lucas, Ann

Swidler, and Kim Voss. 1996. *Inequality by Design: Cracking the Bell Curve Myth.* Princeton, NJ: Princeton University Press.

Ford, Earl S., Robert K. Merritt, Gregory W. Heath, Kenneth E. Powell, Richard A. Washburn, Andrea Kriska, and Gwendolyn Haile. 1991. "Physical Activity Behaviors in Lower and Higher Socioeconomic Status Populations" *American Journal of Epidemiology* 133:1246–55.

Fox, A. J., P. O. Goldblatt, and D. R. Jones. 1985. "Social Class Mortality Differentials: Artefact, Selection, or Life Circumstances?" *Journal of Epidemiology and Community Health* 39:1–8.

Freedman, Vicki A. and Linda G. Martin. 1998. "Understanding Trends in Functional Limitations Among Older Americans." *American Journal of Public Health* 88:1457–62.

Fremont, Allen M. and Chloe E. Bird. 2000. "Social and Psychological Factors, Physiological Processes, and Physical Health." Pp. 334–52 in *The Handbook of Medical Sociology,* 5th ed., edited by Chloe E. Bird, Peter Conrad, and Allen M. Fremont. Upper Saddle River, NJ: Prentice-Hall.

Gaziano, J. Michael, Julie E. Buring, Jan L. Breslow, Samuel Z. Goldhaber, Bernard Rosner, Martin VanDenburgh, Walter Willett, and Charles H. Hennekens. 1993. "Moderate Alcohol Intake, Increased Levels of High-Density Lipoprotein and Its Subfractions, and Decreased Risk of Myocardial Infarction" *New England Journal of Medicine* 329:1829–34.

Gecas, Viktor. 1989. "The Social Psychology of Self-Efficacy." *Annual Review of Sociology* 15:291–316.

Gerstel, Naomi, Catherine Kohler Riessman, and Sarah Rosenfield. 1985. "Explaining the Symptomatology of Separated and Divorced Women and Men: The Role of Material Conditions and Social Networks." *Social Forces* 64:84–101.

Gill, Jaswinder S., Alexander V. Zezulka., Martin J. Shipley, Surinder K. Gill, and D. Gareth Beevers. 1986. "Stroke and Alcohol Consumption." *New England Journal of Medicine* 315:1041–46.

Glaser, Ronald and Janice K. Kiecolt-Glaser. 1998. "Stress-Associated Immune Modulation: Relevance to Viral Infections and Chronic Fatigue Syndrome." *American Journal of Medicine* 105:35s–42s.

Glaser, Ronald, Bruce Rabin, Margaret Chesney, Sheldon Cohen and Benjamin Natelson. 1999. "Stress-Induced Immunomodulation: Implications for Infectious Diseases?" *JAMA* 281:2268–71.

Glenn, Norval D. and Charles N. Weaver. 1982. "Further Evidence on Education and Job Satisfaction." *Social Forces* 61:46–55.

Glick, Paul C. 1984. "Marriage, Divorce, and Living Arrangements: Prospective Changes." *Journal of Family Issues* 5:7–26.

Gordon, Michael E. and Richard D. Arvey. 1975. "The Relationship between Education and Satisfaction with Job Content." *Academy of Management Journal* 18:888–92.

Gore, Susan. 1978. "The Effect of Social Support in Moderating the Health Consequences of Unemployment." *Journal of Health and Social Behavior* 19:157–65.

Gottfredson, Linda S. 1985. "Education as a Valid but Fallible Signal of Worker Quality: Reorienting an old Debate about the Functional Basis of the Occupational Hierarchy." Pp. 123–69 in *Research in Sociology of Education and Socialization* (vol. 5), edited by Alan C. Kerckhoff. Greenwich, CT: JAI.

Gove, Walter R., Michael M. Hughes, and Carolyn B. Style. 1983. "Does Marriage Have Positive Effects on the Psychological Well-Being of the Individual?" *Journal of Health and Social Behavior* 24:122–31.

Grover, Steven A., Katherine Gray-Donald, Lawrence Joseph, Michal Abrahamowicz, and Louis Coupal. 1994. "Life Expectancy Following Dietary Modification or Smoking Cessation: Estimating the Benefits of a Prudent Lifestyle." *Archives of Internal Medicine* 154:1697–1704.

Guralnik, Jack M. and Robert J. Kaplan. 1989. "Predictors of Healthy Aging: Prospective Evidence from the Alameda County Study." *American Journal of Public Health* 79:703–8.

Guralnik, Jack M., Keneth C. Land, Dan Blazer, Gerda G. Fillenbaum, and Laurence G. Branch. 1993. "Educational Status and Active Life Expectancy among Older Blacks and Whites." *New England Journal of Medicine* 329:110–16.

Gurin, Patricia, Gerald Gurin, and Betty M. Morrison. 1978. "Personal and Ideological Aspects of Internal and External Control." *Social Psychology* 41:275–96.

Gutzwiller, Feliz, Carlo La Vecchia, Fabio Levi, Eva Negri, and Vincent Wietlisbach. 1989. "Education, Disease Prevalence, and Health Service Utilization in the Swiss National Health Survey." *Preventive Medicine* 18:452–59.

Hadley, J., E. P. Steinberg, and J. Feder. 1991. "Comparison of Uninsured and Privately Insured Hospital Patients: Condition on Admission, Resource Use, and Outcome." *JAMA* 265:374–79.

Harnish, Jennifer D., Robert H. Aseltine, Jr., and Susan Gore. 2000. "Resolution of Stressful Experiences as an Indicator of Coping Effectiveness in Young Adults: An Event History Analysis." *Journal of Health and Social Behavior* 41:121–36.

Hayes, Diane and Catherine E. Ross. 1986. "Body and Mind: The Effect of Exercise, Overweight, and Physical Health on Psychological Well-Being." *Journal of Health and Social Behavior* 27:387–400.

Hayes, Diane and Catherine E. Ross. 1987. "Concern with Appearance, Health Beliefs, and Eating Habits." *Journal of Health and Social Behavior* 28:120–30.

Hayflick, L. 1998. "A Brief History of the Mortality and Immortality of Cultured Cells." *KEIO Journal of Medicine* 47:174–82.

Helmert, U., B. Herman, K.-H. Joeckel, E. Greiser, and J. Madans. 1989. "Social Class and Risk Factors for Coronary Heart Disease in the Federal Republic of Germany. Results of the Baseline Survey of the German Cardiovascular Prevention Study." *Journal of Epidemiology and Community Health* 43:37–42.

Helsing, K. J., S. Moysen, and George W. Comstock. 1981. "Factors Associated with Mortality after Widowhood." *American Journal of Public Health* 71:802–9.

Herbert, T. B. and S. Cohen. 1993. "Stress and Immunity in Humans: A Meta-Analytic Review." *Psychosomatic Medicine* 55:364–79.

Herrnstein, Richard J. and Charles Murray. 1994. *The Bell Curve: Intelligence and Class Structure in American Life*. New York: Free Press.

Hertzman, Clyde, John Frank, and Robert G. Evans. 1994. "Heterogeneities in Health Status and the Determinants of Population Health." Pp. 67–92 in *Why*

Are Some People Healthy and Others Not? edited by Robert G. Evans, Morris L. Barer, and Theodore R. Marmor. Hawthorne, NY: Aldine de Gruyter.

Heyns, Barbara. 1974. "Social Selection and Stratification within Schools." *American Journal of Sociology* 79:1435-51.

Heyns, Barbara. 1978. *Summer Learning and the Effects of Schooling.* New York: Academic.

Hiroto, Donald S. 1974. "Locus of Control and Learned Helplessness." *Journal of Experimental Psychology* 102:187–93.

Hodson, Randy. 1989. "Gender Differences in Job Satisfaction: Why Aren't Women More Dissatisfied?" *Sociological Quarterly* 30:385–99

Hollingshead, A. B. and Redlich, F. C. 1958. *Social Class and Mental Illness: A Community Study.* New York: Wiley.

Hollingsworth, J. Rogers. 1981. "Inequality in Levels of Health in England and Wales, 1971–1981." *Journal of Health and Social Behavior* 22:268–83.

House, James S., James M. Lepkowski, Ann M. Kinney, Richard P. Mero, Ronald C. Kessler, and A. Regula Herzog. 1994. "The Social Stratification of Aging and Health." *Journal of Health and Social Behavior* 35:213–34.

Hughes, Michael M. and Walter R. Gove. 1981. "Living Alone, Social Integration, and Mental Health." *American Journal of Sociology* 87:48–74.

Hyman, Herbert H. and Charles R. Wright. 1979. *Education's Lasting Influence on Values.* Chicago, IL: University of Chicago Press.

Hyman, Herbert H., Charles R. Wright, and John Shelton Reed.1976. *The Enduring Effects of Education.* Chicago, IL: University of Chicago Press.

Idler, Ellen L. and Y. Benyamini. 1997. "Self-Rated Health and Mortality: A Review of Twenty-Seven Community Studies." *Journal of Health and Social Behavior* 38:21–37.

Idler, Ellen L. and Stanislav V. Kasl. 1991. "Health Perceptions and Survival: Do Global Evaluations of Health Status Really Predict Morality?" *Journal of Gerontology* 46:S55–65.

Irwin, Michael, Carolyn Costlow, Heather Williams, Kamal Haydari Artin, Christina Y. Chan, Diane L. Stinson, Myron J. Levin, Anthony R. Hayward, and Michael N. Oxman. 1998. "Cellular Immunity to Varicella-Zoster Virus in Patients with Major Depression." *Journal of Infectious Diseases* 178:S104–8.

Irwin, Michael, Richard Hauger, Thomas L. Patterson, Shirley Semple, Michael Ziegler, and Igor Grant. 1997. "Alzheimer Caregiver Stress: Basal Natural Killer Cell Activity, Pituitary-Adrenal Cortical Function, and Sympathetic Tone." *Annals of Behavioral Medicine* 19:83–90.

Jacobs, Jerry A. and Ronnie J. Steinberg. 1990. "Compensating Differentials and the Male-Female Wage Gap: Evidence from the New York State Comparable Worth Study." *Social Forces* 69:439–68.

Jacobs, Jerry A. and Ronnie J. Steinberg. 1995. "Further Evidence on Compensating Differentials and the Gender Gap in Wages." Pp. 93–124 in *Gender Inequality at Work,* edited by Jerry A. Jacobs. Thousand Oaks, CA: Sage.

Jacobsen, Bjarne K. and Dag S. Thelle. 1988. "Risk Factors for Coronary Heart Disease and Level of Education." *American Journal of Epidemiology* 127:923–32.

Jencks, Christopher. 1972. *Inequality: A Reassessment of the Effect of Family and Schooling In America.* New York: Basic Books.

Johansson, J.-E., L. Holmberg, S. Johansson, R. Bergström, and H.-O. Adami. 1997. "Fifteen-Year Survival in Prostate Cancer: A Prospective, Population-Based Study in Sweden." *JAMA* 277:467–71.

Johnson, Robert J. and Fredric D. Wolinsky. 1993. "The Structure of Health Status Among Older Adults: Disease, Disability, Functional Limitation and Perceived Health." *Journal of Health and Social Behavior* 34:105–21.

Kaiser Foundation Health Plan. 1976. "Health Examinations." *Planning for Health* 19:2–3.

Kaplan, Howard B., Cynthia Robbins, and Steven S. Martin. 1983. "Antecedents of Psychological Distress in Young Adults: Self-Rejection, Deprivation of Social Support and Life Events." *Journal of Health and Social Behavior* 24:230–44.

Kaplan, Sherrie. 1987. "Patient Reports of Health Status as Predictors of Physiologic Health Measures in Chronic Disease." *Journal of Chronic Disease* 40(supp.): 27–35.

Kaprio, Jaakko, Markku Koskenuo, and Heli Rita. 1987. "Mortality after Bereavement: A Prospective Study of 95,647 Widowed Persons." *American Journal of Public Health* 77:283–87.

Katsillis, John and Richard Rubinson. 1990. "Cultural Capital, Student Achievement, and Educational Reproduction: The Case of Greece." *American Sociological Review* 55:270–79.

Kawachi, I. and B. P. Kennedy. 1997. "Health and Social Cohesion: Why Care About Income Inequality?" *BMJ* 314:1037–40.

Kerckhoff, Alan C. 1993. *Diverging Pathways: Social Structure and Career Deflections.* New York: Cambridge University Press.

Kessler, Ronald C. and Jane D. McLeod. 1985. "Social Support and Mental Health in Community Samples." Pp. 219–40 in *Social Support and Health,* edited by Sheldon Cohen and S. Leonard Syme. New York: Academic.

Kim, Kwangkee and Philip M. Moody. 1992. "More Resources Better Health? A Cross-national Perspective." *Social Science and Medicine* 34:837–42.

King, S. E. and D. Schottenfeld. 1996. "The 'Epidemic' of Breast Cancer in the U.S.: Determining the Factors." *Oncology* 10:453–62.

Kitagawa, Evelyn M. and Philip M. Hauser. 1973. *Differential Mortality in the United States: A Study in Socioeconomic Epidemiology.* Cambridge, MA: Harvard University Press.

Knowles, John H. 1977. "The Responsibility of the Individual." Pp. 57–80 in *Doing Better and Feeling Worse. Health in the U.S.,* edited by J. H. Knowles. New York: W. W. Norton.

Kohn, Melvin. 1976. "Occupational Structure and Alienation." *American Journal of Sociology* 82:111–30.

Kohn, Melvin L., Atsuhi Naoi, Carrie Schoenbach, Carmi Schooler, and Kazimierz M. Slomczynski. 1990. "Position in the Class Structure and Psychological Functioning in the United States, Japan, and Poland." *American Journal of Sociology* 95:964–1008.

Kohn, Melvin and Carmi Schooler. 1982. "Job Conditions and Personality: A Longitudinal Assessment of Their Reciprocal Effects." *American Journal of Sociology* 87:1257–86.

Kohn, Melvin and Kazimierz M. Slomczynski. 1993. *Social Structure and Self-*

Direction. A Comparative Analysis of the United States and Poland. Cambridge, MA: Blackwell.

Kreindel, S., R. Rosetti, R. Goldberg, J. Savageau, J. Yarzebski, J. Gore, A. Russo and C. Bigelow. 1997. "Health Insurance Coverage and Outcome following Acute Myocardial Infarction: A Community-Wide Perspective." *Archives of Internal Medicine* 157:758–62.

Kunst, Anton E., C. W. Looman, and J. P. Mackenbach. 1990. "Socio-Economic Mortality Differences in The Netherlands in 1950–1984: A Regional Study of Cause-Specific Mortality." *Social Science and Medicine* 31:141–52.

Kunst, Anton E. and Johan P. Mackenbach. 1994. "The Size of Mortality Differences Associated with Educational Level in Nine Industrialized Countries." *American Journal of Public Health* 84:932–37.

Lagasse, Raphael, Perrine C. Humblet, Ann Lenaerts, Isabelle Godin, and G. F. Moens. 1990. "Health and Social Inequalities in Belgium." *Social Science and Medicine* 31:237–48.

Lahelma, Eero and Tapani Valkonen. 1990. "Health and Social Inequalities in Finland and Elsewhere." *Social Science and Medicine* 31:257–65.

Lantz, Paula M. and Karen M. Booth. 1998. "The Social Construction of Breast Cancer Epidemic." *Social Science and Medicine* 46:907–18.

Lantz, Paula M., P. L. Remington, and P. A. Newcomb. 1991. "Mammography Screening and Increased Incidence of Breast Cancer in Wisconsin." *Journal of the National Cancer Institute* 83:1540–46.

LaRocco, James M., James S. House, and John R. P. French. 1980. "Social Support, Occupational Stress, and Health." *Journal of Health and Social Behavior* 3:202–18.

Lauderdale, Diane S. 2001. "Education and Survival: Birth Cohort, Period, and Age Effects." *Demography* 38:551–61.

LaVecchia, C., E. Negri, R. Pagano, and A. Decarli. 1987. "Education, Prevalence of Disease, and Frequency of Health Care Utilization: The 1983 Italian National Health Survey." *Journal of Epidemiology and Community Health* 41:161–65.

LeDoux, Joseph. 1996. *The Emotional Brain: The Mysterious Underpinnings of Emotional Life.* New York: Touchstone.

Lee, P. and D. Paxman. 1997. "Reinventing Public Health." *Annual Review of Public Health* 18:1–35.

Leigh, J. Paul. 1983. "Direct and Indirect Effects of Education on Health." *Social Science and Medicine* 17:227–34.

Leon, Arthur S., John Connett, David R. Jacobs, and Rainer Rauramaa. 1987. "Leisure-Time Physical Activity Levels and Risk of Coronary Heart Disease and Death: The Multiple Risk Factor Intervention Trial." *Journal of the American Medical Association* 258:2388–95.

Liang, Jersey. 1986. "Self-Reported Physical Health among Aged Adults." *Journal of Gerontology* 41:248–60.

Libby, Peter. 2002. "Atherosclerosis: The New View." *Scientific American* 286(5): 47–55.

Lieberson, Stanley. 1985. *Making It Count: The Improvement of Social Research and Theory.* Berkeley: University of California Press.

Liu, Kiang, Lucilia B. Cedres, Jeremiah Stamler, Alan Dyer, Rose Stamler, Serafin Nanas, David M. Berkson, Oglesby Paul, Mark Lepper, Howard A. Lindberg,

John Marquar, Elizabeth Stevens, James A. Schoenberger, Richard B. Shekelle, Patricia Collette, Sue Shekelle, and Dan Gardside. 1982. "Relationship of Education to Major Risk Factors and Death from Coronary Heart Disease, Cardiovascular Diseases, and All Causes." *Circulation* 66:1308–14.

Lomas, J. and A. P. Contandriopoulos. 1994. "Regulating Limits to Medicine: Towards Harmony in Public- and Self-Regulation." Pp. 253–83 in *Why Are Some People Healthy and Others Not?* edited by Robert G. Evans, Morris L. Barer, and Theodore R. Marmor. Hawthorne, NY: Aldine de Gruyter.

Loscocco, Karyn A. 1990. "Reactions to Blue-Collar Work: A Comparison of Women and Men." *Work and Occupations* 17:152–77.

Lund, Laura, and William E. Wright. 1994. "Mitofsky-Waksberg vs. Screened Random Digit Dial: Report on a Comparison of the Sample Characteristics of Two RDD Survey Designs." Paper presented at the Center for Disease Control's 11th Annual Behavioral Risk Factor Survey Conference, June, Atlanta, GA.

MacIntyre, Sally. 1997. "The Black Report and Beyond: What Are the Issues?" *Social Science and Medicine* 44:723–45.

Maddox, George L. and Elizabeth B. Douglas. 1973. "Self-Assessment of Health: A Longitudinal Study of Elderly Subjects." *Journal of Health and Social Behavior* 14:87–93.

Magnus, K., A. Matroos, and J. Strackee. 1979. "Walking, Cycling, or Gardening, with or without Seasonal Interruptions, in Relation to Acute Coronary Events." *American Journal of Epidemiology* 110:724–33.

Manson, Joan E., Walter C. Willett, Meir J. Stampfer, Graham A. Colditz, David J. Hunter, Susan E. Hankinson, Charles H. Hennekens, and Frank E. Speizer. 1995. "Body Weight and Mortality among Women." *New England Journal of Medicine* 333:677–85.

Marieb, Elaine Nicpon. 1994. *Essentials of Human Anatomy and Physiology.* Redwood City, CA: Benjamin/Cummings.

Marmor, Theodore R., Morris L. Barer, and Robert G. Evans. 1994. "The Determinants of Population Health: What Can Be Done to Improve a Democratic Nation's Health Status?" Pp. 217–32 in *Why Are Some People Healthy and Others Not?* edited by Robert G. Evans, Morris L. Barer, and Theodore R. Marmor. Hawthorne, NY: Aldine de Gruyter.

Marmot, M., M. Kogevinas, and M. A. Elston. 1987. "Social/Economic Status and Disease." *Annual Review of Public Health* 8:111–35.

Marmot, Michael G. and J. Fraser Mustard. 1994. "Coronary Heart Disease from a Population Perspective." Pp. 189–214 in *Why Are Some People Healthy and Others Not?* edited by Robert G. Evans, Morris L. Barer, and Theodore R. Marmor. Hawthorne, NY: Aldine de Gruyter.

Matthews, Karen A., Sheryl F. Kelsey, Elaine N. Meilahn, Lewis H. Kuller, and Rena R. Wing. 1989. "Educational Attainment and Behavioral and Biological Risk Factors for Coronary Heart Disease in Middle-Aged Women." *American Journal of Epidemiology* 129:1132–44.

Mayer, Susan E. 1997. *What Money Can't Buy: Family Income and Children's Life Chances.* Cambridge, MA: Harvard University Press.

McEwen, B. S. 1998. "Stress, Adaptation, and Disease: Allostasis and Allostatic Load." *Annals of The New York Academy of Sciences* 840:33–44.

McEwen, B. S. 2000. "The Neurobiology of Stress: From Serendipity to Clinical Relevance." *Brain Research* 886:172–89.

McKeown, T. 1979. "The Direction of Medical Research." *Lancet* 2:1281–84.

McKinlay, John B. and Sonja M. McKinlay. 1977. "The Questionable Contribution of Medical Measures to the Decline of Mortality in the United States in the Twentieth Century." *Milbank Memorial Fund Quarterly* 55:405–28.

Mechanic, David and Stephen Hansell. 1987. "Adolescent Competence, Psychological Well-Being and Self-Assessed Physical Health." *Journal of Health and Social Behavior* 28:364–74.

Memmler, Ruth L., Barbara Janson Cohen, and Dena Lin Wood. 1996. *The Human Body in Health and Disease*, 8th ed. New York: Lippincott Williams and Wilkins.

Midanik, Lorraine T., Arthur L. Klatsky, and Mary Anne Armstrong. 1990. "Changes in Drinking Behavior: Demographic, Psychosocial, and Biomedical Factors." *International Journal of the Addictions* 25:599–619.

Millar, Wayne J. and Donald T. Wigle. 1986. "Socioeconomic Disparities in Risk Factors for Cardiovascular Disease." *Canadian Medical Association Journal* 134:127–32.

Miller, B. A., E. J. Feuer, and B. F. Hankey. 1991. "The Increasing Incidence of Breast Cancer Since 1982: Relevance of Early Detection." *Cancer Causes and Control* 2:67–74.

Miller, Michael K. and C. Shannon Stokes. 1978. "Health Status, Health Resources, and Consolidated Structural Parameters: Implications for Public Health Care Policy." *Journal of Health and Social Behavior* 19:263–79.

Mirowsky, John and Paul N. Hu. 1996. "Physical Impairment and the Diminishing Effects of Income." *Social Forces* 74:1073–96.

Mirowsky, John and Catherine E. Ross. 1986. "Social Patterns of Distress." *Annual Review of Sociology* 12:23–45.

Mirowsky, John and Catherine E. Ross. 1989. *Social Causes of Psychological Distress.* Hawthorne, NY: Aldine de Gruyter.

Mirowsky, John and Catherine E. Ross. 1991. "Eliminating Defense and Agreement Bias from Measures of Sense of Control: A 2x2 Index." *Social Psychology Quarterly* 54:127–45.

Mirowsky, John and Catherine E. Ross. 1998. "Education, Personal Control, Lifestyle and Health: A Human Capital Hypothesis." *Research on Aging* 20: 415–49.

Mirowsky, John and Catherine E. Ross. 1999. "Economic Hardship Across the Life Course." *American Sociological Review* 64:548–69.

Mirowsky, John, Catherine E. Ross, and Marieke Van Willigen. 1996. "Instrumentalism in the Land of Opportunity: Socioeconomic Causes and Emotional Consequences." *Social Psychology Quarterly* 59:322–27.

Morris, J. N. 1990. "Inequalities in Health: Ten Years and Little Further On." *Lancet* 336:491–93.

Mossey, Jana M. and Evelyn Shapiro. 1982. "Self-Rated Health: A Predictor of Mortality among the Elderly." *American Journal of Public Health* 72:800–8.

Nagi, Saad Z. 1976. "An Epidemiology of Disability among Adults in the United States." *Milbank Memorial Fund Quarterly* 54:439–68.

Nakao, Keikeo, Robert W. Hodge, and Judith Treas. 1990. "On Revising Prestige Scores for all Occupations." GSS Methodological report no. 69. Chicago: NORC.

National Center for Health Statistics. 1989. *Deaths Attributable to Smoking, U.S., 1988.* Hyattsville, MD: Public Health Service.

National Center for Health Statistics. 1992. *Advance Report of Final Mortality Statistics, 1989.* Hyattsville, MD: Public Health Service.

National Center for Health Statistics. 2002. *National Vital Statistics Reports. Deaths: Final Data for 2000.* Hyattsville, MD: Department of Health and Human Services.

National Institutes of Health. 1998. "Socioeconomic Status Across the Life Course." NIH Guide PA-98-098 (http://grants.nih.gov/grants/guide/pa-files/PA-98-098.html).

National Institutes of Health. 2000. "Health Disparities: Linking Biological and Behavioral Mechanisms with Social and Physical Environments." NIH Guide ES-00-004 (http://grants.nih.gov/grants/guide/rfa-files/RFA-ES-00-004.html).

Neale, Anne Victoria, Barbara C. Tilley, and Sally W. Vernon. 1986. "Marital Status, Delay in Seeking Treatment and Survival from Breast Cancer." *Social Science and Medicine* 23:305–12.

Newcomb, P. A. and P. M. Lantz. 1993. "Recent Trends in Breast Cancer Incidence, Mortality, and Mammography." *Breast Cancer Research and Treatment* 28:97–106.

Nunn, Clyde A., Harry J. Crockett, Jr., and J. Allen Williams, Jr. 1978. *Tolerance for Nonconformity.* San Francisco, CA: Jossey-Bass.

O'Rand, Angela M. 1996. "The Precious and the Precocious: Understanding Cumulative Disadvantage and Cumulative Advantage Over the Life Course." *Gerontologist* 36:230–38.

Oakes, Jeannie. 1982. "Classroom Social Relationships: Exploring the Bowles and Gintis Hypothesis." *Sociology of Education* 55:197–212.

Oxford English Dictionary 2000. Online edition, 2d ed. New York: Oxford University Press. Retrieved November 1, 2000 (http://library.ohio-state.edu/search/t?the+oxford+english+dictionary+online).

Paffenbarger, Ralph S., Robert T. Hyde, Alvin L. Wing, I.-Min Lee, Dexter L. Jung, and James B. Kampert. 1993. "The Association of Changes in Physical Activity Level and Other Lifestyle Characteristics with Mortality among Men." *New England Journal of Medicine* 328:538–45.

Pamuk, Elsie R. 1985. "Social Class Inequality in Mortality from 1912–1972 in England and Wales." *Population Studies* 39:17–31.

Pamuk, Elsie R. 1988. "Social-Class Inequality in Infant Mortality in England and Wales from 1921 to 1980." *European Journal of Population* 4:1–21.

Pappas, Gregory, Susan Queen, Wilbur Hadden, and Gail Fisher. 1993. "The Increasing Disparity in Mortality between Socioeconomic Groups in the United States, 1960 and 1986." *New England Journal of Medicine* 329:103–9.

Parchment, Winsome, Gerson Weiss, and M. R. Passannante. 1996. "Is the Lack of Health Insurance the Major Barrier to Early Prenatal Care at an Inner-City Hospital?" *Women's Health Issues* 6:97–105.

Pascarella, Ernest T. and Patrick T. Terenzini. 1991. *How College Affects Students.* San Francisco, CA: Jossey-Bass.

Pearce, N. E., P. B. Davis, A. H. Smith, and F. H. Foster. 1985. "Social Class, Ethnic Group, and Male Mortality in New Zealand, 1974–78." *Journal of Epidemiology and Community Health* 39:9–14.

Pearlin, Leonard I., Morton A. Lieberman, Elizabeth G. Menaghan, and Joseph T. Mullan. 1981. "The Stress Process." *Journal of Health and Social Behavior* 22: 337–56.

Perez-Campo, R., M. Lopez-Torres, S. Cadenas, C. Rojas, and G. Barja. 1998. "The Rate of Free Radical Production as a Determinant of the Rate of Aging: Evidence from the Comparative Approach." *Journal of Comparative Physiology* 168:149–58.

Pike, Jennifer L., Tom L. Smith, Richard L. Hauger, Perry M. Nicassio, Thomas L. Patterson, John McLintick, Carolyn Costlow, and Michael R. Irwin. 1997. "Chronic Life Stress Alters Sympathetic, Neuroendocrine, and Immune Responsivity to an Acute Psychological Stressor in Humans." *Psychosomatic Medicine* 59:447–57.

Pincus, E. 1998. "Social Conditions and Self-Management Are More Powerful Determinants of Health Than Access to Care." *Annals of Internal Medicine* 129: 406–11.

Pruessner, Jens C., Jens Gaab, Dirk H. Hellhammer, Doris Lintz, Nicole Schommer, and Clements Kirschbaum. 1997. "Increasing Correlations between Personality Traits and Cortisol Stress Responses Obtained by Data Aggregation." *Psychoneuroendicrinology* 22:615–25.

Qian, Zhenchao and Samuel H. Preston. 1993. "Changes in American Marriage, 1972 to 1987: Availability and Forces of Attraction by Age and Education." *American Sociological Review* 58:482–95.

Quinn, Robert P. and Martha S. Baldi de Mandilovitch. 1977. *Education and Job Satisfaction: A Questionable Payoff.* NIE Papers in Education and Work, no. 5. Washington, DC: U.S. Department of Health, Education and Welfare.

Quinn, Robert P., Graham L. Staines, and M. R. McCullough. 1974. *Job Satisfaction: Is There a Trend?* Washington, DC: Department of Labor.

Reynolds, John R. and Catherine E. Ross. 1998. "Social Stratification and Health: Education's Benefit beyond Economic Status and Social Origins." *Social Problems* 45:221–47.

Riessman, Catherine Kohler and Naomi Gerstel. 1985. "Marital Dissolution and Health: Do Males or Females Have Greater Risk?" *Social Science and Medicine* 20:627–35.

Rindfuss, Ronald R., S. Philip Morgan, and C. Gray Swicegood. 1984. "The Transition to Motherhood: The Intersection of Structural and Temporal Dimensions." *American Sociological Review* 49:359–72.

Roche, Alex F., Roger M. Siervogel, William C. Chumlea, and Paul Webb. 1981. "Grading Body Fatness from Limited Anthropometric Data." *American Journal of Clinical Nutrition* 34:2831–38.

Rodin, Judith. 1986a. "Aging and Health: Effects of the Sense of Control." *Science* 233:1271–76.

Rodin, Judith. 1986b. "Health, Control, and Aging." Pages 139–65 in *The Psychology of Control and Aging,* edited by Margaret M. Baltes and Paul B. Baltes. Hillsdale, NJ: Lawrence Erlbaum Associates.

Rogers, Richard G., Robert A. Hummer, and Charles B. Nam. 1999. *Living and Dying in the USA: Behavioral, Health, and Social Forces of Adult Mortality.* New York: Academic.

Rogers, Richard G. and Eve Powell-Griner. 1991. "Life Expectancies of Cigarette Smokers and Nonsmokers in the United States." *Social Science and Medicine* 32:1151–59.

Rogot, Eugene, Paul D. Sorlie, and Norman J. Johnson. 1992. "Life Expectancy by Employment Status, Income, and Education in the National Longitudinal Mortality Study." *Public Health Reports* 107:457–61.

Romelsjo, Anders and Finn Diderichsen. 1989. "Changes in Alcohol-Related Inpatient Care in Stockholm County in Relation to Socioeconomic Status During a Period of Decline in Alcohol Consumption." *American Journal of Public Health* 79:52–56.

Romelsjo, Anders, Deborah Hasin, Mike Hilton, Gunnel Bostrom, Finn Diderichsen, Bo Haglund, Johan Hallqvist, Gunilla Karlsson, and Leif Svanstrom. 1992. "The Relationship between Stressful Working Conditions and High Alcohol Consumption and Severe Alcohol Problems in an Urban General Population." *British Journal of Addiction* 87:1173–83.

Roos, Noralou P. and Leslie L. Roos. 1994. "Small Area Variations, Practice Style, and Quality of Care." Pp. 231–52 in *Why Are Some People Healthy and Others Not?* edited by Robert G. Evans, Morris L. Barer, and Theodore R. Marmor. Hawthorne, NY: Aldine de Gruyter.

Rosen, S. 1986. "The Theory of Equalizing Differences." Pp. 641–92 in *Handbook of Labor Economics,* edited by O. Ashenfelter and R. Layard. New York: Elsevier.

Rosenbaum, James E. 1984. *Career Mobility in a Corporate Hierarchy.* New York: Academic.

Ross, Alan O. 1991. "Memories and Reflections." Pp. 183–224 in *The History of Clinical Psychology in Autobiography,* edited by C. E. Walker. Pacific Grove, CA: Brooks/Cole.

Ross, Catherine E. 1989. "The Intersection of Work and Family: The Sense of Control and Well-Being of Women and Men." Paper presented at the Family Structure and Health Conference. August, San Francisco.

Ross, Catherine E. 1995. "Reconceptualizing Marital Status as a Continuum of Social Attachment." *Journal of Marriage and the Family* 57:129–40.

Ross, Catherine E. and Chloe E. Bird. 1994. "Sex Stratification and Health Lifestyle: Consequences for Men's and Women's Perceived Health." *Journal of Health and Social Behavior* 35:161–78.

Ross, Catherine E. and Joan Huber. 1985. "Hardship and Depression." *Journal of Health and Social Behavior* 26:312–27.

Ross, Catherine E. and John Mirowsky. 1983. "Social Epidemiology of Overweight: A Substantive and Methodological Investigation" *Journal of Health and Social Behavior* 24:288–98.

Ross, Catherine E. and John Mirowsky. 1988. "Child Care and Emotional Adjustment to Wives' Employment." *Journal of Health and Social Behavior* 29:127–38.

Ross, Catherine E. and John Mirowsky. 1989. "Explaining the Social Patterns of Depression: Control and Problem-Solving—or Support and Talking." *Journal of Health and Social Behavior* 30:206–19.

Ross, Catherine E. and John Mirowsky. 1992. "Households, Employment, and the Sense of Control." *Social Psychology Quarterly* 55:217–35.

Ross, Catherine E. and John Mirowsky. 1995. "Does Employment Affect Health." *Journal of Health and Social Behavior* 36:230–43.

Ross, Catherine E. and John Mirowsky. 1996. "Economic and Interpersonal Work Rewards: Subjective Utilities of Men's and Women's Compensation." *Social Forces* 75:223–46.

Ross, Catherine E. and John Mirowsky. 1999. "Refining the Association between Education and Health: The Effects of Quantity, Credential, and Selectivity." *Demography* 36:445–60.

Ross, Catherine E. and John Mirowsky. 2000. "Does Medical Insurance Contribute to Socioeconomic Differentials in Health?" *Milbank Quarterly* 78:291–321.

Ross, Catherine E., John Mirowsky, and William C. Cockerham. 1983. "Social Class, Mexican Culture, and Fatalism: Their Effects on Psychological Distress." *American Journal of Community Psychology* 11:383–99.

Ross, Catherine E., John Mirowsky, and Karen Goldsteen. 1990. "The Impact of the Family on Health: The Decade in Review." *Journal of Marriage and the Family* 52:1059–78.

Ross, Catherine E., John Mirowsky, and Shana Pribesh. 2001. "Powerlessness and The Amplification of Threat: Neighborhood Disadvantage, Disorder, and Mistrust " *American Sociological Review* 66:568–91.

Ross, Catherine E. and Barbara F. Reskin. 1992. "Education, Control at Work, and Job Satisfaction." *Social Science Research* 21:134–48.

Ross, Catherine E. and John R. Reynolds. 1996. "The Effects of Power, Knowledge and Trust on Income Disclosure in Surveys." *Social Science Quarterly* 77: 899–911.

Ross, Catherine E. and Jaya Sastry. 1999. "The Sense of Personal Control: Social Structural Causes and Emotional Consequences." Pp. 369–94 in *Handbook of the Sociology of Mental Health,* edited by C. S. Aneshensel and J. C. Phelan. New York: Plenum.

Ross, Catherine E. and Marieke Van Willigen. 1997. "Education and the Subjective Quality of Life." *Journal of Health and Social Behavior* 38:275–97.

Ross, Catherine E. and Chia-ling Wu. 1995. "The Links between Education and Health." *American Sociological Review* 60:719–45.

Ross, Catherine E. and Chia-ling Wu. 1996. "Education, Age and the Cumulative Advantage in Health." *Journal of Health and Social Behavior* 37:104–20.

Rotter, Julian B. 1966. "Generalized Expectancies for Internal vs. External Control of Reinforcements." *Psychological Monographs* 80:1–28.

Rozanski, A., J. A. Blumenthal, and J. Kaplan. 1999. "Impact of Psychological Factors on the Pathogenesis of Cardiovascular Disease and Implications for Therapy." *Circulation* 99:2192–2217.

Sagan, Leonard A. 1987. *The Health of Nations: True Causes of Sickness and Well-Being.* New York: Basic.

Sandvik, Leiv, Jan Erikssen, Erik Thaulow, Gunnar Erikssen, Reidar Mundal, and Kaare Rodahl. 1993. "Physical Fitness as a Predictor of Mortality among Healthy, Middle-Aged Norwegian Men." *New England Journal of Medicine* 328:533–37.

Sapolsky, Robert M. 1998. *Why Zebras Don't Get Ulcers: An Updated Guide to Stress-Related Diseases, and Coping.* New York: W.H. Freeman.

Schultz, Theodore. 1962. "Reflections on Investment in Man." *Journal of Political Economy* 70:1–8.

Seeman, Melvin. 1959. "On the Meaning of Alienation." *American Sociological Review* 24:783–91.

Seeman, Melvin. 1983. "Alienation Motifs in Contemporary Theorizing: The Hidden Continuity of Classic Themes." *Social Psychology Quarterly* 46:171–84.

Seeman, Melvin and Susan Lewis. 1995. "Powerlessness, Health and Mortality: A Longitudinal Study of Older Men and Mature Women." *Social Science and Medicine* 41:517–26.

Seeman, Melvin, Alice Z. Seeman, and Art Budros. 1988. "Powerlessness, Work, and Community: A Longitudinal Study of Alienation and Alcohol Use." *Journal of Health and Social Behavior* 29:185–98.

Seeman, Melvin and Teresa E. Seeman. 1983. "Health Behavior and Personal Autonomy: A Longitudinal Study of the Sense of Control in Illness." *Journal of Health and Social Behavior* 24:144–60.

Segovia, Jorge, Roy F. Bartlett, and Alison C. Edwards. 1989. "The Association between Self-Assessed Health Status and Individual Health Practices." *Canadian Journal of Public Health* 80:32–7.

Seligman, Martin E. P. 1975. *Helplessness: On Depression, Development, and Death.* San Francisco, CA: Freeman.

Selye, Hans 1976. *The Stress of Life,* rev. ed. New York: McGraw-Hill.

Sewell, William H. and Robert M. Hauser. 1975. *Education, Occupation, and Earnings.* New York: Academic.

Sharp, Kimberly, Catherine E. Ross, and William C. Cockerham. 1983. "Symptoms, Beliefs, and the Use of Physician Services among the Disadvantaged." *Journal of Health and Social Behavior* 24:255–63.

Shavit, Yossi and David L. Featherman. 1988. "Schooling, Tracking, and Teenage Intelligence." *Sociology of Education* 6:42–51.

Shea, Steven, Aryeh D. Stein, Charles E. Basch, Rafael Lantingue, Christopher Maylahn, David S. Strogatz, and Lloyd Novick. 1991. "Independent Associations of Educational Attainment and Ethnicity with Behavioral Risk Factors for Cardiovascular Disease." *American Journal of Epidemiology* 134:567–82.

Siskind, V., R. Copeman, and J. M. Najman. 1987. "Socioeconomic Status and Mortality: A Brisbane Area Analysis." *Community Health Studies* 11:15–23.

Smith, Jack C., James A. Mercy, and Judith Conn. 1988. "Marital Status and the Risk of Suicide." *American Journal of Public Health* 78:78–80.

Smith, R. 1979. "Compensating Wage Differentials and Public Policy: A Review." *Industrial and Labor Relations Review* 32:339–52.

Spaeth, Joe L. 1976. "Cognitive Complexity: A Dimension Underlying the Socioeconomic Achievement Process." Pp. 103–31 in *Schooling and Achievement in American Society,* edited by W. H. Sewell, R. M. Hauser, and D. L. Featherman. New York: Academic.

Stampfer, Meir J., Graham A. Colditz, Walter C. Willett, Frank E. Speizer, and Charles H. Hennekens. 1988. "A Prospective Study of Moderate Alcohol Consumption and the Risk of Coronary Heart Disease and Stroke in Women." *New England Journal of Medicine* 319:267–73.

Stedman's Medical Dictionary. 2000. Montvale, NJ: Medical Economics company, Inc. Retrieved November 1, 2000. (http://www.pdrel.com/pdr/pdrel/stedlev1. htm?srch=health).

Surgeon General. 1982. *The Health Consequences of Smoking.* Rockville, MD: Public Health Service.

Taylor, S. E., R. L. Repetti, and T. Seeman. 1997. "Health Psychology: What Is an Unhealthy Environment and How Does It Get under the Skin?" *Annual Review of Psychology* 48:411–47.

Tcheng-Laroche, Francoise and Raymond Prince. 1983. "Separated and Divorced Women Compared with Married Control. Selected Life Satisfaction, Stress, and Health Indices from a Community Survey." *Social Science and Medicine* 17:95–105.

Thibodeau, Gary A. and Kevin T. Patton. 1997. *The Human Body in Health and Disease,* 2d ed. New York: Mosby.

Thoits, Peggy A. 1982. "Conceptual, Methodological, and Theoretical Problems in Studying Social Support as a Buffer Against Life Stress." *Journal of Health and Social Behavior* 23:145–59.

Thoits, Peggy A. 1995. "Stress, Coping, and Social Support Process: Where Are We?" *Journal of Health and Social Behavior* (Special Issue):53–79.

Toscano, Guy. 1997. "Dangerous Jobs." *Compensation and Working Conditions* (Summer):57–60.

Toscano, Guy and Janice Windau. 1994. "The Changing Character of Fatal Work Injuries." *Monthly Labor Review* (October):17–28.

Townsend, P., N. Davidson, and M. Whitehead. 1992. *Inequalities in Health and the Health Divide.* London: Penguin.

Tsevat, Joel. 1992. "Impact and Cost-effectiveness of Smoking Interventions." *American Journal of Medicine* 93:43S–47S.

Tsevat, Joel, Milton C. Weinstein, Lawrence W. Williams, Anna N. Tosteson, and Lee Goldman. 1991. "Expected Gains in Life Expectancy from Various Coronary Heart Disease Risk Factor Modifications." *Circulation* 83:1194–1201.

Umberson, Debra. 1987. "Family Status and Health Behaviors: Social Control as a Dimension of Social Integration." *Journal of Health and Social Behavior* 28:306–19.

Umberson, Debra. 1992. "Gender, Marital Status and the Social Control of Health Behavior." *Social Science and Medicine* 34:907–17.

Umberson, Debra and Kristi Williams. 2000. "Family Status and Mental Health." Pp. 225–53 in *Handbook of the Sociology of Mental Health,* edited by Carol S. Aneshensel and Jo C. Phelan. NY: Plenum.

U.S. Bureau of the Census. 1995. *The Statistical Abstract of the United States 1995.* Washington, DC: U.S. Government Printing Office.

U.S. Congress, Office of Technology Assessment. 1992. *Does Health Insurance Make a Difference?* Background paper OTA-BP-H-99. Washington, DC: U.S. Government Printing Office.

U.S. Preventive Services Task Force. 1989. *Guide to Clinical Preventive Services.* Baltimore, MD: Williams and Wilkins.

Van Itallie, Theodore B. 1985. "Health Implication of Overweight and Obesity in the United States." *Annals of Internal Medicine* 103:983–88.

Veevers, Joan E. 1979. "Voluntary Childlessness: A Review of Issues and Evidence." *Marriage and Family Review* 2:1–26.

Venters, Maurine H. 1986. "Family Life and Cardiovascular Risk: Implications for the Prevention of Chronic Disease." *Social Science and Medicine* 22:1067–74.

Verrilli, D. and H. G. Welch. 1996. "The Impact of Diagnostic Testing on Therapeutic Interventions." *JAMA* 275:1189–91.

Wagenknecht, Lynne E., Laura L. Perkins, Gary R. Cutler, Stephen Sidney, Gregory L. Burke, Teri A. Manolia, David R. Jacobs, Kiang Liu, Gary D. Friedman, Glenn H. Hughes, and Stephen B. Hulley. 1990. "Cigarette Smoking Is Strongly Related to Educational Status: The CARDIA Study." *Preventive Medicine* 19:158–69.

Wagstaff, Adam, Pierella Paci, and Eddy Van Doorslaer. 1991. "On the Measurement of Inequalities in Health." *Social Science and Medicine* 33:545–57.

Waite, Linda. 1995. "Does Marriage Matter?" *Demography* 32:483–508.

Waite, Linda J. and Maggie Gallagher. 2000. *The Case for Marriage.* NY: Doubleday.

Waksberg, Joseph. 1978. "Sampling Methods for Random Digit Dialing." *Journal of the American Statistical Association* 73:40–46.

Wallace, Douglas C. 1997. "Mitochondrial DNA in Aging and Disease." *Scientific American* 276(8):40–47.

Weaver, Charles N. 1978. "Sex Differences in the Determinants of Job Satisfaction." *Academy of Management Journal* 20:265–74.

Weber, Max. 1968. *Economy and Society.* Translated by E. Fischoff, H. Gerth, A. M. Fenderson, F. Kolegar, C. W. Mills, T. Parsons, M. Rheinstein, G. Roth, E. Shils, and C. Wittich, edited by G. Roth and C. Wittich. New York: Bedminster.

Weiss, Robert S. 1984. "The Impact of Marital Dissolution on Income and Consumption in Single-Parent Households." *Journal of Marriage and the Family* (February):115–27.

Wennberg, J., E. Davis, M. A. Kellett, J. D. Dickens, Jr., D. J. Malenka, L. M. Keilson, and R. B. Keller. 1996. "The Association Between Local Diagnostic Testing Intensity and Invasive Cardiac Procedures." *JAMA* 275:1161–64.

Wheaton, Blair. 1980. "The Sociogenesis of Psychological Disorder: An Attributional Theory." *Journal of Health and Social Behavior* 21:100–24.

Wheaton, Blair. 1985. "Models for the Stress-Buffering Functions of Coping Resources." *Journal of Health and Social Behavior* 26:352–64.

Wiley, David E. 1976. "Another Hour, Another Day: Quantity of Schooling, a Potent Path for Policy." Pp. 225–65 in *Schooling and Achievement in American Society,* edited by William H. Sewell, Robert M. Hauser, and David L. Featherman. New York: Academic.

Wilkinson, Richard G. 1986. "Occupational Class, Selection and Inequalities in Health: A Reply to Raymond Illsley." *Quarterly Journal of Social Affairs* 2:415–22.

Wilkinson, Richard G. 1986. *Class and Health. Research and Longitudinal Data.* London, England: Tavistock.

Wilkinson, Richard G. 1997. "Socioeconomic Inequalities in Morbidity and Mortality in Western Europe." *Lancet* 350:516–17.

Williams, David R. 1990. "Socioeconomic Differentials in Health: A Review and Redirection." *Social Psychology Quarterly* 53:81–99.

Williams, David R. and Chiquita Collins. 1995. "U.S. Socioeconomic and Racial Differences in Health: Patterns and Explanations" *Annual Review of Sociology* 21:349–86.

Winkleby, Marilyn A., Darius E. Jatulis, Erica Frank, and Stephen P. Fortmann. 1992. "Socioeconomic Status and Health: How Education, Income, and Occupation Contribute to Risk Factors for Cardiovascular Disease." *American Journal of Public Health* 82:816–20.

Winship, Christopher and Robert D. Mare. 1992. "Models for Sample Selection Bias." *Annual Review of Sociology* 18:327–50.

Winship, Christopher and Larry Radbill. 1994. "Sampling Weights and Regression Analysis." *Sociological Methods and Research* 22:230–57.

World Health Organization. 2000. *Constitution of the World Health Organization.* Retrieved November 1, 2000 (http://dixit.terminotics.com/dixitdemo/Code/consult/ViewWHRTerm.asp?ILG=GB&ID=238822).

Wray, Linda A., A. Regula Herzog, Robert J. Willis, and Robert B. Wallace. 1998. "The Impact of Education and Heart Attack on Smoking Cessation among Middle-Aged Adults." *Journal of Health and Social Behavior* 4:271–94.

Yergan, J., A. B. Flood, P. Diehr, and J. P. LoGerfo. 1988. "Relationship Between Patient Source of Payment and the Intensity of Hospital Services." *Medical Care* 26:1111–14.

Index

Academic performance, 173, 177
Accumulation (*see also* Cumulative advantage)
  behavioral, 16, 142
  biological, 16, 142–145
  critical events and, 144
  defining, 16, 141
  desirable accumulators and, 143–144
  resource, 203–204
  socioeconomic, 16, 141–142
  undesirable accumulators and, 16–17, 143–144
ACTH, 86
Actuarial life expectancy, 48
Adenosine triphosphate (ATP), 162–164
Adrenal cortex, 86
Adrenocorticotropic stimulating hormone (ACTH), 86
Age
  education's effect on health and, 19, 159
  income and, 159–161
  physical impairment and, 42
  senescence and, 19, 161–165
  subjective health and, 37–38
Aging, Status and the Sense of Control (ASOC) survey
  baseline sample, 207–208
  data, 50, 55–56, 126
  economic well-being measures, 212
  employment aspects, 212–213
  follow-up sample, 208
  health measures, 208–209
  healthy lifestyle indicators, 210–211
  sense of personal control index, 210
  status of origin, 213
  supportive relationships, 211
  work aspects, 212–213

Agreement bias, 61
Alarm phase, 86–87
Alcohol consumption, 57–58, 135
Alienation, 63–64
Allostasis, 145
Allostatic load, 17, 144–145
Amplifying effects of education on health
  cumulative, 200
  feedback amplification, 17, 147–154
  life expectancy, 161–165
  overview, 146
  question raised by, 158–159
  socioeconomic life cycle, 159–161
  structural amplification, 154–158
  trend toward, 165–168
Amygdala, 163
Armed Forces Qualification Test, 52
ASOC study (*see* Aging, Status and the Sense of Control study)
ATP, 162–164
Atrophy, 165
Authority, 123
Autonomy of work
  education and, 118–121
  health and, 121–123
  subjective health and, 122–123

Bandura, Albert, 62
Behavioral accumulation, 16, 142
Berg, Ivar E., 173
Biological accumulation, 16, 142–145
Biological senescence, 19, 161–165
Blood glucose levels, 86
Body fat, 17, 143, 147
Body weight, 55–57, 135
Bourdieu, Pierre, 178–179
Bowles, Samuel, 176

Brown, Julia S., 131
Bureau of Labor Statistics, 102

Cancer mortality, 137
Cancer survival, 137–138
Cardiovascular disease, 87, 144
Cascading sequences, 18, 155–158
CCH survey, 85, 213–214
Children and economic hardship, 9, 81–82
Chronic disease, diagnoses of serious
    health measures and, 44–46
    income and, 78, 81
    stress and, 86–87
Cigarette smoking, 53–54, 135, 146
Cognitive ability, 188–189
Coleman, James S., 187–188
Collins, Randal, 172
Community, Crime and Health (CCH) sur-
    vey, 85, 213–214
Compounding effect of education on
    income, 72–75
Control (see Personal control)
Cortisol, 86–87, 163–165
Creativity of work
    education and, 118–121
    health and, 121–123
Credentialist view, 20, 171–174
Critical events, 144
Cultural capital, 178–179
Cultural self-development, 178
Cumulative advantage
    accumulating effects and
        behavioral, 16, 142
        biological, 16, 142–145
        critical events and, 144
        defining, 16, 141
        desirable accumulators and, 143–144
        resource, 203–204
        socioeconomic, 16, 141–142
        undesirable accumulators and, 16–17,
            143–144
    amplifying effects and
        cumulative, 200
        feedback amplification, 17, 147–154
        life expectancy, 161–165
        overview, 146
        question raised by, 158–159
        socioeconomic life cycle, 159–161
        structural amplification, 154–158
        trend toward, 165–168
    biological senescence and, 19, 161–165
    defining, 16, 140–141

education and, 140, 146, 165–169
life expectancy and, 161–165
life span and, 161–165
overview, 16–17
question raised by, 158–159
socioeconomic life cycle and, 159–161

Defense, 61
Dendrites, hippocampal, 164
Depression, 63
Desirable accumulators, 143–144
Deviation-amplifying feedback, 11, 17–18,
    147, 149
Disability, 108
Divorce, 127–128
DNA, 162–163
"Double-negative" feedback, 17, 148
Drinking alcohol, 57–58, 135

Earnings (see Income)
Economic hardship
    children and, 9, 81–82
    education and, 9, 79–81
    health and, 69, 79–84
    health insurance and, 10, 94
    marriage and, 9, 82
    partners and, 9, 82
    privation and, 9, 82–84, 200–201
    stress and, 9–10, 84–87
Economic resources (see Income)
Economic status, 28 (see also Socioeconomic
    status)
Economic well-being, 12, 96–97, 97–98, 132,
    133
Education (see also Specious views of educa-
    tion)
    academic performance and, 173, 177
    allostatic load and, 17, 144–145
    amplifying effects on health
        cumulative, 200
        feedback amplification, 17, 147–154
        life expectancy, 161–165
        overview, 146
        question raised by, 158–159
        socioeconomic life cycle, 159–161
        structural amplification, 154–158
        trend toward, 165–168
    autonomy of work and, 118–121
    body weight and, 55–57
    Bowles and Gintis's interpretation of,
        176
    cognitive ability and, 188–189

as component of socioeconomic status, 28
compounding effects on income, 72–75
creativity of work and, 118–121
cumulative advantage and, 140, 146, 165–169
disability and, 108
divorce and, 127–128
drinking alcohol and, 57–58
economic hardship and, 9, 79–81
economic well-being and, 97–98
employment and, 184
exercise and, strenuous, 54–55
family resources and standards and, 187–189
genetics and, 185–186
health improvement and
    access to, in improving health, 31
    achieving good health and, 26
    age and, 19, 159
    learned effectiveness theory and, 25–26, 30–31, 50, 70
    reasons for, 14–15, 197
health measures and
    chronic disease, diagnoses of serious, 44–46
    longevity, expected, 46–49
    overview, 49
    physical impairment, 37–42
    subjective health, 35–38
    vitality, 41–44
    well-being, 41–44
human capital theory and, 50–52
income and, 8, 29, 72–75, 80–81, 201
income versus, 25
intelligence and, 189–191
intergenerational, 180–182, 191–192
interpersonal relationships and, 31, 126–129
learned effectiveness theory and
    access to lucrative positions, 198
    health improvement, 25, 30–31, 50, 70
    overview, 25–26
    personal control over lifestyle and circumstances, 198–200
    socioeconomic status, 28–30, 198
levels of, average, 36–37
life span and, 161–165
lifestyle and, designing healthy, 7, 52–53, 58–59
marriage and, 15, 126–127
neighborhood resources and standards and, 187–189

parental, 180–182, 191–192
performance-based placement and, 177
personal control and, 64–65
physical impairment and, 39–43, 174
productive activities and
    employment link, 13, 105–108
    occupation link, 13–14, 114–115
    work link, 14, 118–121
as resource, 27, 30–31
skills developed by, 26–27, 51–52
smoking and, 53–54, 146
social status and, 1
social support and, 128–130
socioeconomic status and, 6, 25, 72–75, 180, 198
as solution, 22–23, 195–196, 206
stratification system and, 30
subjective health and, 36–38
unemployment and, 107–108
widowhood and, 127, 129, 158
Emotional support and marriage, 133–134
Employment (*see also* Occupation; Work)
    education and, 184
    full-time, 13
    health and, 13
    income and, 75
    link to productive activities
        education and, 13, 105–108
        health, 13, 108–114
    status, 28, 99–102
Engels, Friedrich, 104–105, 111
Exercise, strenuous, 54–55, 135
Explicit tracking, 175–177

False satisfier view, 21, 182–185
Family resources and education, 187–189
Feedback amplification
    deviation-amplifying feedback, 11, 17–18, 147, 149
    occurrence of, 17
    personal control, 17, 147–154
    physical impairment, 147–154
Fight-or-flight response, 85–86, 96, 162

GDP, 205
Genetics, 185–186
Gerontology, 39
Giesy, Barbara, 131
Gintis, Herbert, 176
Glucose, 86
Gross domestic product (GDP), 205

Health (*see also* Subjective health)
   autonomy of work and, 121–123
   creativity of work and, 121–123
   defining, 6–7, 32–33
   differences in, 27–28, 158–159
   economic hardship and, 69, 79–84
   economic well-being and, 97–98
   education in improving
      access to, in improving health, 31
      achieving good health, 26
      age and, 19, 159
      learned effectiveness theory and,
         25–26, 30–31, 50, 70
      reasons for, 14–15, 197
   education's correlation with measures of
      chronic disease, diagnoses of serious,
         44–46
      longevity, expected, 46–49
      overview, 49
      physical impairment, 37–42
      subjective health, 35–38
      vitality, 41–44
      well-being, 41–44
   employment and, 13
   gross domestic product and, 205
   income and socioeconomic status and,
      75–79
   lifestyle and, 28, 69–70
   marriage and, 15–16, 129–132, 138–139
   measuring, 7, 34–35
   money fallacy and, 11, 22, 194–195
   personal control and, 11, 95–97
   policymakers' view of improving, 31
   population, 88–89
   productive activities and
      employment link, 13, 108–114
      occupation link, 13–14, 115–117
      overview, 12
      work link, 14, 121–123
   realizations from research and
      education has pervasive, cumulative,
         self-amplifying benefits, 200
      education is a solution, 206
      lack of education turns low income
         into privation, 200–201
      learned effectiveness provides personal
         control over lifestyle and circum-
         stance, 198–200
      learned effectiveness tops access to
         lucrative positions, 198
      no one loses when someone gains con-
         trol, 203–205, 204–206

   overview, 197–198
   resource accumulation and substitution
      imply structural amplification,
         203–204
   structural amplification concentrates
      problems, 201–203
   self-direction toward, 6, 197–198
   social status and, 1, 3–6
   social surveys of, 34–35
   socioeconomic status and, 5, 14, 28–30,
      98–99, 124–125
   traditional focus on medicine and, 2–3
Health care
   income and access to, 87–95
   insurance and, private and public, 10–11,
      91–95
   marriage and, 135–138
   Medicare, 19, 160–161
   national systems, 89
   population health and, 88–89
   preventive, 90, 136–137, 146
   socioeconomic status and, 89–91
Health insurance, private and public, 10–11,
   91–95
Heart attack (as critical event), 144
Helplessness, 26, 63
Herrnstein, Richard J., 189, 191
Heyns, Barbara, 188
Hippocampus, 163–164
Hiroto, Donald S., 63
Homeostatic mechanisms, 147
Hormones, stress, 17, 86–87, 163–165
Household income (*see* Income)
Human capital theory
   education and, 50–52
   increase of human capital and, 191–192
   learned effectiveness theory and, 25, 50,
      52–53
   personal control and, 60
Hydrocortisone, 86–87, 163–165
Hypothalamus, 147

Ideological project and counterproject,
   193–194
Implicit tracking, 177–179
Income
   age and, 159–161
   chronic disease and, diagnoses of serious,
      78, 81
   education and, 8, 29, 72–75, 80–81, 201
   education versus, 25
   employment and, 75

low, 154
marriage and, 75
personal control and, 95–97
physical impairment and, 77, 80
skewed distribution of, 73–74
socioeconomic status and
    access to health care, 87–95
    economic hardship, 79–87
    education, 72–75
    health, 75–79
subjective health and, 75–79
Inequality, social, 22, 193–194
Injuries, work-related, 114–117
Insurance, private and public medical,
        10–11, 91–95
Intelligence quotient (IQ), 52, 189–191
Intergenerational education, 180–182,
        191–192
Interpersonal relationships and education,
        31, 126–129 (*see also* Marriage; Social
        support)
IQ, 52, 189–191

Job, 104 (*see also* Occupation; Work)
Job satisfaction, 184

Learned effectiveness theory
    education and
        access to lucrative positions, 198
        health improvement, 25–26, 30–31, 50,
            70
        overview, 25–26
        personal control over lifestyle and cir-
            cumstances, 198–200
        socioeconomic status, 27–29, 28–30,
            197, 198
    human capital theory and, 25, 50,
        52–53
    self-direction toward health and, 6,
        197–198
Learned helplessness, 26
Lieberson, Stanley, 171
Life expectancy, 46–49, 161–168
Life span, 161–165
Lifestyle
    designing healthy
        drinking alcohol and, 57–58
        education and, 7, 52–53, 58–59
        exercise and, strenuous, 53–54, 54–55
        overweight and, 55–57
        smoking cigarettes and, 53–54
        walking and, 54–55

health and, 28, 69–70
marriage and, 135
minimalist, 195
personal control and, 8, 65–70, 198–200
subjective health and, 59
Literacy, 31 (*see also* Education)
Locus of control, 61–62 (*see also* Personal
        control)
Logistic regression models, 106
Longevity, expected, 46–49, 161–168

Mammography, 90
Marriage
    cancer survival and, 137–138
    divorce and, 127–128
    economic hardship and, 9, 82
    economic well-being and, 133
    education and, 15, 126–127
    emotional support and, 133–134
    health and, 15–16, 129–132, 138–139
    health care and, 135–138
    income and, 75
    lifestyle and, 135
    orderly life and, 134–135
    physical impairment and, 130, 132
    social support and, 133–134
    subjective health and, 130–131
    widowhood and, 127, 129
Marx, Karl, 104–105, 111, 175–176, 178
Mayer, Susan E., 84
Medical Assistants (occupational category),
        102
Medical care and services (*see* Health care)
Medical insurance, private and public,
        10–11, 91–95
Medicare, 19, 160–161
Mental well-being, 43–44
Mirowsky-Ross measure of sense of per-
        sonal control, 61
Misfortune, amplification of, 158
Mitochondria, 162–163
Money fallacy, 11, 22, 194–195
Mortality statistics, 15, 48, 137
Murray, Charles, 189, 191
Musculoskeletal impairment, 67

National health care systems, 89
National Health Service (Great Britain),
        89
Neighborhood resources and education,
        187–189
Neuroendocrine accumulators, 144–145

Obesity, 55–57, 135
Occupation (*see also* Employment; Work)
   categories of, 102–103
   conditions and demands of, 103–105
   job satisfaction and, 184
   link to productive activities
     education, 13–14, 114–115
     health, 13–14, 115–117
   risky, 114–117
   status of, 103
Orderly life and marriage, 134–135
Organ reserve, 164
Overweight, 55–57, 135

Parental education, interaction between
     personal and, 180–182, 191–192
Partners and economic hardship, 9, 82
Path model of personal control, 66–70
Personal control
   education and, 64–65
   feedback amplification and, 17, 147–154
   health and, 11, 95–97
   human capital theory and, 60
   income and, 95–97
   lifestyle and, 8, 65–70, 198–200
   Mirowsky-Ross measure of, 61
   path model of, 66–70
   powerlessness versus, 61, 63–64
   sense of, 11, 60–61
   win-win situation of, 204–206
Physical impairment
   age and, 42
   education and, 39–43, 174
   feedback amplification and, 147–154
   health measures and, 37–43
   income and, 77, 80
   marriage and, 130, 132
   musculoskeletal, 67
   sensory, 67
   subjective health and, 37
Physical well-being, 43–44 (*see also* Health)
Pituitary gland, 86, 162
Plaque, arterial, 87, 144
Population health, 88–89
Poverty, 133, 154 (*see also* Privation)
Powerlessness, 61, 63–64
Predestination, intelligence as, 189–191
Preventive medical care, 90, 136–137, 146
Primary prevention, 136
Private health insurance programs, 91–95
Privation, 9, 82–84, 200–201 (*see also*
     Poverty)

Problem solving skills, 27, 52
Productive activities
   employment link to
     education and, 13, 105–108
     health and, 13, 108–114
   measuring
     employment status, 12, 99–102
     occupational status, 12, 103
     occupations, 12, 102–103
     overview, 12–13
     work, 12, 103–105
   occupational link to
     education, 13–14, 114–115
     health, 13–14, 115–117
   preconceptions about, 98–99
   self-expression, 123–125
   work link to
     authority and, 123
     education and, 14, 118–121
     health and, 14, 121–123
     overview, 117–118
Progressive adjustment regression models,
     69–70
Psychosocial crisis, 17–18, 149–150
Public health insurance programs, 91–95

Regeneration, 164
Relationships, 31, 126–129 (*see also* Mar-
     riage; Social support)
Reproductionist view, 20–21, 174–182
Resource accumulation, 203–204
Resource substitution, 18, 155, 197, 203–204
Retirement, 19, 109
Risky occupations, 114–117
Rodin, Judith, 148
Rotter, Julian B., 62–63
Rotter scale, 62

SAT scores, 173
Schooling (*see* Education)
Screening programs, 90, 136–137
Secondary prevention, 136
Seeman, Melvin, 63
SEI, 103
Self-amplification, 200
Self-blame, 61
Self-efficacy, 62–63
Self-expression, productive, 123–125
Senescence, biological, 19, 161–165
Sensory impairment, 67
Smoking cigarettes, 53–54, 135, 146
Social inequality, 22, 193–194

Social Security, 19, 160–161
Social status, 1–6 (*see also* Socioeconomic status)
Social support (*see also* Interpersonal relationships; Marriage)
  education and, 128–130
  marriage and, 133–134
Social surveys of health, 34–35
Socioeconomic accumulation, 16, 141–142
Socioeconomic Index (SEI), 103
Socioeconomic life cycle, 159–161
Socioeconomic status
  components of, 28, 71
  defining, 71
  education and, 6, 25, 72–75, 180, 198
  education as learned effectiveness and, 28–30, 198
  health and, 5, 14, 28–30, 98–99, 124–125
  health care and, 89–91
  income and
    access to health care, 87–95
    economic hardship, 79–87
    education, 72–75
    health, 75–79
  productive activities and
    employment link to, 13, 105–114
    measuring, 99–105
    occupational link to, 13–14, 114–117
    preconceptions about, 98–99
    self-expression, 123–125
    work link to, 14, 117–123
  research on, 25–26, 29–30, 71
Spaeth, Joe L., 188
Spearman-Brown Prophecy Formula, 36
Specious views of education
  credentialist, 20, 171–174
  education as solution, 22–23, 195–196, 206
  false satisfier, 21, 182–185
  ideological project and counterproject and, 193–194
  money fallacy and, 11, 22, 194–195
  overview, 20–21, 170–171
  reproductionist, 20–21, 174–182
  spurious correlation, 21, 185–193
  zero-sum fallacy and, 22, 195
Spouses and economic hardship, 9, 82
Spurious correlation view, 21, 185–193
Status reproduction fallacy, 179–182
Stratification system, 30 (*see also* Socioeconomic status)
Stress
  alarm phase and, 86–87

biological accumulation and, 144–145
chronic, 86
chronic disease and, 86–87
cumulative effects of, 145
economic hardship and, 9–10, 84–87
fight-or-flight response to, 85–86, 96, 162
hormones, 17, 86–87, 163–165
physical response to, 17, 86–87, 163
plaque and, 87
psychosocial crisis and, 17–18, 149–150
threats and, 9–10, 86, 96, 162
unconditioned response to, 96
viral infections and, 87
Structural amplification
  cascading sequences, 18, 155–158
  concentration of problems and, 201–203
  of misfortune, 158
  overview, 18, 154–155
  resource accumulation, 203–204
  resource substitution, 18, 155, 203–204
Subjective alienation, 63–64
Subjective health
  age and, 37–38
  autonomy of work and, 122–123
  education and, 36–38
  health measures and, 35–38
  income and, 75–79
  lifestyle and, 59
  marriage and, 130–131
  physical impairment and, 37
  Spearman-Brown Prophecy Formula and, 36
Surveys (*see* Aging, Status and the Sense of Control [ASOC] survey; Community, Crime and Health [CCH] survey)

T-lymphocytes, 86–87
Threats, 9–10, 86, 96, 162
Tracking
  explicit, 175–177
  implicit, 177–179

Undesirable accumulators, 143–144
Unemployment, 107–108
U.S. Bureau of Census, 102
U.S. Department of Education, 191
U.S. Department of Labor, 102–103

Vitality, 41–44 (*see also* Health)

Walking, 54–55
Weber, Max, 178

Weight, body, 55–57, 135
Well-being, 41–44 (*see also* Health)
Widowhood, 127, 129, 158
Williams, David R., 90–91
Win-win situation, 204–206
Work (*see also* Employment; Occupation)
  autonomy of, 118–121
  as component of socioeconomic status, 28
  creativity of, 118–121
  injuries related to, 114–117

job satisfaction and, 184
link to productive activities
  authority and, 123
  education and, 14, 118–121
  health and, 14, 121–123
  overview, 117–118
  term of, 104–105
World Health Organization, 35, 41

Zero-sum fallacy, 22, 195